James Anderson was born in Burnley in 1982 and played for Burnley CC before making his first-class debut for Lancashire in 2002. The following winter he made his England debut in Australia. Since then, he has gone on to play 77 Tests for England before the tour of New Zealand in 2012–13, taking almost 300 Test wickets, helping the side to two Ashes series wins. He has also played more than 160 one-day internationals, and he is now England's all-time leading international wicket-taker, having overhauled Sir Ian Botham's record of 528. He was named one of *Wisden*'s Five Cricketers of the Year in 2009 and was England Player of the Year in 2012.

Richard Gibson, who worked with James Anderson on the writing of this book, is a freelance journalist and regular contributor to several national newspapers. His previous collaborations include David Lloyd's bestselling *Start the Car: The World According to Bumble* and Graeme Swann's *The Breaks Are Off.*

JIMMY
My Story

JAMES ANDERSON
With Richard Gibson

**SIMON &
SCHUSTER**

London · New York · Sydney · Toronto · New Delhi

A CBS COMPANY

First published in Great Britain by Simon & Schuster UK Ltd, 2012
This paperback edition published by Simon & Schuster UK Ltd, 2013
A CBS COMPANY

1 3 5 7 9 10 8 6 4 2

Simon & Schuster UK Ltd
1st Floor
222 Gray's Inn Road
London WC1X 8HB

www.simonandschuster.co.uk

Simon & Schuster Australia, Sydney
Simon & Schuster India, New Delhi

A CIP catalogue for this book is available from the British Library.

ISBN: 978-0-85720-707-4
Ebook ISBN: 978-1-47112-831-8

Typeset by M Rules
Printed and bound by CPI Group (UK) Ltd, Croydon, CR0 4YY

In memory of my grandparents – Bob, Doreen,
Danny and Mary.

I owe you so much.
Not only were you a huge support to me,
you proved amazing role models who taught me
that there is nothing more important in this life
than family. If I can keep my own family as
close-knit, I will be a very happy man.

Contents

1

Grumpy

One of life's preconceptions is that fast bowlers are all made from exactly the same stock: leaders of men, ultra-confident, with rippling muscles, rhino-hide skin and superhero strength. The alpha males of the cricketing jungle, the cocks of the walk; some have been rumoured to be partial to slabs of raw meat.

Traditionally they've been bred tough, as labourers in coal mines or on building sites. From an English perspective, you will know the kind of characters I'm talking about here: Harold Larwood, the godfather of the art, and Fred Trueman, a man whose clan reveres him as the best fast bowler Yorkshire has ever produced (which therefore also made him the best in the world, of course) and who spent every waking hour living up to his nickname, Fiery Fred. Darren Gough and Andrew Flintoff are their modern equivalents.

Well, I'd better make the confession now. This fast bowler's wired up differently. Living proof that not all fast bowlers are chiselled from granite, possess the necessary physical prowess to wrestle polar bears to the death or the personality traits of what folk might call a man's man. Call me a bespoke model, if you like, but those archetypal characteristics passed me by. To be fair, it's hard to make aggression look convincing when you've spent your adolescence aiming to avoid it as the class short-arse. You see, until a ludicrous growth spurt at the age of fifteen, I stood about 5 ft tall, and, unlike my predecessors, I've never had to worry about whether my bum looked big in whites.

There was no pull-yourself-up-from-your-bootstraps start for me either, coming from a well-to-do, middle-class family from Brierfield, just outside the Lancashire town of Burnley. My dad's lighting equipment was not strapped to a helmet. I am the son of an optician, not a miner.

Some people are almost born to be fast bowlers because of the size and shape they are blessed with. But it was not until the fifth form at school that it appeared likely that I would make Burnley's first team let alone England's. Of course, I'd never stopped dreaming, much the same as other cricket-mad lads – I always thought 'James Anderson, international cricketer' had a nice ring to it, and I regularly pretended to be an England player when I was battling against my mates David Brown and Gareth Halley on my mum and dad's drive.

Now if you're interested enough about me to be reading this, you either like your sportsmen to be dour or you believe there's more to me than you see on the field. Because, let's face it, there's not much getting away from the fact that I do a rather fine line in grumpy whenever I cross the white line. You see, I am fully aware that the general public's impression of me is that I am quite a cantankerous sod. Granted, it's hardly without foundation. Unfortunately, that is my game face; my work clothes; my uniform. In case this one passed you by, in addition to being the modern equivalent of cavemen, fast bowlers are GRUMPY SO AND SOs. We spend half our working lives with our feet up, and, let's be honest, when that is one half of your job description, you ain't going to be wearing a permanent smile across your clock when the other half is spent in sweltering heat a couple of hours after your batsmen have been dismissed for jack.

However, despite the gurning looks and less than complimentary words I offer towards the blokes standing with wooden weapons in their hands who step into my office, I can confirm two things in these initial pages. Firstly, I thoroughly enjoy what I do. Love it, in fact. Secondly, there really is another side to me away from what you see on a cricket field. The more established I have become as an England player, the more comfortable I have become in showing other sides to my personality, the side that my wife Daniella and daughters Lola and Ruby know, or the one that is familiar to my close mates within the team, such as Graeme Swann and Alastair Cook.

But, equally, I take my work very seriously. Probably more seriously than you realize. To such an extent, in fact, that I actually practise being confrontational, aggressive and generally in-yer-face. I analyse my own performances, not just in terms of my bowling but how I have conducted myself. Because, I have discovered, I tend to be more effective as a bowler when I am chuntering at opponents or involved in a full-on and frank exchange of views than when I am not.

Us fast bowlers tend to have an attribute that gives us an edge over our opponents, and mine is actually being something of a mardy bum. Because I have not got express pace like Shoaib Akhtar, nor am I built like a brick outhouse like Chris Tremlett, or look down from 6 ft 7 in like Steve Finn, I need something else in my armoury as a fast bowler to help give me that edge over the batsmen.

In international sport you are always looking for that extra something that gives you an advantage in a contest. A lot of the time the skill alone will play the biggest part, but when you come across someone who is just as good a match, if not better than you, you need that little bit more, that other thing. My thing is the chat.

Obviously not everyone is susceptible to a verbal duel and so I choose my players wisely, or at least I like to think I do. My aim is to get under their skin and bring them out of their comfort zones. For example, there would be no point in getting into a verbal challenge with someone like Ricky Ponting, an opponent who soaks it up, becomes more determined and plays better because of a bit of niggle. Nor, if I came up against him, would I joust with Kevin Pietersen because he is another batsman who thrives on it.

For different reasons, I wouldn't really go at someone like Sachin Tendulkar – and that has nothing to do with his superior ability or elevated status in the game. He just doesn't get drawn into it, so you are expending your energy for nothing. Whenever we've played against India in recent years, I would be more likely to have a go at Rahul Dravid, another of their supremely talented players, for the simple reason that he would have a go back. Because, in general, as soon as opponents start talking back to you in between deliveries, they have been drawn out of their comfort zone, knocked out of kilter, lured into an area not natural to them.

Batsmen do not generally head into the middle looking for a chat. They tend to have a quiet focus on the job in hand, so I feel I am on top whenever they do start chirping, and as though I am the only one who can win that battle, generally. Let's face it: when a batsman starts talking back he is concentrating on something else other than the red spherical leather object I am about to hurl down at him. Think how heavily the odds are stacked against the batsmen. It takes just one ball to get them out, and that ball will arrive at some point; lose focus and it might come sooner than anticipated, so they're on to a loser in my book.

The most obvious example of that came during the 2010–11 Ashes when Mitchell Johnson was at the crease. Having the last laugh in a verbal exchange can seldom have been more publicized thanks to the popularity of YouTube.

To set the scene on the occasion in question, during the third Test in Perth I was very friendly towards Mitchell when he arrived in the middle. Now our Mitch had not played in the second Test in Adelaide, and I had missed him, so I simply inquired as to where he had been and what he had been up to. I was genuinely interested.

Yet I must admit it was a bit of a surprise when he came back with: 'Just been doing a few photo shoots, mate.' After getting dropped, surely his time would have been better spent in the nets striving to get back into the Australia team. It was an observation I thought I had better share with him, and as far as I was concerned my quip put me 1-0 up early in the contest.

Throughout his stay at the crease, words were exchanged back and forth, until he truly snapped, wandering a few yards towards me, where I stood at the start of my run-up, to inquire: 'Why are you chirping now, mate, not getting wickets?'

Now I am not a bloke renowned for his sense of timing but I couldn't have followed up any better. My next delivery beat Ryan Harris's defensive push and castled his stumps. Cue elaborate celebration towards Johnson, and a not-so-subtle suggestion from me that he button it. Of course, it was a pretty decent reply, that. However, to be fair, Mitchell had the best comeback of the lot when he followed up his half-century with 6 for 40 to set the series-levelling win up for them.

I can be pretty stubborn, and don't generally do backing down when engaged in a duel, which explains my actions during the first Test of that 2010–11 Ashes series. I had been having an exchange with Shane Watson, and although he was keeping me out, I felt as though I was in the ascendancy. For some reason, at a certain point in the proceedings something triggered a memory of what Mike Atherton had once told me. That you always win the battle as a batsman because you can stand your ground, and have a right to do so, whereas the bowler eventually has to turn around and saunter back to his mark. In one-upmanship, the batsman's won.

Even the prospect of Watson thinking he was on top riled me, so when after one delivery we got into a bit of a stare-off, I refused to back down. He stood there, gazing right at me, not moving, so I did exactly the same back. There was no way I was willing to blink first, so instead of turning around I started walking backwards, maintaining eye contact as I went.

A few yards back I considered that it could end really awkwardly, if I collided with the umpire or tripped on the back of one of my boot heels, but I kept going in reverse all the way, and, unusually, he refused to break his stare either. This was strange because Watson is a bit of an obsessive-compulsive about walking away from the crease between deliveries.

This time, however, he remained steadfast and, naturally, I considered that making him do something different was taking him out of his routine. To be honest, I will upset a batsman in any way that I can. Until I've seen the back of them. Having maintained his attention all the way back to my mark, without so much as a flinch from either of us, I shoved my hand out towards Alastair Cook at mid off in anticipation of him lobbing the ball into my palm.

Cookie, having latched on to what I was doing, later informed me it was the most pressured he had ever felt executing an underarm throw! He just had my right hand, arched like a claw, to aim at but thankfully I managed to see the ball coming out of the corner of my eye, and maintained my necessary degree of cool by refusing to turn my head. My gaze was fixed on Watson as I ran all the way to the crease, its termination only coming as my head dipped in delivery stride.

I have never been one to back down and, without a doubt, my best attribute is an inherent will to win. Since I can remember, I have been obsessed with winning. Whatever I do, whether it's an international cricket match or a game of darts or cards with the lads waiting for the rain to stop, it has to be competitive. And if it's competitive, I want to come out on top. As a boy I wanted to win at everything, and that competitiveness has never left me.

Earlier in my career, I guess, I so wanted to do well that my aggression often stemmed from frustration more than anything else. If things were not going as I wished, and I was bowling badly,

I would be mad with myself and end up taking that anger out on opponents.

It has only been in recent years, since working with Mark Bawden, the England team psychologist, that I have been able to control and channel that aggression positively. Mark has effectively helped me use my competitive edge to ensure I am operating at the very top of my game. So, whereas in the past it has revealed itself in its basest form, my antagonistic streak might actually be considered creative.

Mark's take on my on-field personality has encouraged me not to worry too much about image – although I am acutely aware that I have a responsibility not to go too far, and sometimes get a bit too close to the mark. I perform at my best, and this is something Mark and I both recognize, when I create a direct battle between myself and a certain batsman. So that the contest extends beyond each ball that I send down, and each one that the batsman repels, to the words we exchange.

I have never been shy of offering advice to batsmen but what I can say unequivocally is that I am so much better at delivering it these days. In the past, I might have let the verbals take over from the main show. Now, however, I actively ensure that as soon as I have a go at someone, it is forgotten, so that when I turn around and walk back to my mark, I become completely focused on the next ball. There is a technique to clearing your mind of everything external.

When I am out on the field, with ball in hand, I constantly think about whether sledging someone will aid the team cause. Obviously, first and foremost I think about where I am bowling the ball, exclusively so when, with a clear head, I am trudging back to my mark between deliveries. And if I have said something to the batter, rather than dwell on the context, I am then thinking about the ball I have just bowled, and where the next ball should be going.

There has to be clarity about your game plan, and developing the skill of switching on and off, and becoming wiser in selecting who to undermine and how, can improve a bowler's effectiveness. It certainly has in my case.

Being this clinical about it takes no little amount of practice, and there is no doubt in my mind that the mental side of the game is something that you can get better at. After each day's play in a Test match, or after each one-day or Twenty20 game, I will sit down with Mark and he will ask me where I thought I was in terms of filtering my aggression, and verbally exchanging with opponents. If I think I overstepped a line, and I often do, I will say so – the same goes if I could have lured someone in more – and we will effectively mark my performance.

Reviewing how you have felt on the field can be a cathartic process. For example, if you have not felt at ease in a match for whatever reason and can identify why, it can be stored away for the future. And generally knowing in what kind of mood you perform at your best is important. Some people need to be pumped up and confrontational while others need to be quiet and focused, and knowing what mood you need to be in to be at your optimum can be important for the team.

This is where Mark comes into his own. It was no coincidence to me that Mark was working intensely with Alastair Cook when he went through that golden period of form around the 2010–11 Ashes. His development since has partly been down to attempting to replicate ideal conditions for him to flourish. To score 766 runs against Australia in one series suggests his mindset was perfect.

Knowing what every single member of the team needs to perform at his best is such an important part of a coach's job in my eyes, and I also believe that team-mates have a responsibility in this regard. You should know how every single member of your team ticks within your group environment. Take me, for example. If I have had a bad day with the ball, I generally want ten minutes to myself to collect my thoughts. Those ten minutes are an important part of my daily schedule, so everyone leaves me alone. In that period, the last thing I want is people coming up and asking me whether they can fetch me a drink.

Understanding your team-mates is really important as far as I am concerned, and if you can create optimum conditions for each and every individual the team will perform better. Ultimately, we all want to be part of a successful side, and that is why I try to get to know everyone else as best as I can. In cricket we all have little idiosyncrasies – whether it is a superstitious way of getting dressed or a particular pre-match routine or in the way we prepare or unwind – and Mark Bawden is brilliant at examining what works and what doesn't for certain individuals. Getting to know things like this helps to create the best possible environment for each player to perform in. One thing I've always tried to establish is how different guys like others to act when they've just got out. Once back in the changing room, some people just want quiet, others immediately want a chat. The language you choose to use can be important as well. If you are a bit jokey, some might not take that so well; conversely, others might not want you to be too serious.

Good captains and coaches should be able to adapt the way they talk to individuals, too. There are times when it is crucial for a captain to be able to gee up a bowler – when a partnership needs breaking or you are approaching the end of a long, hard day. Finding the right tone to motivate, or even fire up, the bloke you're chucking the ball to is the skill of a captain. Andrew Strauss developed this priceless knack at the end of a long day, when he needed a three-over burst from someone, and I was rarely unhappy when I'm his chosen victim.

There is no exact formula when it comes to making successful cricket teams but one ingredient I feel is essential, and yet is remarkably overlooked, is an appreciation of the different personalities within a team. Cricket accepts all sorts of backgrounds, upbringings, cultures and beliefs, and although you don't have to be best mates with everyone, as you've been selected to work together why not get to know each other better? It's something I try to do whenever someone new comes into the England team, and in turn I would like them to get to know me as a person as well. I am naturally a bit guarded when I first meet people, but I make it my duty to be as welcoming as I can, and find out how the new guy likes to act both within the team environment and outside it. What annoys me more than anything is people who don't take the time to do this. Cricket is an individual as well as a team sport, and what works for one guy doesn't necessarily work for the next.

My personal feeling is that the England team that rose to the top of the world Test rankings was generally committed to getting to know each other better, and this played a crucial part in our collective success.

We've also made it a policy to toast individual milestones – if someone has scored a hundred or taken a five-wicket haul, for example – with a beer at the end of a Test match day's play. It means that we stay around the dressing room for an extra half an hour and, as frustrating as that is for our wives sitting waiting at the hotel, from the team's point of view it is very good bonding time. Having others celebrate on-field success with you emphasizes the value of the performance to the group as a whole, and in talking about the day's play you might find some analysing it in a different way or the conversation moving into different subject areas. Fundamentally, that wind-down session is prime getting-to-know-you time.

This is one of the things introduced not long after Andrew Flower and Andrew Strauss began their coach–captain alliance in 2009, and one that made their England team a more inclusive one than previous outfits.

I know the value of a team that looks to integrate new members because I have always struggled somewhat myself when I have joined a new one. Because in my youth I was naturally reserved and tended to keep my own counsel until I got to know people better, I have always acted the same whenever I have been part of a new team. I guess I have not changed much in terms of temperament – painfully quiet some would say – since I first walked into the dressing room as a first-team player with Burnley Cricket Club. It took me months to come out of my shell as a teenager in the Lancashire League, but that is just indicative of the fact that no matter what team I have gone into I have never initially felt comfortable.

It was not that Burnley was an unfriendly club, just that I tend to keep my distance as a default position. And I certainly didn't have much to say to opposition batsmen either when I made my debut at fifteen. After all, it's quite brave to be lippy when you don't know where the ball is going. If you follow up some chat by spraying the ball everywhere you tend to look a bit stupid.

Over a couple of years I learned about fast bowling on the job against good league batsmen. Almost overnight I went from being fairly average for my age – I did a bit of batting and a bit of bowling in eight-a-side Under-13 cricket, and wasn't great at either – to having the ability to bowl quick. Previously I had trundled in but, as I grew taller, the shock to the system hit me: I could bowl seriously fast, I just didn't know what to do with the ball or how to control it.

For a shy schoolboy, playing against men – and international cricketers in some cases – was a big test. So was dealing with playing in front of a crowd. Before my debut against East Lancashire in May 1998, I had not previously played in a cricket match where people actually came to watch. Sure, the odd mum or dad would have been milling around at junior games but not actual supporters – or, more aptly, barrackers.

There would be a few people on every week for our home games, anything between 20 and 120 for a regular league game, the same group congregating behind the bowler's arm. Matches during early or late season would draw larger crowds still because Burnley football supporters used to park their cars in the cricket club car park for matches at Turf Moor, then stick around for a beer in the clubhouse before heading home if it was a nice afternoon. On those days, you could have quite a few hundred watching.

As a 15-year-old I was liable to spray it about – any kid at that age is, really – and that precipitated cries of 'bowl it straight' or 'get him off' from the regular hecklers. Those with a few bevvies on board were never shy of offering their own assessments, and although public condemnation took a little bit of getting used to, despite being erratic my confidence remained intact thanks to regular wickets.

Confidence is a precious commodity for any cricketer but particularly for a young fast bowler. You're meant to be all macho, of course, but it's just as easy to become little boy lost when things start going against you. As I have said, not all pace bowlers are packaged the same way. Some are delivered on to the scene in a box marked FRAGILE.

2

Roots

Most people dismiss Burnley as an absolute shithole, but as a free-man of the borough I am obliged to defend its honour. A town traditionally founded on its mill industry, these days people are less inclined to recognize its influence. From a modern perspective, it's a place that's very passionate about, and arguably defined by, sport.

As with many northern towns, its major sports team gives it something of an identity. When people think of Burnley, they tend to think of the football club's rich history as a founder member of the Football League and the famous claret and blue colours.

The population is about 90,000 and yet for big matches the football club can attract gates of 20,000. You won't find a better ratio of fans per population in the country, and that tells you something of the feeling from the local people towards the team, and to sport in general.

I have a lot of affection for the two grounds down at Turf Moor – the football and cricket clubs are adjacent – as that was where I spent the majority of my youth. In the summer, the cricket club became like a second home, netting with the juniors in midweek and during school holidays, and scoring for the second XI, for whom my dad was captain, at weekends.

During the winter months, a lot of my family would make the pilgrimage down to the football. Later, as a teenager I worked on the gate as a weekend job. Throughout my youth, in addition to my natural affection for Burnley I had a soft spot for Arsenal, and Ian Wright was one of my sporting heroes, so it was a great thrill when he came up to play for a season. Chris Waddle had a run as player-manager in the late 1990s, and Paul Gascoigne featured half a dozen times in a brief spell at the end of his career, as Burnley threatened bigger and better things.

Over recent years, the success of the football club and its promotion to the Premier League, albeit for the briefest of stays, provided a real boost for the town at a time when most of its publicity was negative. The rise of the British National Party and the race riots of the early noughties dragged it into the national consciousness for all the wrong reasons, so it was a positive thing that sport was able to restore some pride in the region.

One of the main reasons I enjoyed growing up in Burnley was family, and ours is a rather large one. Both my dad, Michael, and mum, Catherine, had two brothers, so I had plenty of cousins to knock about with, and did so weekly at our Friday get-togethers. As we all lived in relatively close proximity, we would congregate at Nana Doreen's house. She would cook a huge potato pie or something like that, and everyone would catch up. I used to love Fridays.

Me and my cousin, Lee, would charge round playing football in the winter, cricket in the summer. It was something I looked forward to all week. Every December we would congregate at their house for Christmas dinner. We would eat until it wasn't physically possible to eat any more. Nana kept bringing out food from the kitchen like a magician pulling a never-ending handkerchief out of his pocket. After opening presents the kids would watch in amazement as Grandad Bob fell asleep at four o'clock in the afternoon and snored his way through to about seven. This was an ongoing joke with me and my sister Sarah.

On Mum's side, we would all go to church on a Sunday and then walk to my Grandma Mary and Grandad Danny's house. Grandma would cook a chicken, and I'll never forget that smell of food as you walked through the door. As a young boy it was like a magnet to me and just kept sucking me in. I remember those days so fondly, none more than on one Boxing Day gathering when Grandma came to me and asked me if I liked my Walkman, not realizing that we had yet to open our presents!

It's quite a northern thing, I suppose, for entire families to meet up on a weekly basis but I always found it comforting. After Nana and Grandad passed away, the honours were passed down to the next generation, and Fridays have become pizza night. Even now that family time is special to me. In one way, having such a wonderful family lessened my need for contact with my contemporaries and meant I rarely felt the need to seek or develop other friendships.

I had a privileged upbringing on the border of Brierfield, two and a half miles north-east of Burnley's town centre, and being so close-knit helped. I've never been someone who has found making friends easy, and so my cousins were my real mates, forming the social network upon which I relied.

Socializing was problematic for me from a young age. For one, I have always been extremely quiet and lacked self-confidence. To such an extent that I was already a bit of a recluse by the time I went to St Theodore's High School at the age of eleven.

I was short, skinny and didn't really have much in common with the other lads, so found it hard to get along. There were no real common interests between myself and the majority of the lads at St Theodore's and because I showed no desire to hang out on street corners, or engage in other anti-social activity, I was viewed as different. And just as with kids of this same description up and down the country, being different made me a target for bullying when I got to secondary school. The bullying primarily took the form of name-calling, and actually began in middle school. I had quite big teeth as a young lad and so used to get called Goofy or Rabbit. Being vertically challenged, there were references to my height, too.

At first it didn't really bother me but with time this wore me down. As an adult, in the environment I am most used to – the dressing room – banter flies around and Graeme Swann would think there was something wrong if a day went by without me taking the piss out of the size of his (humongous) chin. But when you're young, cruel comments about your physical appearance can be very hurtful.

There were a few occasions when I tried to stand up for myself and came off worse for it, most notably on a school skiing trip when I was fourteen. I'd had enough of getting picked on, decided to have a go back at the lad who was giving me the most serious grief, and received a headbutt for my trouble.

I am sure this kind of behaviour happens everywhere. There is always a group of lads that is feared, and make it their policy to belittle people. And, like others who become victims of these mindless idiots, I lived in fear of them.

It meant that from Monday to Friday I just tried to get through the hours of 8.30 a.m. to 3.30 p.m. as best I could. My life consisted of cricket in the summer, then in the winter I would go on the football at the weekend and spend the rest of my time ticking off the days until the new year and the start of indoor nets.

It was not as though I was happy being such an obvious outsider at school, and I did go through a stage in fifth form of desperately trying to fit in with one of the in-crowds. There was a park across Ormerod Road and at lunchtime I would go there with quite a few lads and smoke. Peer pressure got to me to such an extent that I ended up doing something that I really didn't enjoy, with people I didn't really enjoy spending time with, simply in a bid to be liked. You see, part of me has always wanted to belong.

Even then cricket was the focal point of my life, and, because there was no cricket at school, time spent at Turf Moor became my refuge. Well, I say there was no cricket at school but that is not strictly true. There was the compulsory annual match when we entered the Lancashire County Cup.

This was always one of those games when the majority of our team took their ties and blazers off and played in the rest of their uniform. When it was our turn to bat it was like Russian roulette, as you attempted to pick out the barbaric, buckled pads that hurt least from the team kitbag. These monstrosities had been gouging lads' legs since the 1960s.

I was one of the few St Theodore's boys who played for a club, and although I didn't stand out at Burnley I was much better than anyone else at school, and therefore was team coordinator. Teachers did the organizing on annual match days, which mainly consisted of telling me to get off after bowling a couple of overs, and allowing someone else a go.

Back at home, if sport was on the telly I was glued to it. It had been this way for me for years – from the age of six, I reckon – something I would think quite unusual. Even more so when you consider I would sit there and watch an entire fifteen-frame snooker match. Dad showed the same level of enthusiasm, and that is undoubtedly where I inherited it all from. We both liked just about anything going that was competitive. Sport was always my escapism, even at primary school. Because my other communication skills were not the best, it was through playing that I expressed myself, I guess. My mum used to chuckle at the dedication I showed for re-enacting Olympic events – the hurdles might only have been cardboard and the javelin a bamboo stick but the skills were the same. I've always been pretty well coordinated, and I would regularly be found chucking a ball from hand to hand, or throwing one against a wall indoors or outdoors. My bedroom was home to various self-set training drills: I would throw a mini-football or tennis ball against the wall and as it rebounded I would practise either diving headers or diving catches, my bed acting as my crash mat. There was plenty of energy that needed releasing and I've always enjoyed throwing myself about.

When it wasn't a ball, it would be a dart or a snooker cue in my hand. Even at seven and eight when others were interested in *Star Wars*, Lego or Meccano kits, I was sports obsessed. Only when I got into that lazy teenage stage did I develop a liking for computers but even then I was always active outside the house.

At junior school, I played short tennis in an indoor centre down the road, and football for the local team, Brierfield Celtic, in addition to cricket for Burnley's junior teams. At St Theodore's I played basketball. I was the shortest guy in the team and that meant I played centre. I loved it.

As a footballer, I started off at eight as a central defender, made my way to left wing and finished upfront, scoring a number of goals in my final two seasons before joining Lancashire CCC's professional staff. My first sporting impact overseas actually came as a footballer. Brierfield travelled to France one summer to play in a rather large tournament, the size of which was enough to stupefy a 12-year-old. To this day I have no idea why the free kick I bent into the top corner that week was disallowed. I was too shy to ask. Later on, I hooked up with Burnley Belvedere, a sports club incorporating rugby, football and cricket teams, just over the back of where we lived.

Despite the football, though, and the collection of Burnley and Arsenal kits, there was only one shirt I ever wanted to pull on. I always dreamed of playing cricket for England.

Unless I was on the field of play, I tended to keep myself to myself but I was a lot different with my family to how I was with strangers. The fundamental characteristics of my personality have never changed: it has meant I am always cautious when meeting someone for the first time, and don't tend to give much away. Some people express themselves quite openly, whereas I have always been quite guarded.

Yet ask my uncles and they would give you quite a different picture. They would tell you that within the family environment I always wanted to be the centre of attention. I was the complete show-off by all accounts. Once in public view, though, I reverted to type.

However, I have always craved the role of showman despite it being a role that you would expect to upset my stomach. No surprise then that as a 3-year-old I took centre stage as Joseph in the nursery Nativity and threw up down the back of an angel. Throughout my early career I was almost a walking paradox: quiet and reserved, I nevertheless wanted to be the big noise, for all eyes to be on me.

From a career perspective, I have always loved playing in sold-out stadiums. I have never liked games in front of 300 people; give me a packed MCG any day. Growing up I was always content in my home surroundings, and in my working life I have become accustomed to performing in front of huge audiences. It gives me a real buzz taking a crucial wicket in front of a full house at an Ashes Test or in a World Cup match.

My growth spurt at fifteen had its obvious benefits for my cricketing ability but was so severe – as with England footballer Steven Gerrard, it turned me from a small frame to a 6-ft-tall teenager inside twelve months – that it left me in quite a lot of pain at times. It also meant I went from being one of the smallest in my year to one of the tallest.

The physical change coincided with the bullying stopping – funny that, eh? – although I still struggled to fit in as we moved into the sixth form. The common room was split neatly into the people who tried to be cool and those the cool people considered to be geeks. Much as I do now in the England dressing room, with the young guys and the established players, I held my own in conversation on both sides of the divide. Whether it's talking R & B with Steven Finn or real estate with Andrew Strauss, I can generally get by.

And get by I did. Although I flitted between the two groups, I was never comfortable in either environment. There were a number of us who dwelt in that middle ground, and the truth is I never really got close to anyone at St Theodore's in seven years. I guess if I'd formed any close friendships then we would still be in touch but suffice it to say I cut all ties once I left.

Social networking sites like Facebook allow for reacquaintance, of course, and every now and again someone gets on my case, asking me for a signed England shirt, but apart from that I have no real interaction with anyone from my school days. My best mate was David Brown, who I played with at Burnley, and who went on to play county cricket with Gloucestershire and Glamorgan, but, like my cousins, he lived in a different part of town so went to another school.

Academically, I wasn't great. Sitting in a classroom for an hour at a time getting talked at was my idea of torture, really, as I've always felt the need to be active. Things tend to sink in better for me in an informal environment. For example, I have always been a quick learner from coaches. Perhaps it's because they don't sit down and talk *at* you, and their teaching is more interactive, that I respond better.

Not that my relationship with Nasser Hussain, my first England captain, was particularly interactive. Some compared him to an old-school headmaster yet I thrived under his guidance. Although he might not have been everyone's cup of tea, being the intense and fiery character he was, he was brilliant for me. He was always there, lingering on my shoulder, during my first few months as an international cricketer.

Not everyone was fond of his form of leadership but as a 20-year-old plucked from obscurity to take a place on a tour of Australia, he was exactly what I needed. I always felt like he wanted to help me, and, crucially, that he backed my ability. After all, he was the England captain who gave me my first chance.

From the outset, it felt like Nasser was pushing me towards the one-day team when I was called in from academy duty in December 2002. He was always the one who came and talked to me, always the one offering advice. He left me in no doubt that he rated me, whereas I was never sure that anyone else felt that way at the time.

On several occasions, although he was the team leader and one of the mature players, he found the time for me, which, as a young lad coming in, I really appreciated. By his own admission, he could be confrontational or irritable and some of the other lads didn't always enjoy being around him because he was also hard-nosed, bordering on aggressive at times. But I always appreciated time in his company, and having him as captain.

The unmistakable thing about Nasser was his will to win, and how driven he was to make his England team the best it possibly could be. He was always seeking perfection. To such an extent that in one of my early England appearances, a one-day game in Perth, with Sri Lanka needing around 100 runs to win with just two wickets intact, while the rest of the team gathered in a huddle for a drinks break, he maintained his position at mid off, arms folded, chuntering to himself, unhappy that someone had dropped a catch. It was not good enough just to win. He wanted to win properly.

Perhaps I saw some of me in him – I have always believed that if a job is worth doing you should do it to your absolute best. If there is a picture to be hung on the wall at home, I will check a hundred times that the nail has gone in properly and the frame hangs straight. And I mean a hundred times.

Sometimes he couldn't help himself in his quest for perfection. Another incident of note came in South Africa at the 2003 World Cup when, in my best international display to date, I had figures of 4 for 23 from 9.4 overs against Pakistan in Cape Town. It was at this juncture that Nasser opted to come up and tell me: 'Whatever you do from this ball, just don't go for four, it will ruin your figures.'

Cue a rank ball down the leg side that went to the fence, and screams of 'Oh no! Oh Christ!' from somewhere over my left shoulder. Abdul Razzaq took me for two more from my final delivery, so Nasser's warning had gone unheeded.

Others might have been completely narked by that kind of treatment but to me he was like a friendly sergeant major. And I owed him a lot because he always backed me, and little things like that are so important for a young cricketer.

He also sought to take some of the pressure off me, including setting my field for me on my Test debut, against Zimbabwe at Lord's in May 2003. Normal practice is for an opening bowler to discuss field setting with his captain before the first over, but it was probably due to my tender years that he set mine for me that evening, and neglected to post a fine leg. Three times I was clipped to leg for four by Dion Ebrahim in one over, making a pig's ear of my early figures, and he couldn't have been more apologetic when he ran across at the end of the over. 'Sorry, that was all my fault,' he told me. 'You just concentrate on getting into a rhythm.'

It was impossible not to feel how much Nasser wanted you to do well, and because of that you wanted to reciprocate. He also had a very dry sense of humour that I enjoyed. I thought him a funny bloke then, and still have a laugh with him whenever I see him now. Our relationship was always good on and off the field.

The same could be said of my relationship with Michael Vaughan, my other captain during my early England years, since he has retired. Unfortunately, however, despite our cordiality now, I didn't enjoy Vaughan as a captain.

As I say, sometimes as a young fast bowler you just need to know that the bloke you're pounding into the crease for has his arm around your shoulder, if not physically, then metaphorically at least.

Unfortunately, that is not something I ever felt playing under Vaughan. In contrast, I actually felt alone and isolated when I most needed support. The prime example was when I was recalled for the fourth Test against South Africa at the Wanderers in 2005.

I had spent the first few weeks of that tour, and subsequently the first three Tests, out of favour and therefore bowling at a single stump during lunch breaks, before and after play. My tour was one big net, my head was nowhere near international cricket, and because I had been so far removed from the selection equation for the opening matches I wasn't even thinking about playing.

Of course, there will be those who counter that I should have been, that I was on an England tour and the natural extension of that was that it was my job to be ready. Nevertheless, when I was preferred to Simon Jones, and thrown into this game, it was a sudden shock. I was underprepared. By this time, it was five months since my last first-class action. Unsurprisingly, I didn't bowl very well.

Steve Harmison and Matthew Hoggard shared the new ball, and although I started okay as first change, it wasn't long before I began dragging it down short and wide. No two ways about it, I got clattered everywhere, didn't really know what I was doing with the ball, or where it was going, and was soon shot of confidence.

When you feel like that, bowling is a real slog and even starts to feel unnatural. Vaughanie wandered up to me at one point during a spell and asked: 'What's up, mate? Radar gone?'

'Yeah, I think it has,' I said, desperate for some backing. All I received was a pat between the shoulder blades and an instruction to 'keep going'.

'Thanks for that,' I thought.

My feeling is that a good captain should know how to talk to each and every one of his team as individuals. I don't think Vaughan ever had that in him, and it is the major reason I've not held him in as high regard as others have. You see, from my experience he was not as good a captain as others made out. He was captain of a truly great team in 2005.

Good captains get players to perform above themselves at times by putting their players at ease, and although a lot has been made of Vaughan's laconic style, I never felt comfortable playing under him. I never felt like he rated me: the language that he used with me was seldom positive and I didn't like that. My judgement is formed from personal experience and while people might accuse me of forming it out of frustration at being out of favour for long stretches – admittedly the majority of his reign coincided with a time when I was struggling – I also had a good run in the team between 2007 and 2008 and flourished.

Even then, during times of sustained personal success, I still didn't take to him as a captain. All I really wanted was for him to believe in me and my ability.

3

Red Rose Blooming

This will probably not come as a surprise, me being a sports-mad lad, from a sports-mad family, from a sports-mad town, but I felt just as passionately about Lancashire County Cricket Club as Burnley FC in my youth. I grew up as a Lancashire supporter, and when my desire to become a professional cricketer strengthened it was always Lancashire that I wanted to play for.

There would be a group of us – including my dad, and my uncle Mark – that headed down to Old Trafford to watch the odd Sunday League match, and to as many big cup games as we could get to. During the 1990s we were spoilt for big matches because Lancashire possessed a fine one-day team that progressed to quarter- and semi-final stages on a regular basis. We didn't tend to go to as much Championship cricket because I was either playing myself or at school, yet it still felt like we spent our whole summers down there.

I used to love watching them play, and I was the proud owner of the first one-day replica shirt sold by the club, having received it as a birthday present one year. It was actually predominantly white, with LANCASHIRE emblazoned across it in blue and red letters. All the counties had similar kits that year – the name and the colours being the only difference.

Lancashire's success in that period earned me my first ever trip to Lord's, as a 12-year-old, for the Benson & Hedges Cup final against Kent in 1995, a match that was won despite Aravinda de Silva scoring a brilliant hundred. It was a bit of an adventure from the North West. Dad drove down, we found somewhere to park and had a decent walk to the ground. We sat at the Nursery End, just to the left of where the media centre is now positioned. In those days, an English cup final had that real sense of occasion about it, like the FA Cup equivalent at Wembley, the Boat Race or the Grand National, and I remember quite a few incidents from it vividly – Lancashire made 274 for 7 and David Fulton's response was to walk out in a sun hat and pull one of Wasim Akram's first balls to the boundary. But Lancashire kept taking wickets at crucial times and although De Silva obviously played well, it was all but over when he holed out to Graham Lloyd going for his fourth six.

Afterwards we strolled on the sacred Lord's turf – a few more excitable supporters ran on the second the thirty-five-run win was clinched – savouring the moment and the atmosphere. We wandered about in front of the pavilion to witness the trophy presentation, and I clearly recall thinking how much I wanted to be up there, part of a successful team like that, playing in front of that many people. Twenty-odd thousand to see you play for Lancashire at the home of cricket – it was the stuff of dreams to a Burnley lad.

As a Lancastrian, and this applies to Yorkshiremen, too, the club badge is revered from a young age. There's a huge passion for the two roses counties and you grow up wanting to wear a rose on your chest – red if you're from God's County, and white if you live among the queer folk over the hills.

The emotional attachment to Lancashire includes animosity towards Yorkshire – that goes with the territory – similar to the fierce rivalry that exists between Burnley and Blackburn football clubs. There is a real us and them feel about it all, and that

Lancashire team I started watching in the 1990s was chock-full of local lads. Apart from Wasim, the club's overseas player, the others were generally from within the county boundaries, and that gave young lads hope that they could follow on in future years.

Yorkshire were obviously even stricter than Lancashire up until the early 1990s but the distinct sense of identity that side brought was part of the attraction. That sense of identity got lost a little bit with the introduction of Kolpak players, and a more frequent movement of players from county to county, but from my experience of a Championship fixture in 2011 there remains an unmistakably competitive and parochial edge to Lancashire v Yorkshire games. There were plenty of Lancashire-born players in our team and Yorkshire-born in the opposition and we felt that edge. When you play professional sport you actually want that edge to be there and rivalry makes games like that extra special.

Fact is that Wasim Akram was a world superstar but my hero from that Lancashire team was actually Peter 'Digger' Martin. I just used to love the way he bowled. For a big man he had a pretty cool approach to the crease, and because he swung the ball away at pace he was someone I wanted to model myself on when I bowled. I also admired Glen Chapple. He probably won't like being reminded of this but I wasn't even a teenager when I watched him from the stands, running in to bowl, with Digger or Wasim at the other end.

In future years it was rather strange for me to be a part of the Lancashire attack with these guys. I ended up playing with Peter at the end of his career, and then for a decade with Chappie. Undoubtedly they helped with my grounding at the club, and taught me good habits in the way they went about their business. The side they had been a part of, and the one I joined latterly, was a very successful one with some great local players like Neil Fairbrother, Mike Watkinson and Ian Austin. As a young lad you really felt like they passed down the knowledge.

My interest in cricket developed through Dad, who, as I've said, was Burnley's second XI captain. Mum used to push me around the outfield in my pram, so it was always destined to play a huge role in my life. As soon as I could toddle about, I used to go down and watch him play every Saturday, then, when I was old enough, I was coerced into becoming team scorer. Scoring is a rite of passage for most sons of cricket-playing fathers, I guess, and my dad also came to watch me for the club's youth teams.

At Under-13 level, we played eight-a-side cricket in which you batted in pairs. My batting partner was my cousin Lee, who was also a left-hander. Not only did they put me with him because we were related but because we complemented each other. Although I was technically okay, I couldn't hit it off the square, and am still in the process of learning to do that, while he smacked it everywhere. Neither did my medium-pace bowling stand out at that age. I had always bowled but never got it off the straight, really, or had any pace either. In comparison to my contemporaries, I was very much run of the mill, and would bowl first or second change.

Nevertheless, I was always keen and went to Lancashire trials on an annual basis from the age of eleven onwards. Each year I would make the pilgrimage to Old Trafford, and each year it would end in rejection. In fact, it was only after shooting up those several inches, when my bowling had developed considerably in pace, that I made the breakthrough, and only then because of the persistence of one of the mums from our cricket club. Mrs Valerie Brown – mother of David and Michael, who went on to play for Middlesex, Hampshire and Surrey – knew John Stanworth, who ran the Lancashire age-group teams, because her boys had been playing in the system for years.

'This lad is well worth a look at,' she instructed him. 'He's quick.'

I had played in a tournament for Lancashire B at Ampleforth College at Under-15 level but until Mrs B's quiet word I was not on the radar at Old Trafford. Year on year, the same guys had been selected; they played all the way through from eleven upwards, they knew all the coaches and in turn the coaches knew all the parents. It felt something of a closed shop, so I was grateful for the door being opened in the form of a special trial.

About two years earlier, when discussing potential career paths, I told my parents I wanted to be a professional cricketer, and eventually to play for England. The only problem was that I didn't know whether I was good enough. Mum told me they believed in me and would support me in trying to achieve my goal.

The season after my first-team debut for Burnley, I turned seventeen, and began representing Lancashire at Under-17 and Under-19 levels. Mum only ever got into sport because me and my dad would have it on the TV permanently at home – she hardly had a choice in the matter – but once things got serious for me, her interest naturally increased. She'd always watched me play football on Sundays, and cricket now followed.

Goodness knows how neglected my sister Sarah felt through it all. Dad and Grandad used to drive me everywhere throughout my teens, and then when we met up on Friday nights for dinner, talk would naturally turn to cricket once more. Even now she's no fan of the game, quite frankly hates it in fact, and who can blame her? From my point of view, it was handy that Dad, who worked for himself, could take days off to go to places like Leicester and Chelmsford to watch me play. Lately my family, Sarah included occasionally, tend to restrict themselves to watching me at weekends.

These days I would like to think that I have mastered my art but I was at completely the opposite end of the scale when I made my Burnley first XI debut against East Lancashire on 9 May 1998, when, despite all my team-mates' enthusiastic encouragement, fast bowling was pretty new to me. In those early days, I was just getting used to my extra height and so whanged it down with as much velocity as I could muster. When I got it straight I was dangerous and soon I was doing senior club cricketers, who had played the leagues for years, for pace.

The truth of the matter was that occasionally the deliveries I produced were good enough to account for some very good players indeed and before much longer there was a collection of famous international cricketers among my prize scalps. The first professional player I dismissed came in that summer of 1998: West Indian all-rounder Roger Harper, who was playing for Nelson, caught behind first ball. He was one of three wickets for me in quick succession that sent the opposition from twenty-nine without loss to 30 for 3. I made a bit of a habit of getting the professionals out first nut, in fact, and had Martin Van Jaarsveld in that very manner in a game against Lowerhouse in 1999.

At that time, I was making a considerable impression on the Lancashire League, and one player who was not destined to forget me was Australian batsman Brad Hodge, overseas professional for Ramsbottom, at the start of the summer of 2000. Because I was so erratic at times, I was as likely to bowl a beauty as a beamer, so when I forced him to punch one off his face he was not best pleased.

Of course, as a kid of seventeen, bowling to an established Australian state player with a big reputation, I was nervously apologetic.

'I'm ever so sorry about that,' I mumbled.

In contrast, he was typically Australian.

'Fuck off,' was the extent of his reply, and I couldn't get the fact I had hit him on the glove out of my mind as I trudged back to my mark. It spooked me for the rest of the match, and I felt terrible. I might have come close to knocking seven bells out of him with that loose delivery but it was me who was intimidated by the ferocity of his response.

Years later, when Brad arrived on Lancashire's staff as overseas player, he had not forgotten. The very first words he greeted me with were: ''Ere, you're that —t that beamed me . . .' They do say that first impressions count.

Our own pro, Ant Botha, who went on to have a successful career with Derbyshire and Warwickshire, would bowl the bulk of our overs with a great deal of success from the other end, and while he was a steadying influence on the attack, I was anything but.

Primarily it was my pace that got me noticed, and indeed led to opportunities higher up the spectrum. Because I couldn't swing the ball at all back then, I held the seam as straight as I could and concentrated on bowling fast.

Not long afterwards, after establishing myself in Lancashire's Under-19 team, I enjoyed a personal battle with Sajid Mahmood. Whenever we bowled in tandem, I would study how far the wicketkeeper was standing back and try to work out which one of us was hitting the gloves harder, which one was making the ball carry further. Edging that duel was my badge of honour, and it wasn't until I had played a few second XI games and got a contract at Old Trafford that Mike Watkinson taught me to swing it.

Although fast bowling was pretty new to me, I just did what came naturally in those days rather than model my action on anyone else. I always liked watching Allan Donald. He had such a sleek approach and delivery stride but I never tried to copy him.

Well, I tell a lie. I actually tried to copy just about everyone's action on the domestic and international scene (playing in the street against David and Gareth at least). It was a bit of a party piece. I could do a mean Gus Fraser as a teenager while my impression of Dominic Cork was so convincing that I imitated him throughout a twenty-over contest for Burnley Under-18s and barely went for a run. Phil DeFreitas, being a Lancashire player, was another one of my favourite bowlers to mimic, and I also used to bowl properly useful left-arm spin.

Yes, that's right: properly useful left-arm spin. In fact, I still do bowl left-arm spin, and really fancy myself at it. Now it won't have escaped your notice that I am a right-arm pace bowler but one of the things I have always been good at is visualizing other sportsmen's movements and then re-enacting them, and I have bowled left-arm tweakers since my early teens. It was a talent that developed from the days when we played on the drive. All my mates were right-handed batsmen and because I couldn't bowl leg-spin to save my life, I had to find another way of getting the ball to go away from the bat. So I practised and practised left-arm stuff.

Every now and again when there aren't too many prying eyes around, I bowl it in the nets while on tour with England. I don't do it very often because it is frowned upon – some people think I am taking the piss – but I got Ian Bell out in one of my early exhibitions, in Durban, and genuinely believe with regular practice I could bowl left-arm spin in a first-class match. It feels so natural.

When Australia coach John Buchanan claimed in the aftermath of their 2001 Ashes victory that the next target in cricket was for individuals to become multi-skilled and push the boundaries of possibility by learning to bat and bowl with both hands, his claims were dismissed as something emanating from cloud cuckoo land but in the decade since we have seen the emergence of switch-hitting, while David Warner arrived on the scene laying claim to be the first ambidextrous batsman. Anyone who has seen him switch-hit will take his claim seriously. He is better equipped left-handed but can strike it pretty well the other way around, too. Now if batsmen are allowed to jump into a different stance as they take strike, why shouldn't bowlers be allowed to revert from right-arm over seam to left-arm round spin indiscriminately?

Because rules is rules and the laws of the game don't allow it, is the answer. But I reckon it is because people have yet to challenge it. In this instance, unfamiliarity breeds contempt, and why shouldn't cricketers switching from one to the other be a thing of the future? Samit Patel bowls left-arm spin but throws right-handed, so why not be able to bowl both ways? I don't think it's so strange (although for some reason I do get freaked out by the number of right-arm fast bowlers, like Darren Gough and Glen Chapple, who write left-handed).

Imitating others is something I have been good at throughout my life. For example, I have never had a golf lesson but I have got a really good swing, picked up exclusively from watching golfers on TV as a kid. Oh, and there is something about it that I find perfectly normal but others might consider unusual or even freaky. I bat left-handed, or at least try to, but when it comes to golf I am a right-hander. It stems from the fact that almost all those golfers on telly were right-handed, so naturally when I first swung a club I did it that way.

Nowadays, whenever Monty Panesar is around the England set-up, I watch what he does, store an image in my head where his arms and legs go in relation to each other, and how he releases the ball, then try to copy that in a way that feels most natural to me. There is a lot of downtime on tours and people get bored, so you end up doing stuff like this to occupy yourself. Oh, and I am by no means the only one to have tried this kind of thing. Peter Martin used to bowl left-arm spin in the nets – he just wasn't as good as me, that's all!

What Martin and Chapple were good at, however, was guiding me as a young bowler when I made my first-team breakthrough in 2002. Both Kyle Hogg and I were handed contracts on the staff off the back of Lancashire Under-19s' successful 2000 season when we were beaten finalists in the inter-county 100-over competition. By that point, I was established in the Lancashire second XI, having made my debut in an innings win over Hampshire at Old Trafford in 1999, shortly after my first appearance at any level for the club. In the penultimate Lancashire twos match of 2001, I took 8 for 90, including my first five-wicket haul, a performance that earned me a first-team debut in the final match of the Norwich Union League at Derby that September. Bad weather reduced it to a twenty-five-over-per-side contest. Michael Di Venuto gave me some tap and I finished with 1 for 33 from my four overs – Steve Stubbings dismissed lbw, my maiden senior scalp.

This rise through the ranks at Lancashire coincided with my first international recognition. On the back of my second-team displays, I was selected for the England Under-19 team and claimed seven wickets on my debut, albeit in defeat to West Indies at Grace Road. Although we lost that series 1-0, there were some prominent players for the future in that side. Matt Prior, Monty Panesar and James Tredwell all featured and a 16-year-old called Tim Bresnan was twelfth man and my room-mate for the final match in three that series. Ian Bell was recalled as captain for that drawn series decider at the Riverside, having spent the summer playing in Warwickshire's first team. He had an air of superiority about him, and an old-school style of captaincy. Hand signals would represent your summons to have a bowl, and he would rarely call you by your name. It was almost a throwback to the gentlemen and players era. Even then he was a veteran – I earned three caps, he earned caps over three years – and international star in the waiting.

There were others like Belly, too, among our group – players who were ahead of their time as teenagers, and touted nationally as the next big things before they had played a senior match – such as the Durham duo Gary Pratt, whose claim to fame was to run Ricky Ponting out in the 2005 Ashes, and Nicky Peng. Matt Prior and I often reminisce about those days. There would be thirty to forty players gathered at a national trial day for the England Under-17 or England Under-18 teams and this select trio would be the targets for pointing fingers, knowing nods and general chat.

'That's Ian Bell over there,' you'd hear lads say, in a tone you suspected young Australians spoke about Don Bradman three-quarters of a century earlier.

'He's quite a player that Nicky Peng, ain't he?' another would pipe up.

Some players naturally develop quicker than others, and Matt and I were playing catch-up, although we were good enough to be selected for the England Under-17 B team that played a match down at a Siberian Abergavenny in 1999.

It was the first time I saw what has subsequently become Matt's odd obsession. He has always been particular about his appearance on the field, and so when the brand new England caps were handed out by the coaching staff, he took it upon himself to ensure each one was perfectly presented. Such is his devotion to him and his team looking smart, that you can still find him sitting in the corner of the dressing room during quiet periods of international matches, bending the peaks so that they are all unquestionably the perfect shape. The curvature has to be precise and he is so anal about this when a new player is called up that he requests to complete the moulding process before they wear it outdoors.

In comparison to some of my peers, I had limited experience, and was therefore thankful for the support of Martin and Chapple as well as senior men like Warren Hegg and Neil Fairbrother during my breakthrough into senior cricket with Lancashire. When I made a decent start to the 2002 season in the second team – including best figures to date of 8 for 54 in the first innings of a draw against Northamptonshire at Crosby – my reward was a County Championship debut against Surrey at Old Trafford on the final day of May.

The first of my four wickets was Ian Ward, caught behind, and they also included Mark Ramprakash, lbw to a yorker first ball in the second innings. Unlike the previous September for my one-day bow in Derby, I was shitting myself in the build-up to this one. There were no nerves against Derbyshire because it was the equivalent of a token appearance. There was nothing to play for, it was a dead rubber and whatever happened there was slightly irrelevant. It was not as if I was performing to retain my place. It was the final game of the season, there was a winter ahead of me in the knowledge that I had made the staff for 2002, so I didn't get so worked up about it.

This was different, though. This was a serious opportunity to impress and as something of a perfectionist I put pressure on myself. Like I say, if something is worth doing, it's worth doing properly. That's my motto.

I clearly did enough against quality opposition to earn further chances, and although I played only one Championship game before July, I was a regular at the back end of the 2002 season. One of my first games was a televised Roses match in which I got a five-wicket haul in the first innings, and two more plus the run-out of Matthew Elliott in the second. We lost the game but from a personal point of view it was memorable. So was the season as a whole, and made especially so by a gesture from Warren Hegg at the very end.

It was the final day of the final match, against Somerset at Taunton, and we had the home team nine wickets down. Hegg, who was captain, knew I had forty-nine first-class victims for the year and made a point of bringing me back on for one final spell. It was a really nice gesture, a touch of class. Thankfully I completed my half-century, and the team's victory, by prising out last man Simon Francis.

There were mentors aplenty for me in that team, in fact, and I will always be grateful to those team-mates who looked after me during my first season. Martin and Chapple would always be available to talk to about bowling, while Neil Fairbrother, at first slip, and Heggy, behind the stumps, were never short of advice. More often than not it was to stop trying to swing the ball, a skill I had been working on with Mike Watkinson over the past twelve months, just get it down the other end as fast as I could. They didn't want me to overcomplicate stuff and just told me: 'Bowl as quick as you can, forget everything else.' I had that youthful elasticity shared by a lot of young fast bowlers when they break on to the scene, and although I was developing my outswinger, their attitude was very much to simplify things during matches. If the ball shaped away then great, if it didn't then I had enough pace to pose batsmen serious problems.

4

England Calling

Even though I was now a fully fledged county cricketer, it had been such a whirlwind start to my career at Lancashire that I had barely stopped for breath, or certainly to stop and think about my debut season – which amounted to a baker's dozen of first-class matches – when I was called on to the England academy programme that winter.

Mike Watkinson, Lancashire's cricket manager, presented me with a letter from Lord's informing me of my selection. I was naturally apprehensive about the trip to Adelaide as I had not previously been away from home for such a long time nor travelled so far but the presence of my team-mate Kyle Hogg proved something of a relief and I went on to thoroughly enjoy the experience. I was settling in rather nicely among the rest of the lads, in fact, when Nigel Laughton, the team manager, came up to inform me that I had been called up to the senior squad. We had just moved to Canberra, it was two days before the academy's first competitive match of the tour, and given that we had literally just unpacked, I considered this was some kind of wind-up.

Playing a trick on the youngest lad is not so out of the ordinary in cricket teams, after all, and some of the senior Lancashire lads had got me only a few weeks earlier on an end-of-season golfing event. Graham Lloyd had offered to drive me up to Gleneagles, and just as we were about to set off from his house, he checked whether I had got my passport.

'What do I need a passport for?' I asked.

'Well, we're going to Gleneagles, aren't we?' he said, in unison with Ian Austin, who had also turned up at his gaff to cadge a ride. 'Yes.'

'And Gleneagles was in Scotland last time anyone checked.'

Of course, naivety won the day and I was on the phone to my mum within seconds, asking her if she could dig it out for me.

'What on earth are you on about?' she asked. 'I think someone's having you on, James.' Cue roars of laughter, and the slapping of thighs. Oh, how we japed.

In subsequent years I have been told stories that some officials at Lancashire even believed England had mixed myself and Kyle up, and picked the wrong one. You see, I'd featured almost exclusively in four-day cricket in 2002, and had only five wickets in three one-day matches to my name by that stage, whereas Kyle had been quite successful. But that is certainly not something that I was ever aware of; and why would I care whether other people were surprised by my inclusion? I was throwing stuff back into my suitcase and heading off to Sydney to join England's Ashes squad.

In one way I was sad to be leaving the academy lot, as it was a really good group that showed its true colours with the number of other lads who were genuinely pleased for me. Gordon Muchall, of Durham, was my room-mate, and it was a fairly young collective, some of whom I had played alongside for England Under-19s. Darren Stevens, then in his late twenties, was the oldest.

One of the things that was good about that tour coinciding with the Ashes was that there were always different players flying in and flying out. Because of the number of injuries, it meant we had people from the academy joining the full tour, moving this way or that. Andrew Flintoff was on his crutches for a while, and Simon Jones came to us before he went home following the horrendous injury he incurred in the first Ashes Test in Brisbane. It meant as a new guy on the scene I got to meet quite a lot of new people, and I actually enjoyed that part of things, although you always wish your meetings could occur in better circumstances.

One thing that hadn't really sunk in, though, until Nigel pulled me over for a quiet word, was that I was part of the group identified as next in line to play for England. There were so many good bowlers on board – Chris Tremlett, Kabir Ali and Alex Tudor – that even if I had considered myself one of the next cabs off the rank, I would have expected others to get the first fare. Of course, now with experience of the clearly defined hierarchical structure the England and Wales Cricket Board (ECB) has in place, it is fairly obvious that we were the understudies to both Test and one-day teams.

But the academy system was still in its infancy. We were only the second intake and although it is now par for the course when you get picked in an England Lions team that you are being groomed for international cricket (you are usually in the same country or pretty close by and shadow the full team's programme in terms of fitness, nutrition and skill drills), it was fairly fresh back then. So even though I was in Australia, on the team's doorstep, I never once felt like I was there because I was next in line.

Unsurprisingly, the England captain has some influence on a tour as to who gets called up, and at the time Nasser Hussain had never seen me bowl a ball. Thankfully, however, he was quite close with Ronnie Irani because, as the story goes, or at least the way a certain former Lancashire and Essex all-rounder tells it, it was Ronnie's influence that got me in. We had played against each other earlier that year, and Ronnie, who was in that one-day party in Australia, had a word or two in Nasser's ear when the list of injured fast bowlers lengthened to include Darren Gough, Simon

Jones and Chris Silverwood. In addition, Andrew Flintoff had failed to recover properly from a hernia operation.

'This is unbelievable,' I thought as I checked into my room at the Sheraton on the Park in Sydney. I'd never stayed in a hotel like it before. It was as plush as you could imagine, and, to cap it all, there was a box of England shirts in the corner. Not any old England shirts. They were *my* England shirts. I just sat on the bed, speechless – no big deal since I still wasn't very talkative in those days – considering how incredible this all felt.

It was not until the next morning at practice that I met everyone, and it felt totally surreal because there were some guys who I had spent so much time watching on TV as I'd grown up. Here were people like Alec Stewart and Nasser Hussain introducing themselves to me. It took quite a while for me to get used to that.

I was not selected for the opening match against Australia at the SCG, but much to my shock I *was* picked for the second at the MCG just a couple of days later. When I'd arrived and thumbed through that England kit in my Sydney hotel room, I'd made a pact with myself to cherish every minute. Even then I don't really think I had factored in the possibility that I would be anything more than a last resort if every other bowler fell over or fell ill. But here I was on 15 December 2002, making my international debut.

I spoke few words in that first week as an England tourist. As you will have gathered now I don't find social interaction straightforward with strangers, so I really only talked when addressed by others. In that situation hiding my nerves was easy but there were plenty of them, I can assure you.

My memory of my international debut is all the more vivid for the torrent of horrendous abuse I received from large sections of the 34,000 Melbourne crowd. Granted, because I didn't have a name on my shirt, I was something of an easy target. 'Where've they dug you up from then?' 'Too embarrassed to admit you play for England, what's-your-name?' 'Hey pal, you're anonymous like your bowling.' They weren't likely to pass up the opportunity of getting stuck into some fresh English meat, especially a 20-year-old piece they'd never heard of before.

This was my first experience of Pommie-bashing and it proved an interesting baptism. I copped loads but all I concentrated on when I was down at fine leg was walking in when the ball was bowled, and then walking backwards, never facing the mob, or even turning in the slightest to do so, back to my fielding position.

For a wide-eyed boy from Burnley that was not necessarily the most intimidating factor of my England bow. More scary than that was that I was now competing against guys that I'd also become accustomed to watching on TV. Standing somewhere between me and those stumps twenty-two yards away were Adam Gilchrist, Matthew Hayden and Ricky Ponting – three of the best batsmen of all time.

It was a hard game first up for me. I claimed Gilchrist as my first international wicket, a drag on from a wide half-volley. However, not for the first time, nor the last for that matter, Australia inflicted a heavy defeat on England but although my figures of 6-0-46-1 were far from flattering, and I had obviously gone for more runs than I would have liked, I walked away from my debut pleased that I had not been overawed and reflecting that I'd actually done okay.

By Christmas 2002, I had played as many one-day internationals as I had one-day games for Lancashire, taken five wickets, and been involved in not one but two England wins. Both came against Sri Lanka, the third team in the triangular VB Series.

We played them twice within seventy-two hours, and, no disrespect to them, because they were a good side, but facing anyone other than Australia provided some respite. We probably caught them a bit cold in the first encounter in Brisbane, and defended a target of 293 comfortably under the lights. Sanath Jayasuriya was my second international wicket, deceived by a slower ball.

Three days later, we were thrust into battle again in Perth on a typically bouncy WACA pitch that gave us another distinct advantage. I was at the crease in the final over of the innings when Paul Collingwood got his first international hundred, and this time our victory margin was even greater. My return of 2 for 23 from eight overs was my best yet.

These two games gave me a good deal of confidence. If my debut series had been exclusively against Australia, things might have felt slightly different for me. Undoubtedly, I would have found that more difficult to cope with. But as I prepared to fly home for Christmas – the Ashes tour was a weird split that year with a chunk of one-day games wedged in between the third and fourth Tests – I knew that I could not have made much of a better start to my England career.

I had clearly made an impression on the England hierarchy, too, because coach Duncan Fletcher asked me to stay out there for the conclusion of the Test series rather than head home for a few days. Unfortunately, however, returning to the UK was non-negotiable for me. My grandma Doreen had been diagnosed with cancer while I was at the academy, and given only weeks to live. She passed away while I was in Australia. When I received the news, I told my family that I would be coming home, but they persuaded me to stay on. Instead, they waited for me to come back before having the funeral – so I was determined to spend that Christmas with them. I didn't even consult my mum and dad about the subsequent offer to stay on for the final two Tests. There are times when your nearest and dearest come first, and this was one of those for me.

As I packed my suitcase to return home, I paused for a moment to look at my England gear. Just over six months earlier, it had been a thrill to play in a second XI Championship match alongside a former international Neil Fairbrother, who was coming back from injury, and now here I was confronted by my very own England attire. Once it becomes the norm, it loses some of its magic, but at the time it filled me with wonder. One of the moments I will never forget is Phil Neale, our long-serving operations manager, walking up to hand me my first England helmet. The feeling was incredible. I treated it like a prized possession for those first few months, whereas nowadays I get through them like loose change because they get clunked, mangled or lost.

My return flight got me back to Sydney in time to see in New Year 2003, and I trained with the other one-day specialists at club grounds around the city while the final Ashes Test took place. Confidence boosted by my 2 for 48 in Brisbane and 2 for 23 in Perth, I was excited rather than daunted by the resumption of VB matches against the Australians. Down in Hobart I maintained my run of picking up a couple of wickets every game, this time claiming the scalps of Gilchrist and Ponting inside the opening half-dozen overs in a match that we really should have won. We were 165 for 0, chasing 272 to win, but somehow conspired to lose by seven runs.

Despite losing to Australia consistently, we began to push them closer in the new year, and the fact that we picked up another bonus point in defeat in Adelaide meant we qualified for the best-of-three-finals ahead of Sri Lanka. That prospect did not look likely when we made only 152 but we managed to take their chase beyond the required forty-over mark to secure the point, and, when they were 104 for 6, with Michael Clarke, on debut, together with Shane Watson, it looked as though we might even overturn their established hold on us.

It was a day-night match on one of the hottest days South Australia had experienced in years, and the Adelaide Oval pitch was extremely dry. It was still ferociously hot – even as the sun was going down around 6.30 p.m. it was something like 40 degrees – as I took the new ball. At the time I didn't think about the temperature a great deal, preferring to concentrate on the job in hand.

I bowled a lot of cutters across the left-handers at the top of the Australian order and although I didn't rip them out, I enjoyed the rhythm I was in. They barely took a run off me, and Nasser just kept me on, checking if I could manage one more every over towards the end, for my full allocation in one burst. My spell of 10-6-12-1 equalled the most economical completed analysis for an England bowler in a fifty-over international, matching the number of runs Ian Botham conceded in a World Cup match against Pakistan on the same ground eleven years earlier.

When you have a low total on the board to defend, but are keeping things tight, it is just a case of keeping going and physically I felt fine. If I had been tiring Nasser would have whipped me out of the attack, and there are certain times when a good captain's skill comes in and he saves a form bowler for a bit later on. In this situation, though, there was a chance there might not be a bit later, and so I needed to keep up the pressure for him and the team. One of the things I've always endeavoured to do is produce a consistency of performance, so that I always bowl as well in the final session or at the end of an innings as I did in the first or at the start. It was only later, after my spell was over, that the conditions took their toll on me. Feeling light-headed, I asked to go back to the dressing room for a sit-down, and never made it back on to the field.

Despite Australia's dominance, and four-year unbeaten hold over us in one-dayers, we actually retained a chance of winning my first series for England until deep into the second of the best-of-three finals. Although we were obliterated in the first final at the SCG, where the Australians took only seventy-four balls to knock off their 118-run target, and did so without losing a wicket, we let a very good position slip badly in the second in Melbourne.

In what was Andrew Flintoff's first game back after a lengthy injury lay-off, we came back strongly from that heavy defeat two days previously, and were on the cusp of victory. Chasing 230, we needed fourteen runs off the final three overs with four wickets in hand and with Fred on strike. But Brett Lee swung the game back their way in dramatic fashion when he bowled him with his first ball back. Lee proved ridiculously fast that day and the ball was scuffed up and looked dark under the lights. I certainly struggled to pick it up when I went in with five balls and six runs required. We lost by five!

Despite feeling personal satisfaction at the start of my international career, however, I did not feel settled. Good performances tend to make others more accepting of you but although I felt terrifically backed by Nasser, the captain, and didn't dislike anyone, I felt that first England team I played for was particularly difficult to integrate into. Admittedly, on the one hand my reserved nature prevented me from pushing myself forward but, on the other, it was not a very welcoming dressing room to outsiders. Whereas these days a lot of work goes into trying to make it a really comfortable environment to walk into, almost the opposite was true back then. Not much work went into that at all. If any.

That was probably something to do with the personnel within the squad. People like Nick Knight, Alec Stewart, Andy Caddick and Darren Gough had all played a lot of international cricket, and appeared to be fully consumed by their own agendas. Now I am not saying for one minute that there was any hostility towards new faces – there certainly was not – it was probably because these players were all so familiar with the international scene, and got on with their own daily routines – cricketers are creatures of habit, after all – but I felt ignored and left to fend for myself in their company. None of them went out of their way to talk to me, put it that way.

Then, when Caddick broke rank to do so after one match, the tone and context of what he had to say shocked me.

'I'm so glad that there's someone coming through that can fill my shoes because I didn't think there was anyone who could,' he told me.

Even as a raw 20-year-old I was shocked that someone could think in that way, let alone say it. His comments were certainly more a reflection of his own ability than a compliment to me, and

I am not sure why an established international cricketer in his thirties wanted to big himself up like that. Perhaps it was because so many players in that group were detached, insecure, aloof.

On that particular tour, there was hardly any mixing. You formed a little social group and stuck together for the whole trip, something I reflect upon with regret. It is the kind of cliquey behaviour outlawed today by the England team under Andy Flower and Alastair Cook. Under their management, spending the entire time with the same group as I did – Adam Hollioake, Ian Blackwell and Gareth Batty – would not have been permitted. Batts knew Adam, who had just been recalled to the England one-day squad mid-tour, from their time together at Surrey, and I suppose our little quartet was one of outsiders. We spent a lot of evenings together, going for dinner and just generally hanging out.

These days, you really could end up going out with anyone from the squad. Things have become a lot more inclusive, so that someone will announce 'I'm off to the Gallery Café tonight to eat, who fancies it?' A few will say yes, and then those who have said no will either have room service or discuss going somewhere else with each other. It's all fairly relaxed, and although you do tend to hang around with some people more than others, there is a good deal of mixing and you will almost be guaranteed to be out with every other member of the team over the course of a week or so. In comparison, in 2002–3, you might not have spent time with certain guys throughout the entire trip.

I am not sure the lack of invites from others that winter was particularly great for Blacky, who I got to know a little bit during our time at the academy. For one, the result was he had to put up with my company 24/7. Secondly, I am a bloke who can eat anything and not put on weight (*disclaimer – correct at time of going to press in case of developing lardy tendencies and fast bowler's arse in my thirties*). Unfortunately, the same couldn't be said for him. He tends to pile on the pounds.

It was like Groundhog Day, particularly once we were parted

from Batts and Smokey, who were not selected for the World Cup in South Africa. 'We'll watch a film and get room service again then, shall we?' We became like an old married couple, although others like James Kirtley would join us from time to time.

Forget the fact I was playing for England at cricket: I was also an Olympic-standard trougher, and so I would order big steaks, burgers, whatever I fancied, and Blacky thought nothing of ordering the same thing, or something similar. After all, if one England cricketer was eating what he liked when he liked, why shouldn't another? He was a pretty laid-back character, not the gym's greatest fan and one who believed it took all shapes and sizes.

An issue developed with his fitness that winter when he got heavier while on England duty, and the price he paid in the long term was that he was overlooked. To be fair to him, he adhered to the fitness regime he was set during the winter of 2002–3. I saw that for myself. Some people have to eat salad and train three hours every day to lose weight, and Blacky was one of those. But as they say, real men don't eat salad.

If you look at him now playing for Durham he is in his absolute element. There is not that extra pressure on him to lose weight – which is something he had to contend with at Somerset – they just let him play as freely as he wants. Without being forced into it, he turned up at Chester-le-Street that winter 10 kilos lighter, and contributed massively to back-to-back Championship seasons. There has been considerable success: he's got hundreds in Championship cricket, has opened for them in one-day cricket and has always been a solid left-arm spinner in both forms.

I've kept in touch with Blacky via text – I'll send him a congratulatory message and vice versa – although he was pretty unfriendly towards me with the bat on one of my last visits to the North East with Lancashire, smacking me for a big six.

To someone as quiet as I was, he was a massive help during my first six months with England. He was always good company and a lot closer to my age than the majority of that squad. When I see people on the commentary scene now like Nasser Hussain and Alec Stewart, they're fine, but as southern elder statesmen ten years ago they were quite different from a 20-year-old Lancastrian lad, so I was grateful for Blacky and James Kirtley, who I also found very helpful from a cricket perspective. He might not have played a lot for England at the time but he was quite an experienced county bowler, and he was very willing to pass on any knowledge he could.

While Kirtley was good for tips on bowling in one-day cricket, Duncan Fletcher worked a hell of a lot with me on my batting in those early days. One of his big things as coach was to try to eke out as many runs as possible from the tail-enders, so he spent considerable time trying to improve technique and working on individual game plans.

Duncan was pretty supportive of me in those early days – asking me to stay on in Australia over Christmas was a positive sign – and it was pretty evident to me from an early stage that if you worked hard, and spent time in the gym, he was fine with you. Nor was I likely to upset any apple carts in the dressing room. I wasn't a big voice, never kicked up a fuss, so he was fine with me from that perspective, too. In fact, despite his well-documented frostiness with others, I cannot really recall having an issue with Duncan in my first period of international cricket.

Despite the fact that we were there for a World Cup, I hadn't really thought about our chances when we landed in South Africa that February. Not that I was being selfish; I was simply concentrating on getting the best out of myself, enjoying every minute of my experience because at that stage I had no idea how long it was all going to last. After all, I had come in as an injury replacement in Australia and it was in my head that as soon as the other guys were fit again, that would be it and I would be off. Last in, first out and all that.

With that in mind, I was determined I should enjoy it for what it was. I certainly never got as far as envisaging us winning the

World Cup, or anything like that. I love playing cricket and this was a dream come true so I didn't think too much about anything beyond performing to my best every minute I was out there, no matter how many South Africans or Aussies were shouting abuse at me.

Things started off pretty well for me in that tournament, with a man-of-the-match award for four new-ball wickets against the Netherlands, and, following the defeat of another minnow, Namibia, I was to enjoy the most incredible experience of my England adventure to date. The night in question came in Cape Town, in what proved to be perfect conditions for us.

It was the group match against Pakistan in which Shoaib Akhtar clocked a delivery of 100 mph to Nick Knight. Understandably, I was just relieved I didn't have to go in and bat. Then, under the lights, it started hooping around big time and it was an incredible atmosphere as Pakistan slipped to 17 for 3 in their chase of 247 with yours truly inflicting the damage. After Shahid Afridi had one waft too many at Andy Caddick, I dismissed both Inzamam-ul-Haq and Mohammad Yousuf first ball: Inzamam caught at third slip and Yousuf bowled by a perfect outswinger.

Once again, I bowled my ten overs in one spell, and during the penultimate one I doubled my haul by sending back Saeed Anwar and Rashid Latif. The support we received at Newlands was sensational and what made it all the more special was that this was the first game for England that my dad, uncle, grandad and cousin saw me live. I never knew their whereabouts in the ground but just the knowledge that they were there was enough for me.

Not that I could have picked them out in the sea of brightly lit faces. I was fielding at fine leg, in front of a temporary stand, crammed full of English supporters, from which emanated an incredible noise. Goosebumps covered me at the end of every over as I walked back towards them for another standing ovation. It had been a really solid start to our campaign but the fact that we had forfeited the 13 February fixture against Zimbabwe in Harare nine days earlier meant it had to be to give us half a chance of progressing to the next stage.

We had been due to start our tournament in the Zimbabwean capital but debate over whether an England team should compete in an international match at a time when Robert Mugabe's deplorable regime was at its most barbaric had been raging as far back as my initial call-up for an England squad. In Britain, MPs were lobbying for us to boycott the match but no such instruction from government was forthcoming.

So we spent the week after the opening ceremony in Cape Town in meeting after meeting about what we should do. It was a horrific experience. I had no idea what was going on, and hadn't that kind of thing in mind when I'd signed up to play top-level cricket. Sitting in rooms for hours on end, debating the whys and wherefores of whether we should go to Harare or not was not what I thought it was about. All I remember thinking was 'why are we being asked to decide?' Weren't we supposed to be the ones who did the bidding on the pitch? Weren't there others who should be deciding for us?

In those initial days in Cape Town, we would head off to practice then have a meeting with someone or other afterwards that would drag on for hours. Meetings as a team, meetings with the Professional Cricketers' Association (PCA), meetings with the International Cricket Council (ICC), meetings with security experts. By the end of it our heads were full of so many different stories, so many different opinions, it was hard to know what to think.

I was full of admiration for Nasser Hussain in all this. This was the kind of situation where he showed himself to be a particularly good leader of men. He was of the opinion that we were his players, and that meant both on and off the field. He wanted to take charge, and stood up to an awful lot on our behalf against our own bosses at the ECB, and the ICC who insisted politics should not and could not come into the equation. However, unfortunately cash was also a motivation. At one stage we were asked by our bosses to think of the consequences for the English game if we did not go and the ICC imposed heavy fines as a result. Only later, after it became apparent there was a strong desire to scratch the fixture did the focus alter to trying to negotiate a share of the points rather than hand Zimbabwe a walkover.

I basically sat there while all this played around me. One of the reasons that younger guys in the current England team are made to speak out is so they become, and feel, involved, and are not afraid to do so when there are decisions to be made. But there were so many strong voices raised in these discussions – whereas I'd played only a handful of games, was still only twenty and was a quietish fellow – that I let others do my bidding. I just wanted to go about the business of playing cricket, which is what I thought I was there for. But I was quite clear that we shouldn't go, and in one respect I was lucky because a number of senior players spoke out who communicated exactly what I thought about the situation. When we finally sat around a table and were asked individually whether we wanted to go, I said no.

Confirmation of my own thoughts, if any were needed, came in the form of the death threats we received. These letters threatened those close to us. Although they were later discredited by some, when you have someone writing 'you will be safe out there but how safe will your families be back in England?' it certainly makes you think twice. My reaction was 'why are we even discussing this?'

Matthew Hoggard was affected by it as much as anyone, and became quite emotional about things, concerned about his wife Sarah's wellbeing. Even after the ICC got their security people to come in and inform us that these letters, from a group calling themselves The Sons and Daughters of Zimbabwe, were not authentic, not from a credible organization, and that we should ignore them, we felt we could not. How were we to know what these people were or weren't capable of? To me, the fact they had written them in the first place highlighted they were pretty angry.

We spent a lot of time as a group and with Richard Bevan, of the PCA, and he was of the opinion that we shouldn't go. That feeling was pretty strong around that table by the end of the week in question.

Once the decision to scratch had been made, there was no naivety from us about the task ahead. It was going to be tough to get to the Super Sixes stage but we vowed not to use it as an excuse if we exited the competition prematurely.

Three wins from three proved a good start but India smashed us in Durban – Ashish Nehra's six wickets simply blew us away – which meant we would have to overcome the Australian hoodoo to get through.

We faced the reigning champions on a slow surface at St George's Park in Port Elizabeth and adapted well to the conditions. Just as in the VB Series, however, we fell short at the death despite dominance for long periods of the contest – this time a record unbroken stand for the ninth wicket between Michael Bevan and Andy Bichel denied us.

Australia had been 114 for 7, needing ninety-one runs from 18.1 overs, when Brad Hogg was out and required 70 from 12.2 overs when Brett Lee was run out. Expertly, Bevan, the master finisher of the one-day scene, and Bichel, one of the game's great fighters and buoyed by seven wickets earlier in the day, chipped away at the requirement, until with twenty-three runs needed from twenty-four balls, Nasser brought me back into the attack.

I kept my cool and went for only three from my first five deliveries, but Bevan managed to nick three from my final one. Things remained tense, and after Ashley Giles went for just three from the next over, Nasser had a big decision to make. Either stick with me, or hand the ball to 34-year-old Andy Caddick, who had figures of 9-2-35-4 and whose new-ball spell had left the Australians 48 for 4. History shows that he chose me.

With thirteen required from eleven deliveries, my attempted slower ball was wiped into the electronic scoreboard by Bichel. It was a blow that pretty much sealed the game for Australia and in the aftermath of the two-wicket defeat I was absolutely devastated. Afforded time for reflection, however, I considered the positive aspect of Nasser plumping for me even though he had an over from an experienced bowler like Caddick up his sleeve. Whether it was Caddick not fancying it, or Nasser not fancying him to bowl it, I don't know, and nor did that matter; what did was that he had chucked the ball to a 20-year-old with only a few games behind him. Nasser was an established England captain and he had shown faith in me to do the job, so after getting over the initial disappointment I considered it a real feather in my cap.

It was certainly an experience that helped me in the future but there and then all I wanted to do was get back home and see my family. I had not been back to Burnley for a while, and it was straight down the cricket club when I arrived. It was always a big influence on me, and it was full of friends only too pleased to raise a glass and toast my success.

In contrast to now, that was not something that the England team of ten years ago did. We celebrated beating Pakistan in Cape Town with a few drinks but there was no sense of the team coming together. These days, after a victory, as long as the window of opportunity is there, we will organize to meet up at a designated time in the hotel bar, and everyone has to be there. Afterwards you can do what you want but for half an hour or so you all come together, and reminisce about the game.

5

Rise and Fall

'He never does that when I ask him to,' chuntered Nasser Hussain, as he hobbled back into the away dressing room at Old Trafford in early May 2003.

Seconds earlier, I had struck him flush on the boot with a yorker, the middle victim in my first senior hat-trick, in a County Championship match between Lancashire and Essex, the others being Darren Robinson and Will Jefferson. 'Typical Nasser,' I thought, when I found out what he'd said. His gentle grumpiness made me chuckle.

Of course, getting the England captain out gave me a bit of extra pleasure, but my relationship with him at that stage prevented me taking the mickey out of him to his face after play. It was a bit of a 'junior–senior pro' thing, and while I like nothing more than ribbing team-mates in a good-natured way, I have to be completely comfortable that the person in question likes me before I get into that kind of territory. Nowadays I would be unceremonious in my piss-taking towards him, and he loves that kind of thing, but it was almost like a schoolboy–headmaster relationship in those days.

What my performance that day undoubtedly served to do,

however, was tip the balance for me getting picked in the first Test team to face Zimbabwe the following week.

It was only after being named in the squad that it really hit me that I was now an England cricketer. Now back on home soil, I felt a weight of expectation, whereas abroad throughout the winter I had not considered any to exist. When you are abroad you don't tend to think about the reaction your performances are getting back in the UK. You don't have the British newspapers out there, in those days online versions were few and far between, and Twitter wasn't even a twinkle in Jack Dorsey's eye.

Somehow on our own turf things felt different. Even if you ignore what is written about you, your mum and dad read everything and relay it faithfully, good or bad. Not that what was being written about me was negative. Exactly the opposite, in fact. Because I had done well, I was having my case backed by all and sundry, and that brought added pressure. And the public were expecting things of me, too.

I appeared to do my best to douse those expectations when my first over in Test cricket went for seventeen. I started with a no-ball, and got hit for three fours by Dion Ebrahim, who kept tucking me off his pads gleefully due to the absence of a fine leg. Nasser had set my field and typically of him proved extremely apologetic about things at the end of the over.

That, combined with the fact that things couldn't possibly get any worse, had a settling effect on me but, although I got a wicket in my third over, bowling Mark Vermeulen, it was the only loss Zimbabwe suffered on the second evening as we struggled for breakthroughs as a team.

It was a different story the next morning, though, as the ball started swinging. I was in my element, and because I pitched the ball up, and the tail-enders kept trying to hit through midwicket, the dismissals looked really pretty. Mostly, they missed and I hit the stumps, which is a thing of beauty for any fast bowler. When they did get the outside half of the bat on it, it travelled into the slips. Following on, the Zimbabweans failed to take the contest into a fourth day.

We beat Zimbabwe in both Tests comfortably, as was expected, but the series against South Africa provided a much sterner examination of our credentials, and soon there was even greater focus on me. And not just because of the red streak I sported through my hair. Some suggested I was fond of creating some kind of image but that really was nothing like the truth. The truth was that I was a young lad, who was really into Arsenal, Freddie Ljungberg was one of my favourite players, and I just copied him. Simple as that.

If people only knew how uncomfortable I felt at an appearance for Vodafone in midsummer, and not only because my bright hairstyle clashed with the England sponsor's branding. This kind of thing was completely new to me, and, as I paused for breath in the pits at Silverstone, I considered: 'I can't believe this is happening.' These thoughts summed up how I felt about every little detail of the start of my international career.

It was during the build-up to the British Grand Prix, and I had been asked to do a photo shoot, which I cannot pretend was enjoyable. Everyone involved was pleasant enough but all the attention was still something new and made me feel slightly uncomfortable. Not only was there the usual struggle associated with meeting new people, to make matters worse, I was mildly star-struck by the others involved in the shoot.

Here I was, a 20-year-old, who twelve months earlier had been desperate but yet to make the grade with Lancashire, and now I was not only posing for pictures taken by professional photographers but posing for them alongside Formula One multiple-world champion Michael Schumacher, one of the most recognizable sportsmen on the planet, and someone who had a distinctive aura about him. This was water off a duck's back to him, no doubt, but by nature I found it more than a little intimidating.

The presence of my England team-mates Michael Vaughan and Alec Stewart alongside me hardly had a settling effect either. After all, I'd grown up idolizing them. After more than six months in the dressing room, I was still coming to terms with sitting among these kinds of people, as well as Graham Thorpe and Darren Gough.

At this time Vodafone sponsored both the England cricket team and the Ferrari Formula One team and we were looked after splendidly – it was a relaxed environment, a fun kind of day – yet I still found it quite hard work. Not that what I had to do was difficult. I bowled to Schumacher, and he smacked balls into his team's computer area, which produced the amusing effect of technicians scrambling all over the place in panic.

Here was a realization that as an England cricketer more would be expected of me than just running in to bowl or strapping my pads on occasionally to walk out for a bat. These public appearances were going to be part of my duty from time to time if I was to maintain my place in the team, so I needed to learn to handle them. Looking back, it was actually beneficial to get exposure to all that at such a young age, rather than have it when I was twenty-five or twenty-six, because it opened my eyes to what was required at the top level, and I am not sure I would have coped any better as a debutant at that age. This helped me get the period of struggle out of the way before my mid-twenties.

Back on the field of play, South Africa turned up under Graeme Smith, who was not much older than me yet was already captain of his country, and began the series firmly on the front foot. On the opening day of the scheduled twenty-five in the series, the South Africans were 398 for 1, and Smith was close to completing the first of two double hundreds in consecutive matches. A new broom had swept through South African cricket after they were knocked out of the 2003 World Cup and we were about to experience the same thing.

When, after the drawn first Test at Edgbaston, Nasser stepped down as captain, and was replaced by Michael Vaughan, it was a bit of a bolt from the blue. Yes, Vaughan had been a big member of the side, a senior player, but it was still a bit of a shock that Nasser had gone. He had played such a big part in my fledgling career, and the unerring faith he showed in me meant I shall always be in his debt. I really enjoyed playing under him. Although we were different characters, with different backgrounds, from different eras, I understood him and even got his sense of humour – most of the time at least.

Occasionally he would let his frustration spill out with a kick of the turf or mutterings under his breath but despite that exaggerated animation from mid off I always got the distinct impression he wanted to get the best out of his team and to help his teammates improve. Of course, the way he went about that upset a few people sometimes but that is the lot of a captain – you can't please all of the people all of the time – and I did not have a bad word to say about him. I didn't play under him for that long but in the short time we did have he knew how to get the best out of me. And he made me want to do the best I possibly could for him.

Another significant change came after the heavy second Test defeat at Lord's. Darren Gough was struggling with injury and announced his retirement from Tests at the end of the match. I had become Goughie's new-ball partner in both forms of the game that summer but his departure led to numerous others walking through what seemed like a revolving door. James Kirtley was called up for the next Test at Trent Bridge, where I got another five-for, and he followed up with six wickets in the second when we defended a target of 200 comfortably on an up-and-down pitch.

There were five of us – including Andrew Flintoff – crammed into one team for defeat at Headingley, and, with Martin Bicknell recalled, I was asked to fulfil the unusual role of second change. Kabir Ali also played in that match.

Our bowling attack altered weekly during that series, and Fred and I were the only constants. It was during that summer that I got to know him a little better. The fact that there was another northern lad like me in the England side was quite comforting, although the strange thing was that I hardly knew him at all before the previous winter. Although we were both from Lancashire, it seemed that whenever I was playing he would be away on international duty. Then, at the time I was called up in Australia, he was absent through injury.

One of the things that sticks in my mind about our incredible series-levelling win at the Oval, a result achieved despite the South Africans scoring 484 in the first innings, was Fred hitting Makhaya Ntini for a straight six that smashed the dressing-room window. Now anyone familiar with the Oval will know just what a monstrously big hit that is. He was capable of some amazing feats on the field and that blow was part of an extraordinary assault on the fourth morning.

When Steve Harmison walked to the crease in the first over, we were narrowly in the lead on first innings but the next hour or so completely changed the complexion of the match, and, of the ninety-nine-run stand he shared with Fred for the ninth wicket, Harmy's contribution was precisely three. Marcus Trescothick was also in supreme form at the start of the innings, with a double hundred, and the momentum was never relinquished.

The Oval was a happy hunting ground for us that summer: in addition to the nine-wicket Test win with two sessions to spare, we also comprehensively defeated Pakistan and South Africa in one-day internationals there. The first of those matches thrust me into the record books as the first England bowler to take a hat-trick in an ODI, in finishing off the Pakistan innings.

However, having been the common denominator among the frontline bowlers in that drawn Test series, I felt really fatigued at the end of it. I was also struggling with a knee injury that I had remained determined to keep bowling through while the series was alive. It was especially bad in the middle match at Trent Bridge but my competitive streak, and the fact we sealed victory, kept me going.

By the end of the series I reckon I was down to bowling at around 80 mph. It's funny how your mind works as a young bowler, because even though I knew I wasn't as effective, I didn't want to get dropped. Uncertain whether it was a serious injury or not, I just kept going.

Statistically, my first home international season looked good. I was England's leading wicket-taker in each of the Test series I played, and claimed nineteen victims across nine NatWest Series matches against the South Africans, Pakistan and Zimbabwe. Upon its conclusion, it was an honour to be named the Cricket Writers' Young Player of the Year at an awards dinner in London.

But there were downsides to these exertions. Despite things appearing positive, I was fighting and losing two major battles. Firstly, with my bowling action and secondly with the damage to a tendon in my left knee, which kept me out of the tour of Bangladesh.

My chances of a Test recall were not helped by my own naivety during the tour of Sri Lanka in November 2003. Wet weather had decimated the one-day series: I got only four overs before the rain came in the solitary practice match and, as we managed only eighty-eight in the single ODI possible in Dambulla, I hadn't got a lot of bowling behind me there either.

With cricket activity limited, exercise had to be found else-where. I've always wanted to be active, and will play just about any sport going, so in downtime on tour I tend to keep an ear out for other people organizing games of tennis, squash or golf.

My stupidity was not in agreeing to play squash with James Kirtley on the eve of the first Test match in Galle, but to do so wearing inappropriate footwear. As I was getting ready to head down to the court at the hotel complex, I realized that I had left my trainers at the ground. *Nil desperandum*, I thought. I simply borrowed a pair of someone else's cricket shoes, which had rubber pimples on the soles.

Obviously, they weren't ideal for playing squash in. But I was sure they would do a job for forty minutes or so. In fact, they had served me for about that length of time when I slipped on a sweaty patch on the floor, turning my ankle in the process and causing possibly the worst pain I've ever experienced. It was just horrible. Like a shock had gone straight through me.

My entire body weight pressed down on my ankle as it went from under me, and I was left alone, writhing in agony, as James went to get Dean Conway, the team physio.

It requried both of them both to carry me back to my room. Because of the pain I knew immediately that I would be out for a while, and half expected a rollicking from Duncan Fletcher. Thankfully, one was not forthcoming. After all, all the lads play other sports from time to time, and playing squash is obviously good for improving fitness and agility. Needless to say, I didn't book a re-match in a hurry, though.

Some of my colleagues found it amusing that my chances of playing in the opening match of the series had been blown in such a clumsy way, and of course I found it absolutely hilarious. It was a good result for James, though, as he ended up playing the second Test in Kandy after the selectors opted to make changes.

Despite the joint swelling up something massive, I remained on tour as a scan confirmed no ligament damage. So it was a case of icing it regularly, and getting Dean to work on the sore area. I was soon to learn that the worst thing ever for any sportsperson coming back from injury is when the physio rubs the soft tissues to get any swelling down. That is always more painful than the initial damage itself, and Dean, a former rugby union prop, is a bloke who has got some strength behind him.

So despite not being able to walk, and thinking I was going to be on a plane home sooner than everyone else in the immediate aftermath of my fall, I actually discovered how amazingly robust ankles can be. My recovery meant I was available for the third and final Test in Colombo, although I didn't manage any wickets and we lost the game and the series, to complete what was a frustrating first half of the winter for me.

That was a rare outing for me, in fact, and my appearances became increasingly sporadic over the next couple of years. Although a perennial tourist, it felt like I hardly played at all. That was hard to take, but when you are young you tend to brush it off because you feel there is time on your side, and that being there means you are highly thought of.

But such belief soon wore thin. The truth was that, despite picking me in squad after squad, the England management never really had the confidence to play me over a lengthy period of time. That is certainly how it began to come across. I felt as though I wasn't really getting a fair crack, and that meant I sulked a lot. On the tour of the Caribbean later in 2003–4, I didn't play a game on the Test tour. The following winter, again I made the trip, this time to South Africa, but appeared just once when brought in from cold storage in Johannesburg.

With England caps so limited for me during this period, I made damn sure I enjoyed myself off the field. It was no coincidence that I developed great friendships with guys like Chris Read and Gareth Batty at this stage in my career, as they were also dwelling in a selection hinterland. As much as you say it's a team effort on tour, occasionally it's not; you can get brushed aside when you are twelfth man, second reserve, last resort, and we just tried to help each other through. Being part of a successful set-up was no antidote to being overlooked

Nor did it help that we were beating West Indies so convincingly in a Test series where Michael Vaughan's Fab Four fast-bowling attack clicked into gear. Being part of a successful set-up was no antidote at all.

Back then peripheral figures were just not important, which was quite hard to take. It was bad enough not to be playing but to be treated like a skivvy – 'get me this, get me that' – was not nice. The dynamic meant that if you were not part of the XI you did not feel part of the team; the coaches didn't really give you the time of day either, so a number of us felt in the same boat on tours around that period.

I would like to think that the whole business is more inclusive these days. There is a way of doing things properly and because most guys in our team have been twelfth man on several occasions, and been on tours where they have not played, they tend not to take the piss out of the lads who are doing menial duties for them. Our code of respect for each other means that we make a point of saying thank you for even the smallest tasks like receiving a drink while batting. From first-hand experience, I can say that that is not something that used to happen.

Whenever there is an inevitability that you will not be playing, you tend to look at life on the road differently. Whenever I go on tour now I am 100 per cent focused on the cricket but on those initial trips I would consider that if I didn't play the first game then I was not going to play at all during the entire series unless someone got injured. It meant you had a different focus. Instead of developing tunnel vision regarding the on-field challenges, of bowling to certain players or maintaining your level of performance, inevitably the mind turned to pursuits designed to make the time go quicker.

Don't get me wrong: you would always rather be picked in England squads than not, and, although we are away for marathon spells of time, we are handsomely rewarded for what we are asked to do.

Unfortunately, though, what I was being asked to do increasingly frequently during the course of my first four years as an England cricketer was to bowl at a cone or a single stump. It is indescribably frustrating to spend what feels like your entire life practising for something but never getting a chance at the real thing.

On tour there are so few warm-up matches that if you are not in the first-choice XI, you become a specialist net bowler. Net sessions provide your one chance to expend some energy but they get mind-blowingly tedious after a while, and defeat the object of practice in the end. In my opinion, unless you are doing drill work with a specific purpose, I don't see the point of it. I wasted a lot of time searching for that one perfect delivery during practice sessions with Troy Cooley, the then England bowling coach, before play, or during lunch or tea intervals. For what?

Sure, getting out on the ground makes you feel like you are doing something productive, and breaks the monotony of the day, but I was just getting through a workload for the sake of it. I would plough through mountains of overs trying to fulfil what was being asked of me but there was no endgame in sight. If you bowl with good pace or rhythm, even at one stump, you would hope that the bowling coach would report it back to the head coach. But I am not sure that ever happened.

If I am honest, there were times when it was not always obvious why I wasn't playing under Duncan Fletcher, and that simply added to my frustration. Again, as with other things, communication is something that is much better within the England set-up now than it used to be. If you are left out these days, you are free to go up and ask why it is the case. At the end of the day it is the coach's prerogative whether he tells you or not but generally you will get a reason.

In those days, the hierarchy viewed me as something of a work in progress, and the reason Troy spent so much one-to-one time with me on public display at matches, and in net sessions, was that he was perpetually remodelling my action. Troy was revered as a bowling coach for the work he did with England, particularly during the Ashes summer of 2005 when reverse swing played such a huge part in the success, but I was his one failure.

What people might not realize is that Troy first started analysing and altering my bowling action at the academy, even before I had made my England debut. He was the bowling coach there before being promoted to the full side and so the process of remodelling my action with him continued into my England career.

Later, when I lost form, quite a thing was made about this. Yet the action I had when I first pulled on an England shirt was different from the one I had playing in my last Championship game of the 2002 summer for Lancashire against Somerset at Taunton. Between September and December, Troy began implementing significant changes, concerned that I was going to get a stress fracture of my back. Ironically, it was only later in my career – after I had had one of those dreaded stress fractures – that I reverted to my natural action, and it coincided with a more productive period.

Troy's thinking was to make gradual alterations, primarily in my 'gather' as I hit my delivery stride. Ostensibly, my arm used to be up high when I loaded to release the ball but he wanted to get it down closer to my waist, and eventually to something similar to where Brett Lee's arm was at the same point. The theory was that doing this would increase my pace, accentuate the amount of swing I generated and decrease the chance of injury. Unfortunately, the hooping 90-mph thunderbolts never materialized, and, if anything, both my speed and ability to move the ball through the air dropped off.

If you watch footage from the summers of 2003 and 2004, you'll see that my load gets lower and lower, to a point where it is so low that it looks really uncomfortable and weird. That is exactly how it felt to me at the time. It was totally unnatural. Even when I got that hat-trick against Essex the week before my Test bow, my bowling felt horrible.

And that was the problem: I spent a huge chunk of my early career thinking about what I was doing with my action rather than what I was doing with the ball. You shouldn't be heading into international matches with those kinds of concerns in your head.

But I was young, and had only just played my first season of county cricket when Troy first got hold of me. Now if someone like Troy, with the reputation he had as a bowling coach, tells you that if you carry on in the same vein there won't be too many more seasons ahead because a stress fracture is inevitable, you listen. I have to say that at the time, when I was talked through the bio-mechanics of it, it all made sense, although with the aid of hindsight I have a different opinion now.

Troy's ploy was to alter my arm path, and in turn that led to my back moving in a different way – it was about lining my bottom half up with my top half, so that, rather than my legs being front-on and my chest being side-on, I was always aligned. The theory being that the stress upon the body on impact when landing would be reduced.

Never once have I considered that Troy acted in anything other than good faith but, as with a lot of kids who come through age-group cricket, if you have bowled a certain way over a number of years your body becomes grooved to it. When you try to change to something that does not come naturally, it can be a shock to your body. I had bowled a certain way since I was ten or eleven, I guess, and here I was ten years later, having reached the top of my trade, going against everything that had got me there in the first place.

Ironically, it was only after I had a stress fracture in the summer of 2006 that Mike Watkinson, my coach at Lancashire, and Kevin Shine, Troy's successor as bowling coach, planned my rehabilitation programme and suggested I went back to what felt most natural to me when I began bowling again. So now I am pretty much back to bowling how I did when I first started playing first-class cricket.

Throughout the period of change, I never did feel 100 per cent comfortable with things. My mind was probably in a similar state to that of Liam Plunkett, who also went through a remodelling of his action a year or two later. You run in to bowl, thinking about everything but the fact that there is a bloke down the other end you are trying to get out.

When things were going well, and I felt in good rhythm, I didn't think about it. But when things weren't going well, it always triggered the thought that something in my action must be wrong. But if someone is struggling like that, it is the bowling coach's job to step in and talk things through. I loved Troy and got on with him really well, and because he was so into his biomechanics, and the workings of bowling actions, we talked a lot about that. But I know now that if I had worked with David Saker, Ottis Gibson or Allan Donald at that impressionable age – someone who just concentrated on the ins and outs of the game itself – it would have been more beneficial.

There is time to work on your action and time to work on the game itself and overall I don't think Troy really helped me, even though it was his desired intention.

Because of the start I made to international cricket, my action became a subject of national debate, and I began to receive advice from all quarters. Well-meaning souls would write to me suggesting I try this or try that. Some even sent me photos of different bowlers throughout the ages.

It also led to commentators discussing it at length on television. Most of the focus, however, was on something that was never an issue for me, or for Troy for that matter. A number of people used to question how I knew where the ball was going if I was looking at the floor rather than down the pitch, but that was never a problem, was never going to be a problem and never will be one. I can understand why some might have thought it would be but, if I am being brutally honest, those people who undoubtedly know a lot about cricket don't necessarily know about the technicalities of bowling.

It became something that got blown out of proportion. Bob Willis even claimed I could not last five years in international cricket with an action like mine but Shaun Pollock did exactly the same, so did Jason Gillespie. I am back *au naturel* now and I still look at where I am going to bowl the ball right until the last minute when my head ducks for a split second, always coming back up in time to see whether the ball is hurtling back at me.

Such had been my decline that I started the famous 2005 summer out of the England picture. I hadn't been in the team in the lead-up to the series – things hadn't gone well for me at all out in South Africa the previous winter – so it wasn't as if I was surprised or upset not to be in the reckoning for the Ashes.

It was always going to be hard to break up the fabulous foursome of Steve Harmison, Matthew Hoggard, Simon Jones and Andrew Flintoff even if I displayed my very best form for Lancashire. The quartet first established themselves in the West Indies, complemented each other well and had been the backbone of the team that had won five consecutive series and lost just one match in the process.

So as much as it was a frustrating time for me, the most part of it on the sidelines, I didn't think about my ongoing omission in any negative way. Sometimes you feel that selection has been unjust when it goes against you but this was not one of those occasions.

Despite not being involved, however, I was as hooked on the Ashes as the rest of the nation. I played pretty much the whole season with Lancashire but the Ashes became such a big thing that talk in the dressing room would always turn towards what was happening and the television would get turned on whenever we got a chance.

Chris Tremlett was named in every one of the first four Test squads of that series, so that was fairly indicative of where I stood in the fast-bowling pecking order. But to my shock – because until that point I had not done that well for Lancashire – I was called in for the final Test, along with Paul Collingwood, after Simon Jones was injured.

My selection, it appeared, was based on the fact that I had played Test cricket before whereas Tremlett – who had played some one-day internationals that summer – hadn't. For a match like that they wanted a player with a little bit of experience rather than someone who might suffer from debut nerves. As a fast bowler, I was the attacking option, I guess, with Collingwood, a number seven batsman, being the more defensive alternative. So in the context of the series, with us 2-1 up and merely required to avoid defeat to reclaim the Ashes, it was perfectly understandable why they went for Colly in the end.

You could sense that the Ashes was a big deal everywhere you went, and the build-up to the finale had an amazing amount of media attention around it. I was there for only two days but the buzz around the practice sessions was tangible. You woke up in the morning and it was the first subject being discussed on breakfast television.

After I was released, I rejoined my Lancashire colleagues for a County Championship match against Essex. The TV was on permanently in the away dressing room at Chelmsford, and as soon as we came off for lunch we would be engrossed in the morning session's highlights.

It had been exactly the same wherever you travelled up and down the country that summer. Other teams were watching the Test whenever they were batting. If your thoughts weren't on your own game, they were with England and how they were doing. County cricketers were no different from the general public that summer; from men and women in offices, or kids holed up in their living rooms during school holidays or in the playground at break. Any spare minutes were devoted to a sneak peek or turning on the radio, or logging on to the Internet.

To be honest, it was with a sense of relief that I took my place among the millions of armchair spectators rather than be involved in English cricket's biggest match for decades because even though my competitive nature told me I wanted to get involved, the reality was that even in county cricket I was hardly pulling up any trees. My sixty first-class wickets in 2005 came at more than thirty apiece and I was not happy at all with how I bowled.

My game was absolutely all over the place, my head full of conflicting advice about how to rectify things. Coaches at Lancashire would tell me this, and people within the England set-up would tell me that. It was a difficult time for me to work out where my career was going, and, more importantly, whether it was ever going to get where I wanted it to be. Such was my disillusionment with the game that I was not bothered when, upon release from the squad, I drove out of the Alec Bedser Gate and headed for the A13 and county duty.

It was indicative of the fact that I would have had little confidence in delivering a decent performance in such an important contest. My belief was nowhere near as high as it could have been, and as it has been in subsequent years.

Others' uncertainty over my worth meant I was bypassed in the pecking order by Liam Plunkett for the Test tour of Pakistan a couple of months later, and my perennial struggle to establish myself as an England player took an ignominious twist in the one-day series that followed when the new ICC rules that permitted substitutes meant I got my name into the record books. Having played in the first of back-to-back games in Lahore, which we won, I was subbed out of the second before I'd even stepped on to the field.

I had been retained in the XI but after we slumped to around 100 for 5, just as I was focusing on my preparation for batting, I received a tap on the shoulder from Duncan Fletcher.

'Vikram's now playing,' he told me.

So it was Vikram Solanki and not me who walked out on to the Gaddafi Stadium outfield at the start of the thirty-first over with England 130 for 8. It was the most surreal experience. Everything had been as normal in preparation: I'd had a bowl before play, mentally switched on for the game, and had just started to think about putting my pads on.

Although Vik did get a few runs from an unfamiliar position of number ten, the change made us a bowler light and we were never going to defend a score of 230, Pakistan cruising home to level things with seven wickets and six overs intact.

However, the substitution fad worked in my favour for the final two matches of the series in Rawalpindi. Although I started as

supersub – not so sure what was super about it – for the penultimate match, I was in from the start after Pakistan won the toss and
elected to bat, with Ian Bell suffering the same fate I had a few
days earlier, this time from the very start of the match. The theory
behind naming a fast bowler as substitute was that you could
begin the match with a batting order of greater depth, and then
make an immediate change if you were asked to bowl first. On the
other side of the coin, if you won the toss, the extra batsman provided potential for extra runs.

This was the scenario in the series finale when Andrew Flintoff
was not fit enough to fulfil his usual role as an all-rounder, and was
named in the side as a specialist batsman. I came into the XI at the
halfway stage, after we posted 206, took the new ball and laid
claim to another record. I finished up with four wickets and was
named man of the match in a game that I had not originally been
supposed to play in.

I owed a lot of credit to Marcus Trescothick, who was captain-
ing that game, for this award, as he had shown an unerring belief
in my ability when things got tight at the death. I had nipped one
out with my new-ball spell but it was pleasing from my point of
view that I had been relied upon when the game was in the balance late on. Having dismissed both Shahid Afridi and Abdul
Razzaq in consecutive overs, it was still nip and tuck with Rana
Naved at the crease. And it was when Rana wiped a slower ball
into the stands for six that Tres showed his true worth.

It is important to keep your cool in such a situation but sometimes when the crowd is getting lively that is easier said than done.
Thankfully, what Tres did next completely settled me down, and
showed a distinct degree of confidence in me. I've always thrived
on being backed and I was enthused when, instead of walking
towards me kicking the turf, he said, 'Mate, that's brilliant!'

Not the response you might expect but I was all ears.

'Just bowl that same ball again but a little bit shorter and a little
bit wider,' he added.

I managed to deliver exactly what he recommended and the ball spiralled straight up in the air, and down Paul Collingwood's throat. It was an incredible piece of captaincy, and emphasized what great faith he had in my skills as a bowler. It left Pakistan's last pair needing sixteen off the final nine balls, and the game was ours.

I only played under him for a very short period but I considered Marcus to be an extremely astute captain and motivator. Captaincy is a role that tests individuals' communication skills and the biggest compliment I can pay him is that he got the best out of me on the few occasions I played under him.

Even before Tres was captain he gave me confidence because he displayed an outward impression that he rated me. Someone like Michael Vaughan, when he was among the rank and file, never gave off those kinds of vibes.

Vaughan was always unsure whether or not I was a good bowler. That much was pretty obvious. His assessment of me would have been something like: can bowl well at times but not overly convincing. Whereas Tres was always encouraging, to get the best out of me, something I believe I have always responded to. It was not an approach Vaughan took.

Of course, I was still a relatively young bowler during Vaughan's tenure but I do not believe age had anything to do with his opinion of me. And it is the younger players in a team rather than established senior ones who are most in need of backing by captains. Someone like Tres instilled confidence, and that had a positive effect when he was in charge. When you don't trust your game – as I didn't – you need that sort of backing and it was not something I felt again until Peter Moores took charge as England coach in May 2007.

6

Behind Every Good Man . . .

Other than with my sister Sarah, who is four years younger than me, I had virtually no social interaction with girls until I was sixteen.

It was at that point that I began sixth form, which at our school, in contrast to the first five years, was mixed. Although my junior school was co-educational, the boys would go off to St Theodore's, and the girls off to St Hilda's – and, if you were like me, into hibernation before re-emerging five years later.

Sarah and I got on like any brother and sister. She really knew how to wind me up, especially as the years went by, and it tested my patience something rotten. One day, when I was playing darts in my room, anger spilled over. I tried to throw a dart into the floor near her foot to give her a fright. Unfortunately, my accuracy was found wanting and the point plunged straight into her leg. It was absolutely horrible, and I can't imagine how much it hurt.

This love-hate sibling rivalry was just about the only relationship I had with anyone of the opposite sex prior to one particular Saturday night. The night in question being 21 August 2004. I had had only one serious girlfriend prior to this night – a night that would change my life.

Earlier, I had been part of an England side that had completed a ten-wicket victory over West Indies at the Oval inside three days, sealing a series whitewash and 100 per cent record in Test cricket that summer in the process. It was also the debut of Ian Bell, who I played with England at Under-19 level, and he and I were among a group that headed into central London that evening to let our hair down.

One of our crowd got chatting to a group of girls in a nightclub called Elysium, and one girl in particular caught my eye. As they came over to introduce themselves, I made sure I sat down next to her. I was mesmerized.

Now normally in a social situation like that I would be completely useless. Small talk with girls had never really been me. But add alcohol to the equation and I tend to loosen up with every sip, and on this occasion I was thankful that a resounding win had allowed for multi-sips. Enough of my inhibitions disappeared to allow some of my true personality to be revealed.

However, even allowing for me feeling uncharacteristically confident, Daniella still did all the talking that night. I pretty much gave yes and no answers to whatever she said, but obviously did something right because, when I woke up the next morning, I had her phone number in my back pocket. She was bowled over, she later told me, and to this day I am thankful for the fact that the mutual attraction outweighed the lack of a two-way conversation.

Daniella had absolutely no idea who I was, or who any of the other lads were for that matter. Not a clue. She later revealed, in her naivety, that she didn't realize cricket was a full-time profession and presumed that I had a real job as well! To her cricket was village greens, tea and scones on a Saturday afternoon. No more than a social pastime. She genuinely did not believe that it could be serious.

Not that the world of sport was completely foreign to her. After all, she appeared in a Reebok advert with Ryan Giggs in one of her early modelling jobs, and her late brother had played rugby union to junior international level.

Within our first couple of dates, I knew just about everything about Daniella. She talked, I listened. However, she was economical with the truth about one fact: her age. During our first meeting, she had asked how old I was, and when I told her I was twenty-two, she replied that she was twenty-five. The three-year age gap didn't bother me in the slightest. Nor does the fact that the actual gap is double that.

Daniella could tell that I fancied her but was more than a little taken aback that I had no real interest in chatting. Both my school and professional work environments had been very male-orientated, and us blokes don't do the chinwag thing as naturally as women, do we? I've always tended to think before I speak, whereas Daniella just blurts things out. She loves talking, and they do say opposites attract, don't they?

However, my vow of silence was not destined to last long, and when I was given an ultimatum on our third date, things needed to change. Either I opened up a bit, or that was that, Daniella told me. She was telling me every last spit and cough of her life, and getting very little back in return. Because our conversations were a one-way street, there was personal stuff that she told me about her past that she later admitted she regretted divulging. But every time there was a lull at the end of one story, whereas I would embrace a period of silence, she would begin to feel awkward and continue on to another subject.

Of course, because I liked her so much, her threat shocked me into action. She later said she recognized there was so much more to me, and that was the motivation to call my bluff. From my perspective, all I knew was that I liked being with her, and didn't want to reach the end of this road.

There were still hurdles to overcome, however, even accounting for me opening up to her over the next few weeks. You see, her friends thought this silent treatment signalled that I was rude, and

blatantly didn't like them. This caused a minor difference of opinion between us. My justification was that I was not one to talk for
the sake of talking, and would only do so when I had something
of meaning to offer. Daniella's conflicting view was that I possessed
a social tick that needed addressing.

Once again, I was so keen that I made a real effort, and Daniella
reckoned that in opening up a bit more she realized I was the one
for her. Over several weekends that autumn, she recognized the
emphasis in the quietly confident guy she was dating was changing from quiet to confident. That although I don't always give the
impression outwardly to strangers, I am very self-assured, not
short of opinions and will not be easily swayed.

Between the end of the 2004 domestic summer and the tour to
Zimbabwe and South Africa in November, I headed up to London
most weekends. Daniella was majorly into *The X Factor* at that
time, so our early dates revolved around Steve Brookstein's rise to
prominence. Remember him? Daniella would make a spaghetti
bolognese, and we would enjoy a few glasses of wine. My devotion
to her can be summed up not only by my sitting through that
inane Saturday-night telly but also the fact that I ate every last
morsel of her culinary creations despite the fact I despise onions
and mushrooms. I can't remember when I unleashed that latter rev-
elation upon her but I am guessing I waited until we were married.

In contrast to me, Daniella was fairly outgoing. So were her previous boyfriends, including Oasis frontman Liam Gallagher. She
was in on the London party scene, and as some of her mates ran
nightclubs, we would typically go off to the Wellington, or No. 5
Cavendish later on. This was a different world from the one I was
accustomed to, but Daniella encouraged me to relax a little bit
more.

After getting a few drinks down me, I would be okay around
her circle of friends but that initial hour, breaking the ice with
standard conversation, was habitually difficult for me. Neither can
it have been a barrel of laughs for Daniella, and one sentence stuck

with me throughout our weekends together: 'Look, if you don't start talking, that's it, I'm not going to see you again!'

Such was my desire to make things work with Daniella that I forced myself out of my shell as much as I possibly could, and in the longer term she has been a tremendous help in developing my confidence. I'd had a girlfriend at the age of sixteen but Daniella was my first one since then, and getting through those initial dates was crucial to my long-term happiness.

And it's fair to say that our relationship moved on apace within just three months. I have always been an impulsive person, and so I asked Daniella to come out on the England tour of South Africa over Christmas with the other wives and girlfriends. I am not sure she ever envisaged herself being swept away from her very successful life. Her career with Premier Model Management was one she loved; she was busy with shoots for department stores, for catalogues and for commercials; she spent weeks in various parts of the world, in New York, Milan and Paris; she earned exceedingly good money; she owned her own house in Kensal Green; she was independent but loved by lots of friends.

All in all, Daniella was pretty settled when I asked her to come and spend a fortnight with me over Christmas and New Year. It was not an easy decision for her, as she had an overseas job with a regular client in her diary. In the modelling world – one of the most fickle you will ever come across – turn down work and that's pretty much that. Once you've pissed someone off, you move to the back of the queue, and another girl moves to the front. On the back of her decision, gigs would inevitably dry up. If you show even the slightest inclination that you are not interested, that's how brutal it gets. So in agreeing to accompany me she was gambling with her future career.

But she knew that if she didn't follow her instinct, and decline the assignment, we would hardly see each other in the foreseeable future. I am not sure she was ever one to take risks but thankfully on this occasion she chose one – a flight to South Africa, and me.

There was an additional complication for Daniella, too, as her parents live in Spain and Christmas was an obvious time to go and see them. So she not only had to choose between me and her work but me – a bloke she had been dating for four months – and her family.

It was during that fortnight that I proposed. We went out for dinner one night to a steak restaurant called the Butcher's Shop and Grill in Sandton, Johannesburg, where the England team traditionally stays. It was only a short time since we had first met but I didn't just take a punt – 'This could be it, so I'll go for it' – we hit it off from the start, seemed to complement each other perfectly, and that was that.

My mum and dad got married when they were twenty and they always said they just knew it was right. They just knew – I always kept that with me. I just knew with Daniella, too.

I popped the question when we got back to our hotel room, after dinner. Being a romantic at heart, I was so well prepared that I didn't have a ring, asked on the spur of the moment and failed to get down on one knee. As a bloke, I naturally considered the spontaneity of these actions to somehow constitute a nice touch. In my head I considered it to be cool and original. Daniella said yes, burst into tears, and later told me she couldn't believe how lucky she felt (that was subsequently to prove something of a contrast some years later, of course, when I bunked off to Asia for ten weeks, leaving her to look after two children under three).

The next morning we headed to a Sandton jeweller's for a big South African rock, and I rang Daniella's dad for permission to ask for his daughter's hand in marriage. I had not even met her parents at this stage but I thought letting them know my intention was the right thing to do, particularly since I'd already gone through with it!

My life had pretty much changed overnight, and so had Daniella's. In one way, I wrecked it for her by dragging her up north. She had been doing really well, having established regular work with British Home Stores over a number of years, and modelling is a bit like acting in that you have to take whatever work you can while it's on offer.

We were married in February 2006, at a church in Hale. Long-term friend David Brown was my best man and Gareth Batty and Chris Read, team-mates on England tours over the previous couple of winters, were two of my four ushers. Most of the England team of the time were in attendance at the wedding reception at the Lowry but it just goes to show how things have changed because I didn't even know Graeme Swann and Alastair Cook, the pair I would consider to be my best mates in cricket now; at that time they had yet to join the international set-up.

We honeymooned in New York for a week before I headed off to the West Indies on an A tour. At that particular point in my career, I couldn't even make the England tour squad let alone the England team. I appeared destined to be playing a lot for Lancashire for the foreseeable future, so although Daniella kept her house in London, if we were going to live as man and wife she had to move up to my flat in central Manchester.

That was not an arrangement that lasted for too long, however. In fact, she rejected the idea immediately, and took the lead in our house hunting. To such an extent that she spotted one, and had put two offers in during the space of one Lancashire net session. It was literally a case of her bidding after breakfast and buying it by the end of lunch. I guess she really wanted that house!

Things were actually pretty hard in our first few months of marriage. Daniella had given up everything in her life to be with me, and she was soon to realize exactly how lonely it can be as the wife of an England cricketer. Some people may consider it a glamorous lifestyle, and, yes, it does have its perks, but she didn't know a soul, and being up in the North West wasn't working for her. She had no social scene to fall back on and, because professional cricket and travelling go hand in hand, I was away for the majority of the time, leaving her at home alone.

Initially, the new house gave her a focus for her time: the chance to design and decorate. But once that was done, there was a lot of kicking of heels alone, and she even told me at one point that she couldn't do it any more, that because I was away all the time she didn't get to see me and it wasn't the life that she'd ever wanted.

It was a very hard time for us, and was something that affected my performances, no question. Having spoken to a lot of the lads in the England dressing room, I find that they have been through exactly the same thing. But at the end of the day it is my job, and as we wanted to remain together we found a way around it. With her own work having slowed right down, she spent more and more time travelling around the country with me, and we decided to crack on in a bid to start a family. That was a big commitment for us, and unfortunately didn't come without its own heartache.

Devastatingly, Daniella suffered a miscarriage while I was on a tour of Sri Lanka in 2007–8. Such is the lot of a cricketer's wife that she had to deal with it by herself, finding out the news as I was preparing for a one-day international. She had already received the all-clear at the routine twelve-week scan, but at the nuchal scan the following week there was no heartbeat. She was due to come and meet me in Sri Lanka, from where we were to travel on to the Maldives. Instead, I returned home and we spent a traumatic day in hospital.

For my part, I felt useless, thousands of miles away, and had to suffer in silence. Testosterone-fuelled dressing rooms are not sympathetic places. Naturally, I was upset, and just wanted to be there for Daniella. What she had to endure, and my absence so far from home, highlighted the downside to being an international sportsperson; that was one of the most painful experiences of my life. You have no choice in such a situation, on duty for your country, but to grin and bear it.

Daniella is an amazing person, who has had to deal with horrific personal loss. She was only sixteen when her brother died in a car accident. He was eighteen, and, as an England Under-18 rugby player, had a potential career as a professional sportsman ahead of him. It is a loss that Daniella and her family have to face every single day of their lives.

For many years, Daniella didn't speak about it, finding it hard to do so, but I have always been a good listener, I would hope, and tried to be intuitive about how she might feel. They say time is a great healer but I am not sure something like that ever heals completely.

We were blessed with the arrival of Lola Rose in January 2009, and Ruby Luxe was born in December 2010, both in the middle of busy winters. Having to say hello and then an immediate good-bye to your newborn babies is one of the hardest things we have to do as England cricketers. Of course, it's a privilege to play for England. I've never thought of it any other way, but it does present challenges for you as a husband and father. I am both of those as well as an opening bowler.

And while I'm running in trying to take wickets in 35-degree heat somewhere in the southern hemisphere, Daniella is single-handedly bringing up two children in a city where she knows very few people. During the winter in which Ruby was born, I spent just five weeks out of five months at home.

One upside of the children's arrival has been that it has coincided with Daniella getting to know some of the families of the players at Lancashire. Kerry Chapple, wife of Glen, became a good friend and the kids all tend to play together. Initially, Daniella had struggled to get to know the other partners at Old Trafford because I tended to be away with England in the off-season when the majority of the club's social functions were scheduled.

If anything, fatherhood has made me more responsible, and provided extra focus on what I am trying to achieve in my career. My form certainly showed distinct improvement from the start of 2009 onwards, and, although it is not the sole reason, it has certainly been a major contributing factor.

What with the loss of sleep, and general running around whenever I'm back at home, you would think being a dad would have been draining but it has actually had the opposite effect. It definitely sharpens your focus when you consider that you are not only doing things for yourself any more. The prospect of achieving things for the good of my family spurs me on.

In fact, one of my best performances in the 2009 Ashes came when Lola was just six months old, and I stumbled on to the field for the second day of the Lord's Test having had about an hour's kip. Daniella and Lola came everywhere with me that summer. But, unfortunately, Lola did not settle easily in unfamiliar surroundings, and appeared determined to cry all night on this particular occasion. I might have been tired but I was happy.

My first tour as a married man, in early 2006, had been a fleeting one. It was with the England A side to the Caribbean rather than the full side, and was cut short by some news. Only a week or so had passed, in fact, when injury to Simon Jones led to my call-up for the Test series in India. And, due to a knee injury to Michael Vaughan, I was to have a travelling companion for the thirty-six-hour journey from Antigua to Nagpur via London. One Alastair Nathan Cook.

On the first British Airways flight, he was sitting across the aisle from me, our seats facing in towards each other slightly. Now despite having spent a few days practising alongside him out in Antigua, we had not really conversed with each other up to this point, so I hadn't got to know him at all. On trips like that you initially get drawn to people you have met, or played with before, and so I had spent most of the early days in others' company.

But I had played against Cook a couple of times the previous summer, and because I used to be an angry fast bowler – I'm such a reformed character these days, don't you know? – sledged him. Nor was I the only one who got stuck into him when we met in the contest at Chelmsford that previous September. He had hit a double hundred in a two-day match against the touring

Australians the week before and we thought he had a bit of arrogance about him. Even guys like Mark Chilton, who never said boo to a goose on the field, gave him a send-off when he got out.

The first thing he said to me as we settled for that flight was: 'The last time we spoke, you called me a —t.'

As ice-breakers go, this was right up there with the best of them, and immediately had me on the defensive.

'Oh, I'm really sorry about that,' I mumbled, apologetically. 'It's just that when I'm playing cricket I can be . . . well, grumpy. Hope you didn't take it to heart – I do it to most people.'

Once our opening gambits were out of the way, we hit it off famously and chatted the whole way back to Heathrow, where Daniella and Alice, Cookie's partner, came to spend a few hours with us before our next flight to India. We have been the best of mates pretty much ever since.

Our personalities are not so different. We both have a fear of socializing with people we don't know for a start and, like me, he stumbles and stutters when he speaks in public. Until recently, I'd always struggled to get my words out when faced with a crowd because of a lack of confidence.

Away from cricket, Cookie is also someone I trust implicitly. He's the sort of guy you want as a mate. He's got your back the whole time. He is the bloke in the dressing room who everyone likes, or at least who no one dislikes. Because there is nothing about him to dislike. I don't know anybody who's got anything bad to say about him, and that goes for the whole of world cricket, to be honest. He's such a nice fellow.

He goes about his business in an undemonstrative, quiet way, and he's a great guy to be near in the dressing room because he is secretly very funny. He possesses as good a sense of humour as anyone in the England set-up and because he is quick-witted he often comes up with good one-liners, which, because of his fear of speaking out loud, he whispers to Graeme Swann and me under his breath. He's a godsend in that regard because we simply repeat them and bag all the laughs.

In future years he went on to become my England batting buddy, too. Every batsman has a bowler they work closely with when practising, and I was Cookie's. That period of time also coincided with me becoming the Test team's nightwatchman, and meant we batted together several times. Cricket is strange for throwing up combinations of people who enjoy on-field success together and I definitely responded to being with him in the middle. We had a couple of fifty partnerships, and seemed to click as a pairing. It is strange how these things work out, and I couldn't tell you a particular reason why we gelled. We just did. And although they have done things at a different tempo, Stuart Broad and Graeme Swann have had quite a good record together, too.

Cookie was pretty good for me. Astounded to discover I didn't have a bat contract, he soon rectified that with a word in Mr Gray-Nicolls's shell-like. Within an hour I was the recipient of a phone call from the manufacturers informing me they would be my new sponsors, and within a couple of days I was fully kitted out, and looking like a Cookie clone.

He went through a stage of trying to get me to play exactly like him, too, which included whipping balls from off stump through the leg side. Unfortunately that little experiment didn't work, as ultimately I haven't got the same ability as someone like him. If I had, I wouldn't be a number nine, ten or eleven.

While he can take liberties against bowlers and prosper, it became pretty evident that I could not, so we concentrated on the mental side of batting. With someone like me you have to keep things as simple as possible, so instead of trying to replicate the shots of a batsman, he encouraged me to start thinking like one. If you walk in at number nine or lower, you tend to think a swipe will be worthwhile because no one expects you to get runs. Whereas, in reality, if you think like a top-order player you have more chance of getting in and scoring a few.

Without a doubt, in the successful England team that went nine Test series unbeaten, an ability to score runs from numbers one to eleven was something we prided ourselves on. After all, if you contribute twenty runs batting at number ten, it's worth the same amount to the team as twenty runs from your number three.

Cookie contributed prolifically to England from the start, beginning with a fine debut hundred in Nagpur, but he succumbed, as so many had before him on tours of India, to food poisoning on the morning of the final Test in Mumbai.

You have to be very careful with what you eat on these tours, and I generally struggle because I lose weight ridiculously easily, and find it hard to put it on, which means I have to take supplements. We are actively encouraged to eat local cuisine by nutritionists these days because it is seen as a safer option than asking an Asian chef to cook shepherd's pie, which is always a temptation as it's my favourite meal.

Cookie was paying homage to Armitage Shanks in the early hours, so Owais Shah was thrown in at the last minute, which is something you should always be prepared for in India. In addition to diet, we have it drummed into us about general hygiene – whenever we touch door handles we rub alcohol gel into our palms because germs can be picked up so easily – because there is an 80 per cent chance you will pick up some kind of sickness bug while you're out there.

So Owais, myself and Shaun Udal came into a team that was 1-0 down, and won against all odds. There were probably only four players who would have been in the first-choice XI when the tour party arrived on the subcontinent the previous month. India won the toss and surprisingly asked us to bat first in the kind of extreme conditions that would have been hard work for our bowlers. The sapping humidity took its toll on Owais, whose debut half-century was truncated when his hands cramped up, forcing him to retire hurt.

Matthew Hoggard struggled a bit when we bowled but it was a

disciplined team display with the ball that helped us into a healthy first-innings lead. I began with a stroke of good fortune when I dismissed Rahul Dravid with a strangle down the leg side, and claimed four in the innings. Then, with 300 to defend in the fourth innings, Shaggy Udal had the game of his life with 4 for 14.

Cramping was a feature of the tour, and the conditions were extreme throughout the one-day series that followed. Playing India on their own turf is hard enough going but playing at that time of year made it even more of an uphill challenge. People like Matt Prior regularly had to take on extra fluid to rehydrate after batting in those intense temperatures, and the one game that stands out from the seven came in Jamshedpur, where we won despite it being in the mid-40s. Andrew Strauss retired ill and was immediately hooked up to a drip. Others were suffering, too, and by the end our dressing room resembled a scene from *MASH*.

My problems had nothing to do with the temperature. It turned out that I'd played the entire one-day series in India with a stress fracture of the back. Pain had caused me to complain about it on several occasions but it was diagnosed as no more than stiffness by our medical team and so instead of being nursed through I was subjected to back-strengthening exercises and sit-ups. To be quite honest, this suited me in one sense because I felt in half-decent nick, and was loath to miss a match, particularly as I was in line for my fiftieth cap in the final game in Indore.

Despite being in agony in the build-up, I was desperate to keep going. When I was in the England team early in my career, my attitude was to stay in it come what may, one that arguably hindered as much as helped me. Just as in the Test series against the South Africans in 2003, the fear was that if ever I gave up my place I might never get back in. So I played ignorant to injuries until it literally got too late on both occasions.

When my condition began deteriorating in the final week of that tour I knew I had to let on to the physio Dean Conway. Now some physios take different approaches to others, and someone like Dean, with his rugby background, was of the attitude that more often than not injuries were no more than niggles and that the best course of action was to get back out there. Someone like Kirk Russell, who also worked with the England team during the noughties, erred on the side of caution. With him, you had to be 100 per cent or you couldn't play. It is similar with the team doctors we have had: some, the minute you tell them you are experiencing tightness somewhere in your body, immediately dispatch you for a scan. Others prefer to leave things be for a couple of days and see what develops. Whichever course is taken, by whoever it may be, you have to trust their judgement. It is their field of expertise, not ours, and their opinions and decisions play a crucial part in our careers. Although the longer you play the more you can second-guess, and understand your body. For example, if I go for a long run I know I am going to get tight calf muscles. It happens every time but I still wouldn't tell some doctors as they would send me off to hospital as a precaution.

The sit-ups were supposed to rid me of the supposed stiffness, strengthen my abs and look after my back. But outside match days the pain was horrible. Once I was playing, things eased up because, apart from the odd ball causing mild irritation, the painkillers and adrenalin kicked in.

Only when we got home did a scan reveal the extent of the damage – a massive crack in my lower back. Subsequently, I spent six weeks in a brace, waiting for the bone to heal completely. I watched *Big Brother* in bed and ate rice pudding, frustrated that the extent of the damage had not been picked up sooner.

Not normally one to feel sorry for myself, I got myself on a really downward spiral, until some stern words from Daniella snapped me out of it: 'Stop being a knob' as I recall. It's disastrous for a cricketer to be seriously injured during the English summer but she convinced me to cease wallowing in self-pity and that in the greater scheme of things my lay-off would not be lengthy at all. By midsummer I was slowly building up my fitness again, and was back playing before its end.

There was a feeling that the damage incurred was a combination of the volume of bowling I had got through in recent times, combined with my action. Here it was again, at the centre of everything: my bowling action. Everyone had offered an input between my first and fiftieth one-day caps, and the fact that what I had been told by those involved with England and those who looked after me at Lancashire conflicted only exacerbated the confusion in my head.

But if any good came out of my hellish 2006, it was that suddenly both sides agreed it was time to revert to what felt natural. Kevin Shine, successor to Troy Cooley as England's bowling coach, and Mike Watkinson, at Lancashire, are both pragmatic when it comes to their decision-making. I am not even sure which one of them made the eminently sensible decision to allow me to bowl in the way I had always felt most comfortable, and what my body had become accustomed to, when I emerged as a fast bowler of promise, but the other one acquiesced.

Between them, Winker and Shiney put the plan together and although most of my work was done up at Old Trafford, the three of us would meet occasionally at England practices so that all parties could have a view on how things were progressing. I was receptive to all they suggested and it was a relief to turn back the clock. This was akin to a fresh start and it made the whole process, including all the general rehab, a lot easier.

Had Daniella pushed harder for it, I might have pursued a move to a southern county that year – not something I would have taken lightly but something that I had to consider, nevertheless, as she was so obviously unsettled in Manchester. Word had evidently got out that I might be looking to relocate because a contact within the game rang me during my recuperation to ask whether I would be interested in joining Hampshire.

Daniella was naturally keen, and, as she had gone to college in Southampton, she was familiar with the area. Life is about compromise, I truly believe that, and when we got engaged I knew

I really fancied myself as a top-order batsman until I reached the age of five!

My junior team-mates at Burnley (left to right from top): Gareth Halley, Michael Brown, Steven Holden, David Brown, Jonathan Clare. Four of us went on to play first-class cricket.

The Burnley lads again, in a sing-song (left to right): Andrew Beet, Gareth Halley, me, David Brown and Ian Gade.

Courtesy of James Anderson

With my dad Michael and sister Sarah – looking very cool.

With my dad Michael, my sister Sarah and my mum Catherine.

Courtesy of James Anderson

At home with my three girls, Daniella, Lola and Ruby. My family means so much to me and I cherish the time I spend with them away from cricket.

At Lancashire's pre-season photocall ahead of my first summer as an England cricketer, Old Trafford, April 2003.

Press Association

Like most cricket-loving lads from Lancashire, I grew up wanting to wear the red rose on my chest.

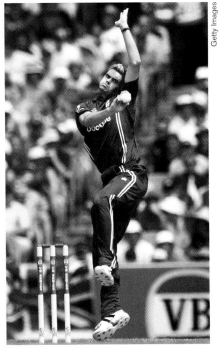

Getty Images

My international debut at the MCG against Australia, 15 December 2002.

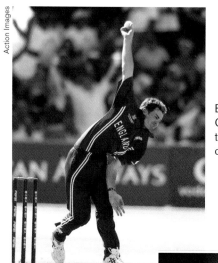

England v Australia, 2003 Cricket World Cup, Port Elizabeth. We came so close to causing an upset but ultimately defeat condemned us to an early exit.

Earlier in the tournament, I was named man of the match for my four for 29 against Pakistan under the Newlands floodlights.

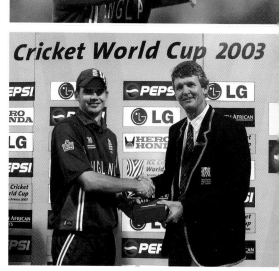

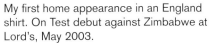

My first home appearance in an England shirt. On Test debut against Zimbabwe at Lord's, May 2003.

With Nasser Hussain (right) before his departure as England captain, England v South Africa, Trent Bridge, August 2003. He was always 100 per cent supportive.

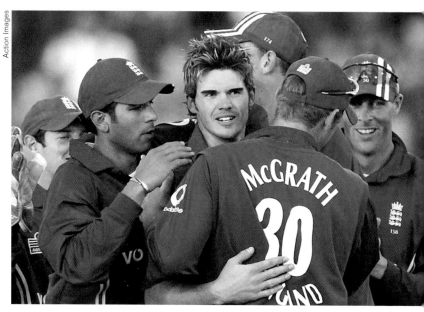

On the way to becoming the first England bowler to take a hat-trick in an ODI, England v Pakistan, the Oval, June 2003.

Nursing an ankle injury, Colombo, November 2003. Some of my colleagues found it amusing that I had been crocked playing squash – and clearly I found it absolutely hilarious.

Although I recovered for the third Test in Colombo, I failed to take a wicket, and we lost the game and series, to complete a frustrating first half of the winter for me.

At the Champions Trophy 2006, Jaipur, India (left to right): Rikki Clarke, me, Jamie Dalrymple, Steve Harmison and Sajid Mahmood.

At the World Cup in the Caribbean, spring 2007. Our lack of tactical nous floored us in a one-day tournament once again.

Celebrating a rare wicket during the 2006-7 Ashes – this was one of my five, Michael Hussey, caught behind early on the third morning of the final Test in Sydney.

Despite this being taken shortly after the Ashes whitewash was complete, during a Twenty20 defeat to the Australians, I consider it to be a great photograph. The SCG is packed to the rafters. Taking wickets in front of a full house always gives me a real buzz.

Training under the watchful eye of Peter Moores, a few months into his tenure as England coach, Sri Lanka, November 2007. Almost from the moment he took over, I felt a new lease of life as an international cricketer.

that relocating had to be a viable option. For the sake of Daniella's happiness, and our marriage, I was willing to look at all avenues and all options. This option would have allowed her to commute to London and continue her career. But she believes in compromise, too, and happily for my career it never came to that.

That phone call was just testing the water, letting me know that Hampshire would love to talk to me if my domestic situation dictated a change, but while it is always good for your self-esteem to hear that someone else is interested in signing you, there were a number of things that came into the equation. The primary one was that I never wanted to move away from Lancashire, and at that stage they were my primary employers.

Another was that I felt in the club's debt. They invested in me as a teenager by handing me my first professional contract, and have provided constant support since. A number of coaches helped me progress to the very top of the sport. There was a sense of carrying on the club's legacy to pass on to the next generation. And because I've played so few games over recent years, I desperately want to give Lancashire something back, either in a playing or coaching capacity.

Things are different since I became centrally contracted and modern England players can live pretty much anywhere in the UK now. So even if we moved south, I would envisage staying put. I would certainly never leave the club unless asked to do so. Due to international commitments, my general availability spans about two games a season, and if I did live in London, say, the chances are that one of those Lancashire games would be against Middlesex, Surrey, Essex or Kent. And if it so happened that both appearances were scheduled for Old Trafford, I would be hopeful of Glen Chapple putting me up for a night or two.

7

Fighting Back

There was even hype about who would be named in the touring squad such was the place of the 2006–7 Ashes in the nation's sporting consciousness. In what was one big PR exercise, the squad was named on the first anniversary of the urn being back in English possession, and I was not the only one selected in the sixteen-man party who was not 100 per cent match fit.

Prior to selection, with Lancashire without a fixture at the start of September, there had been talk of me being loaned to Glamorgan so I could get an extra first-class match in. As it turned out, my only one of the 2006 season came against Hampshire, a few days after the 12 September squad announcement. Neither was the onus on me to get a run-out solely because of my own state of health, I felt, but because there were others in the squad with injuries, too, and the more players they could show were playing before we left for the tour the less their fitness gamble would be scrutinized.

My only other cricket in the past five months had been in six matches over four weekends for Burnley, a spell that gave me much pleasure and culminated in me picking up a Lancashire League winner's medal. Initially selected as a specialist batsman, I gradually upped my involvement and was permitted to bowl in four-over spells in back-to-back matches on 9 and 10 September.

I hit an unbeaten thirty-five against Rawtenstall on the Saturday to take us to a five-wicket win, and was at the crease the following evening when we sealed the title against Haslingden at Turf Moor. John Harvey – brother of Mark who I played with for Lancashire, a league pro for donkey's years, and now Burnley captain – was shaking with nerves at the other end. Not because he was fearful in any way, but because it meant so much to him to knock off the runs and achieve something for his family club. He did that, with fifty-five not out. My main contribution was to calm him down as we eased to our 120-run target.

It meant something to me, too. Truly, it did. Under ordinary circumstances, I would never have got a chance to go back to play for my club side, and even my run-outs for Lancashire have been sporadic since I became centrally contracted in 2007. I left Burnley almost overnight as a teenager and so to return unexpectedly and contribute even in a small way filled me with a sense of pride and achievement. It had been four years since my previous appearance, against Rishton, and it was good to be back playing alongside my old mates.

There were other plans to get me ready physically, too, as I was placed on an all-you-can-eat diet ahead of the Champions Trophy in India. And like Andrew Flintoff had done in his own rehabilitation that summer, I ran up and down Rivington Pike in Lancashire under the supervision of club physio Dave 'Rooster' Roberts. The idea was that bulking me up, particularly given my propensity for losing weight whenever I ventured to the subcontinent, would strengthen my body in readiness for a heavy winter workload.

We started our Champions Trophy campaign in Jaipur, and that is where it ended, effectively if not geographically, following defeats to India and eventual winners Australia, in a one-sided pre-Ashes contest. Under-par scores batting first cost us on both occasions, although I still got some competitive overs and wickets under my belt, and faced a proper workout against Chris Gayle and Dwayne Bravo in a dead-rubber group game against West Indies in Ahmedabad, where we successfully chased down the thick end of 300.

After six months away from England duty I was up and running again, and with Simon Jones still not recovered after breaking down in India in the spring, I was firmly in contention for a spot in the first Ashes Test. Although I hadn't been involved in the summer at all due to my back injury, I had done well in my previous Test appearance – that series-levelling win in Mumbai.

The team had changed a lot since then, across home series against Sri Lanka and Pakistan. Myself, Andrew Flintoff and Ashley Giles had missed the 3-0 win over Pakistan through injury, while Geraint Jones was on the sidelines, having lost out to Chris Read towards the end of the summer. Then there was Marcus Trescothick, who had come home from India with his stress-related illness. Now just a few months later he was prepared to combat his demons on overseas soil once more.

These selection issues were primarily about one thing: getting as many of the successful 2005 Ashes team out in the middle as was possible. The thinking behind it was that it would provide us with some kind of psychological edge but in doing so it actually created a really uncomfortable environment. It was not an enjoyable time.

Whereas the team had been so settled in 2005 – a prime ingredient in success – there was now so much doubt lingering because of these injuries. Having failed to beat Sri Lanka in the first home series of 2006, things picked up and momentum was developed against Pakistan, yet there was an obvious move to recall the old guard as soon as it came around to naming that squad for Australia.

Then there was the captaincy issue. It was something that caused a major debate in the build-up to the squad announcement. Michael Vaughan was still not fit after his knee operation and there were effectively two candidates, both of whom had an equal claim. Flintoff had taken over when Vaughan was forced off the tour of India but when Fred himself was crocked in mid-summer, the captaincy baton had passed to Andrew Strauss for the four-match series against Pakistan. Strauss had won plaudits for both his leadership and the nature of the success in beating the tourists 3-0.

There was impetus at the end of the season and to be honest when, following much deliberation, Flintoff was revealed as captain, it felt strange. The team had just completed such a good set of results, and yet here was a move to alter one of its chief dynamics. It was an emotional decision to appoint Flintoff, in my opinion. The logical one would have been to go for Strauss.

That is easy to say with the benefit of hindsight because Strauss has been such a successful England captain since, but even back then if you had put the pair together and compared the skills they possessed, and the ones needed to be an international captain, Strauss stood out more than anyone else in that team. And he certainly possessed more career captaincy experience than Fred.

With that series against Pakistan behind him, he felt like the leader to everyone from a playing perspective, and the winning culture rediscovered in both Test and one-day formats had a lot to do with him. The team had become accustomed to his captaincy, and was functioning well.

Lots of people had opinions on the subject and although some have conveniently rewritten history to claim a place in the Strauss camp, there was also support for Flintoff within the media and general public. Their counter-argument was fairly simplistic. As Fred was England's talisman, he would lead from the front. It was based in no small part on the fact that he had been so good at standing up to the Australians in 2005, and that such conflict inspired him. Ergo, his efforts would inspire the whole team.

What better way to defend the Ashes once Vaughan was crocked than to have him as the representative presence of the team? Australia feared him and that would negate their chances of undermining the opposition leader as was their wont.

It was true enough that Fred was very much a lead-with-actions kind of captain and those in power clearly recognized the influence his performances had when in charge on the tour of India earlier that year. There were all kinds of disruption on that tour, but he was pretty consistent throughout, with four half-centuries in a row, and plenty of wickets, too, and the 1-1 series scoreline was a phenomenal result.

To be honest, though, even in India there was something not quite right about it all. Yes, he did lead from the front, he was very passionate, but as an England captain you need more than that. You need to be very tactically astute, switched on at all times, your man-management has to be exceptional and when all the attributes needed to be a successful captain were weighed up, in my head Strauss had the edge.

At the time Fred was a good mate, and from a purely selfish point of view I was really pleased that he was chosen because, all things considered, it gave me a better chance of playing. But deep down I always believed Strauss was what you might term the safer, and better, option. In the aftermath of a first 5-0 Ashes whitewash in eighty-six years there was a lot of 'told you so' from outsiders but that did not truly reflect the fairly even pre-tour split in the Flintoff v. Strauss debate.

The Flintoff supporters who championed his ability to unite the dressing room, and provide a dynamic presence within it, were perhaps labouring under something of a false illusion because that 2005 team was just about as cliquey a team as I have ever known. That is not to say it was not a very good team; it undoubtedly was. But it was one of those series when everything clicked and everyone in an England shirt performed to just about their best over the course of five matches. It was a series when every member of the team seemed to dovetail with others at crucial times. When individuals are able to do that, it means that any failures within games can be glossed over. There were a sufficient number of players operating at their maximum to account for off-days for others.

Marcus Trescothick was in amazing form, and was able to set a positive tempo at the top of the innings, Andrew Strauss played well alongside him, Fred batted and bowled unbelievably well, Kevin Pietersen got his first chance to impress at Test level and took it with both hands, culminating in that memorable hundred at the Oval, Steve Harmison bowled with real pace and roughed the Australians up, Matthew Hoggard had that knack of coming up with wickets when they were needed most, and Simon Jones was in the form of his life. It was a case of everyone being in great nick simultaneously. However, it was evident in subsequent months and years that it was a team that possessed more frailty, both mental and physical, than people suspected.

Compared to the 2010–11 team in which pretty much everyone got on, the 2005 team was more about individuals, and the dressing room reflected that. Individuals were having a great time on the field as opposed to a team working hard for each other, backing up the rest of the unit.

Once they had gone through the celebrations, the Trafalgar Square thing, the bus to Number 10 Downing Street and the dishing out of the MBEs, the egos really started coming out. Divisions in the dressing room were inevitable once that happened.

Suddenly, instead of the focus being on performances, it shifted to materialistic things. There was a lot of 'I'm getting this, I have been offered that, I am going on this show tomorrow'. Everyone was trying to trump each other commercially, and, in my opinion, that is one of the reasons why the England team crashed so spectacularly from its zenith at the end of the 2005 summer to a point where we were overwhelmed by uncertainty within a few series.

The downhill course resulted in only one England win out of the next four campaigns immediately after that 2-1 victory over Australia. Consequently, I am not sure we were a very confident group when we landed down under braced for the usual round of

Pommie-bashing. Australians are nothing if not predictable – you could tell they couldn't wait for us to get there – and it was the same old story from opponents like Glenn McGrath, who wheeled out his staple pre-series claim that they were going to win 5-0. Only this time they truly meant it.

We knew they were going to come hard at us because of the hurt we inflicted in 2005, but persuaded ourselves we were prepared for the toughest of asks – to win over there. Deep down, though, I didn't recognize a firm belief in the camp that we could win. Of course, we went there talking a good game publicly but our words, including mine, lacked conviction. My mindset was totally different on the next tour of Australia four years later when each and every one of us believed 100 per cent that we would win. I am now able to distinguish the difference between the two sets of feelings, and they are incomparable.

Preparation was meticulous in the extreme, but the focus of it all wrong. We had endless meetings prior to departure, which contained staggering attention to detail, not on how we were going to take twenty Australian wickets, but on subjects that really didn't matter in the slightest. For example, we discussed the importance of turning up in our number ones – the really smart suits with the England badge – so that we would look the part getting on and off the plane.

'We will change during the flight, and when we get off at the other end, they will still be looking crisp.'

The theory was that because this was a rematch of the greatest cricket series in memory, certainly from England and Australian perspectives, it was going to be scrutinized like no series that had gone before. Millions of eyes (billions if it was being screened through Asia) would be pointed in our direction and we had to make the right impression.

Walk confidently, stand tall – shoulder to shoulder with colleagues rather than in dribs and drabs to emphasize the togetherness of the team – across the tarmac both for boarding and disembarking.

Our exit and entrance for this long-haul flight was choreographed, with no one allowed to begin their descent down the steps of the aircraft before the last member of the squad had addressed the effects of a thirty-hour transit – combs and wax were thrown through hair, pearly whites were flashed in mirrors, shirts were fully buttoned, ties knotted and shoes gleamed with polish. It could have been Oscars night.

The theory was that if we were turned out immaculately, and in tune with one another, we would reek of confidence. If we portrayed the correct image, it would let the opposition would know we meant business.

Let's be honest: all this emphasis on being presentable when we got there was fairly ludicrous. We were a cricket team, yet we were compiling sartorial rather than tactical lists. We were focused on the wrong subject matter.

Compare it to 2010–11 when everything we discussed was cricket-specific. For example, we talked about how we were going to approach the first three warm-up games – targeting victories in each of them – discussed how the frontline bowlers would go to Brisbane during the final one of the three against Australia A in Hobart, details that really matter when it comes down to winning a series like that.

When we arrived in November 2006, it was more in hope than expectation. Things would really have to fall into place for us to do well. Sure, we had players good enough to beat Australia, that much had been proved already, but we arrived with a team as unsettled as my stomach.

Now falling ill on tour goes with the territory when it comes to being an international cricketer, and it tends to be Asian destinations that have hit me most often. Without being too graphic there have been a couple of times in India when I have had it coming out both ends. Whoops, I was too graphic there, wasn't I?

But unfunnily enough, the worst I have ever been was after we landed in Sydney. That night I was sick until there was literally nothing left to come out, and I missed the first practice session because of it. It was only one of those twenty-four-hour bugs, and nothing to do with any failed attempt at David Boon's long-haul booze record, I assure you, but it didn't half throw me about.

Speculation in the media about who would play in the first Test in Brisbane intensified the closer the match got but the plan was always to throw together as many of the successful 2005 side as was possible. It was a policy designed to provide a psychological edge over the Australians; to provide them with the illusion that this was the same England team that had turned them over just fifteen months earlier.

But it was flawed thinking because it was dependent on gambling on the fitness of certain players with minimal cricket under their belts and meant disbanding the team that had developed at the end of the 2006 home summer. Monty Panesar prospered as the first-choice spinner while Ashley Giles was out, Chris Read had been his tidy, dependable self behind the stumps after ousting Geraint Jones, and Sajid Mahmood had also made an impression in the 3-0 win.

Another issue that didn't help in the build-up involved Marcus Trescothick, who came out on tour in the belief that he could overcome the stress-related illness that had forced a break in his international career earlier that year. It was a big deal for him to get on the outbound flight, after what he had been through in India the previous winter, when his illness forced him to return home – we all knew that. Nobody was left in any doubt that including him now was another risk but from a cricket perspective, if there was any chance of getting him there we had to do it, because he was our best player.

It was difficult to know how to deal with him and because none of us wanted to upset him, it was a case of treading on eggshells, not asking him how he was every five minutes, and leaving Ashley Giles, his best mate in the team, to make sure he was okay in the initial days of the tour. Of course, you try to act as normal as possible in that situation but not having experienced that kind of thing before meant we had little real understanding of his condition.

Nevertheless, we still weren't prepared for him breaking down once again. I had yet to join the tour of India when it first happened in Baroda eight months earlier but those who were present suggested it was a very similar scenario in that no one had an inkling it was about to happen. So when Tres did break down in the dressing room during the game against New South Wales in Sydney, it provided a shock, a significant blow to our Ashes chances, and ultimately a deflating feeling. He'd aborted his part in proceedings after a matter of just days.

His importance to the team was multi-faceted. He was an experienced international player, a senior member of the squad, and such experience and knowledge would have been key for us on such a challenging tour. As well as being our most consistent batsman, he provided a lot of good insight on the game, and I am sure he would have been the first port of call on Andrew Flintoff's list of those to turn to for tactical advice. I had discovered first hand what a brilliant cricket brain he possessed in that one-day series in Pakistan the previous winter, but he was also very sensitive in relation to teammates, and maintained a universally positive on-field demeanour.

So we lost good vibes and developed bad ones with a selection policy that did not heed form, and which, to be blunt, benefited me indirectly. Basically, above and beyond the unwavering desire to recall the old guard, the identity of the spinner dictated the make-up of the rest of the attack. In that if Ashley Giles, a solid number eight batsman, played that meant they could pick me as a specialist fast bowler. Duncan Fletcher always liked a robust tail and Gilo's presence ensured that. In contrast, if they picked Monty, they believed they also had to choose a bowler with decent batting ability to accommodate the loss of runs. So Sajid would come in to bat at eight, and I dropped out.

It might be considered strange that the selection of our bowling attack was dependent on how you handled a bat but that is just how it was. It was no secret, and although it didn't cause any ructions within the team, inevitably a feeling developed that if we weren't picking our best XI, how were we meant to be confident about performing? How were we meant to feel backed?

There had been no obvious reaction to my stress fracture following the Champions Trophy excursions and when I bowled a good spell against New South Wales, an Ashes starting berth was as good as mine. Nevertheless, I was a little bit annoyed that the new ball was not in my hand on that opening morning. Bowling first change has never been my strength, still isn't, and the fact I had been picked in that role showed the uncertainty that prevailed at the time.

We started in the worst possible manner, too, when Steve Harmison sent down his infamous double wide first ball and although Fred tried to palm off the fact it had flown directly to him at second slip as coolly as he could, unfortunately it set the tone for the entire series. I was at mid on and therefore right behind the ball's flight path. I haven't seen that happen too many times at any level.

Harmy is a nervy character, a real confidence player and someone who needs to start well to develop confidence. He did anything but, and it sent a shock wave through our team and provided ammunition to a baying crowd. Actually, I take that back because I am not sure they needed any more geeing up, but they certainly jumped on the back of it, using it as a focus for their abuse. They didn't stop for the rest of the day, a day that felt like one of the longest in my Test career. We couldn't manufacture chances and the Aussies batted for what felt like forever across the opening two days.

We were up against one of the best, if not *the* best Test team in history, and they were intent on showing that 2005 was just a blip in their careers. They put their foot on our throat on the opening day of that series and didn't remove it until the final day at Sydney. There was added incentive for guys like Shane Warne, Justin Langer and Glenn McGrath because they knew this represented their career swansongs, and they were committed to making it one big glorious send-off.

When it came to my performances, I bowled like someone who was low on confidence and unsure of his place in the team. This was no coincidence because it was how I felt.

During that first Test, I got pulled a hell of a lot by Ricky Ponting. Sometimes when you switch from country to country you can fall into the trap of getting your length wrong but once you've been around a bit this shouldn't be the case, and I would certainly not hide behind the excuse that I could not locate a length for Australian pitches and conditions. There was no adjustment issue, the problem was quite simple: I just didn't bowl very well. If you play international cricket it is not a problem to switch length for conditions, and it certainly wasn't an issue in the 2010–11 Ashes.

The Australian public were extremely hostile towards the England team and revelled in the fact that their mob were playing much better cricket than we were. From the moment the plane hit the tarmac in Brisbane, following warm-up matches in Sydney and Adelaide, there was a fervour about the place. We were well backed by the Barmy Army and all our England supporters as always, and while they displayed a keen sense of anticipation, the mood from the home fans was much more aggressive.

Perhaps they had seen all the celebrations English cricket had put on in 2005 to commemorate a first Test series win over Australia for eighteen years. There was no question we had made the most of that historic victory and it would have riled them.

The comprehensive 277-run defeat at the Gabba made everyone realize, if they hadn't already, that we were in for a tough few weeks. Australia had piled up 602 for 9 declared in their first innings of the series, opening up a massive 445-run advantage in the process, and had even neglected the opportunity to enforce the follow-on in a bid to keep their bowlers fresh and allow any cracks on the surface to open further for the fourth innings. All the talk was of how Australia wanted to, and were going to, grind us into the dirt as payback.

There was a suggestion that we had got a little star-struck in that first Test but that certainly never entered my head and, ahead of the second in Adelaide, we had a team meeting to try to put it behind us. Duncan Fletcher put the opening result down to us not performing well and Australia playing to their very best. A number of the squad had an input into what had gone wrong, how we would try to put things right, that individual performances had not been good enough and that we would be better prepared this time.

But what happened at the Adelaide Oval effectively knocked the stuffing out of us. It was a really flat pitch, and we got into a position that should have given us confidence going forward; a position from which we really should not have been able to lose. In fact, with 551 for 6 declared on the scoreboard, courtesy of a double hundred from Paul Collingwood and 158 from Kevin Pietersen, we had a platform to push to level the series.

Again, I was overlooked for the new ball but we nipped both openers out cheaply and Australia would have been under serious pressure had Ashley Giles held on to the chance offered to him when Ricky Ponting hooked a Matthew Hoggard short ball to deep square leg. The Australians were 78 for 3 at that stage, and the series could potentially have gone a different way if he had held on. Typically, Ponting cashed in, as the best players tend to, and we somehow conspired to lose a match in which we had set the pace when our batting folded on the final morning.

Even if we had gone on to win that particular match, my own view is that Australia would still have triumphed in convincing fashion. The facts of the matter are that they were a lot better than us, and in a Test series the best team normally wins.

Trailing 2-0 in a flash, we reverted to a team more closely resembling that which had represented England at the back end of the summer for the third Test in Perth, in a bid to claw our way back. I am honest enough to admit that Monty and Saj, who came in at the WACA, should have started the series. In trying to send out that message to the Australians at the start of that series, by recalling the old guard, we managed to send another which did us internal damage – namely that those in possession of the shirts weren't as trusted as others.

In contrast, their big characters came to the fore in that series, and imposed themselves on us. They weren't prepared to take a backwards step and never was it more evident than when Shane Warne got involved in a verbal spat with Paul Collingwood during the final Test in Sydney. Our lads were convinced that Warne had gloved a delivery from Monty through to Chris Read and Colly, fielding at slip, let him know about it.

It turned into a war of words, and Warne got in some low blows by once again mocking the fact that Colly had been awarded the MBE for scoring seven at the Oval in 2005. To be honest, Colly was a bit exposed to it, left on his own; the team that developed a couple of years later would not have let that happen.

In subsequent times if someone got a grilling from an opponent, others would pile in to back him up. I guess Warne's aura, the state of the series and the confidence levels of those in England shirts around him contributed to the silence. But Colly would not have been a lone voice had an opponent started chirping at him in the 2010–11 Ashes.

Warne was something of a master when it came to undermining opponents, and I had been batting with Colly in Adelaide when the Aussie began dishing out stick to him for accepting his medal at Buckingham Palace. His expertise in causing divisions in the opposition team was apparent at one point when Colly blocked one of Warne's deliveries, and I shouted 'well played' down the pitch. Warne looked at me, stopped and asked me:

'What're you doing? I thought you were a decent bloke. Why are you talking to him?'

One of the main differences now is that he would not have stuck into both of us individually. There would be much better protection. Sure, if you looked at his record Warne was intimidating but forget the status of the opponent: it doesn't matter who is having a go at one of the lads. If Sachin Tendulkar abused one of the England team, we wouldn't be of the opinion that because he was the great Sachin we couldn't say anything back to him. There is much more of a team ethos.

Australians have prided themselves on being adept at causing mental disintegration over the years but, with the public also aggressive, the levels it got to on that tour were quite astounding. It even proved a daunting experience for our wives and girlfriends. The home crowds were truly awful to them. They were just there to watch and support their husbands but for the Aussie barrackers they were an easy target, and there was no escape.

Daniella was quite shocked both by the reception she got and the reaction to us as a couple walking down the street in broad daylight. Even while out shopping it seemed like everybody had something to say, and it was never very pleasant. It was just prolific, and downright nasty. Australia is home to some of the most poisonous creatures on earth, and most of them seemed to dwell on the streets of Sydney and Melbourne. The Australian public couldn't have created a more hostile environment in which to play, and we just couldn't wait to get out of there. To such a degree, in fact, that Daniella vowed, having left upon the conclusion of the Test series, never to go back again. I said something similar after I left a few weeks later, although I naturally had to retract my threat given my contractual obligations with the ECB!

There is no doubt that abuse like that has its desired effect, and there is no let-up. It's constant from the moment you arrive to the moment you depart. And to be honest, it wouldn't really have mattered what was said; it just added to the inhospitable nature of that Ashes tour. We were getting a battering on the field by their players and off it by everyone else.

Christmas and New Year passed in fairly sombre mood that year; no one was particularly happy and our families bore the brunt of the lingering disharmony. Cricket tours are not much fun when you are getting beaten heavily every week.

With Matthew Hoggard ruled out through injury, I was recalled for the final Test in Sydney, having been left out for the third Test in Perth and the fourth in Melbourne, and bowled all right as it happened, taking three wickets in Australia's first innings. But with the series gone, we were on a hiding to nothing, and although you claim to be playing for pride, the truth is you would rather not be there in that situation.

Australia had everything you could want in a team: destructive batsmen like Matthew Hayden, Ricky Ponting and Adam Gilchrist, an incredibly accurate bowler in Glenn McGrath, another that bowled in excess of 90 mph in Brett Lee and one of the best, if not *the* best, spinners in the history of the game in Shane Warne.

And their reserves weren't bad either. By this stage in the series, my former Lancashire colleague Andrew Symonds – an incredible but complicated all-round talent – had been called in. Simmo was a really fierce competitor, a great guy to have on your team in terms of his cricket skills but a very unstable individual.

His misdemeanours in Cardiff in 2005 when he was axed by Australia for being the worse for wear during the warm-up of their one-day international against Bangladesh have been well documented, and his big-night reputation was well earned. On one occasion, he rocked up about an hour late for practice and took his place on a bench that ran alongside the Old Trafford nets. He just sat there, sunglasses on, head down, neglecting the opportunity to apologize for being late.

Mike Watkinson, our coach at the time, was fuming but tried to remain cordial. 'Simmo, do you fancy a bat?' he asked him, calmly.

'No point, mate,' he said. 'No point. Be a waste of time.'

Five minutes later he walked off and left for the day. For one game he turned up ten minutes before the start, with no explanation. But like the rest of this Australian team, he was completely in tune for this series.

Being whitewashed by Australia had an inevitability about it, and was as dispiriting an experience as an England cricketer can have, and I am not sure things would have been much different if we had been able to field our 2005-winning side at their peak. We would certainly have struggled like hell to win because these Australian greats were determined to bow out at the top of their game. The best players are always spurred on by challenges, and after Justin Langer confirmed he was to hang up the baggy green at the same time as Warne and McGrath, their challenge was to complete the first 5-0 over England since 1920–21. Whatever we threw at them, they were undeniably at their peak and would have come out on top.

There were to be recriminations for the Test series result in the following weeks, in the shape of a review fronted by Ken Schofield, the former director of the European Golf Tour, whose brief was to assess what had gone wrong, and to plot the best route forward for the England team. It was the first time that Duncan Fletcher's position as coach had been questioned.

My personal relationship with Fletcher was similar to a lot of other people's. Some days you would think he really liked you, and had time for you, but the next you might as well have been someone he had never met before. It was very strange the way he acted with people.

On the coaching side of things, I always found him useful. He helped me with my batting extensively in the early days, although he didn't really talk to me much about bowling. He never really spoke to the bowlers much at all, in fact, which I always considered strange given that he used to bowl himself.

Generally with Fletcher you either loved him or hated him but

I was somewhere in the middle. I neither got on with him, nor rucked with him. He was just odd, and frustratingly so at times. His little social habits mildly annoyed me. One day he would say 'good morning' to you at breakfast, the next he would walk straight past you as if you weren't there.

The people who loved him tended to be the flavour-of-the-month gang, guys who were very friendly with the coaching staff, who always looked to make an impression, and who would do everything asked of them, then a little bit more, sometimes just for the sake of being noticed. In contrast, the guys he didn't naturally bond with were those not so patently obvious in their dedication, or had something different about them. Guys he didn't think he could control were not so popular with him.

I would have been in a minority, maybe even on my own, in that I was somewhere in the middle – or at least that's what I considered myself to be. Because I was relatively young when I came into the England set-up, I didn't have a lot to compare him to, and didn't have particularly strong feelings either way. But what I would say is that I probably got on better with Fletcher during that initial period when Nasser Hussain was captain, as I didn't really enjoy the Fletcher–Vaughan era that followed.

One of the reasons for this is the way I felt I was treated when struggling with my form, and one of the reasons I struggled for form was the fact I was forever tinkering with my action.

Now although the 2006–7 Ashes was not productive for me in the slightest in terms of a statistical return, as a series it had its significance. It was the first Test series I had ever entered with anything like my natural action.

For three years I'd felt like I was trying to impersonate someone else, and although I have already boasted in these pages that I am pretty good at that, I was thankful to be able to be my own man again. The difference in how my action looked between 2003 and 2006 from how it looked in subsequent years was astounding, and that really hit home at one of my early benefit functions in 2012, when Steve Finn was so taken aback by seeing footage of my early England career.

Seeing video reruns, my bowling just looks so unnatural and reminds me how cumbersome it felt at the time. This is going to sound stupid but even when I got two hat-tricks in 2003 – against Essex on the eve of my Test debut, and against Pakistan at the Oval in a one-day international – it felt horrible. The yorker with which I pinged Nasser Hussain on the foot was completely unintentional; as I was so consumed by thoughts of how to get through each stage of my action, I wasn't concentrating on what I was trying to do with the ball.

Of course, I wish I had spoken out more, dug my heels in and insisted on doing things my way because I had bowled quick when I first burst on the scene with Lancashire and that is how I had earned my chance. My speed came from the fact that I was quite wiry and had a fast muscle twitch. In this regard I was not dissimilar to Simon Jones. Neither of us steamed into the crease, and we relied on whippy actions – albeit Jonah with greater reliance on his shoulder – whereas Brett Lee's action was a lot more jerky and muscular.

Changing my action only served to negate all of my natural attributes. I had generated speed through being lithe but the tinkering meant I was no longer snappy at the crease.

The biggest issue I had in that period was that I was playing Tests and one-day international matches where I was running in thinking about every technical stage of my action. For a bowler – and this is something I have come to appreciate the more knowledge I've acquired – it is the worst possible thing you can do. Now I don't even think about anything other than where I am going to bowl the ball. That is a definite reason why I have got better. You should not be road-testing a bowling action during England matches, when you have been nominated as one of the top four in your particular field in the country.

Now this was not entirely Troy Cooley's fault, of course, because the international schedule did not allow anyone to take the necessary step back. If you want to make such drastic changes and completely overhaul an action, you probably need a three-month block of time off and that was never available. But Troy must take a share of the blame, as must I. As a coach, he should have recognized that I needed taking out of the system. And I should have said more at the time.

So when Mike Watkinson and Kevin Shine agreed a U-turn was required in midsummer 2006, and that we would try to revert to something similar to what I had previously found natural, it provided me with a boost in both confidence and energy. Such was my excitement at the prospect that I worked even harder on my rehab. They agreed it was the best way forward, and I wanted to show them they were right.

Although we were not going to get the necessary changes completed overnight, it was a lot more straightforward working backwards towards something my body felt comfortable with and something that had not caused any injuries up until my England debut year of 2002. We started using video cameras to record my bowling, and I could see the difference unfold before my very eyes.

8

A Sobering Winter

There is one night of shame that will be indelibly linked with the winter of 2006–7. It has been referred to ever since simply as the pedalo night. The night that ended with Andrew Flintoff knee-deep in the Caribbean Sea at around 2 a.m., and he and a number of other members of our World Cup squad, including yours truly, in altogether hotter water.

However, this excessive night on the beer wasn't spontaneous and isolated. It had been, excuse the expression, brewing for months. There weren't many England tourists that winter who could paint a saintly picture of themselves when it came to the consumption of alcohol in Australia. When you consider that we were an international sports team, it is shocking to consider what went on during that Ashes trip.

Undoubtedly, some of our guys turned to booze as a direct consequence of what was happening to us on the field against one of the best international teams in history. Things hit new lows for a lot of our Ashes squad that winter, we weren't enjoying the tour either individually or collectively, and we were being comprehensively outplayed by a side intent on putting their name in international cricket folklore.

We were getting abused by crowds to an Olympic standard – in volume at least, both noise and amount, if not content: *'What do you call an Englishman with a hundred next to his name? A bowler'* is a slow burner I grant you and one day soon it might raise a laugh. While their punters got zero marks for originality, however, we got a similar score for our efforts. Goodness knows what level of stick we were getting back home – thankfully we have an out-of-sight, out-of-mind approach to British headlines and news bulletins when on the other side of the world.

But we got the gist of disappointment resonating around the country because we felt it ourselves as we lurched from defeat to defeat. And we sought solace in the bottom of pint glasses.

Our first beer was usually in what the Australians call their rooms – never been sure why they use the plural as they only ever showed us one, and it was the one they got changed in – after matches. Having a drink post-match with the opposition became a feature of the 2005 Ashes and so we upheld the Australian practice of displaying grace in defeat throughout the series, although being there among them became increasingly annoying with each pasting.

To be fair, the Australians displayed great levels of humility throughout that Test series, except that is for Michael Clarke, in the aftermath of Adelaide, where we prised defeat from the gums of a well-chewed draw. While others chatted with opposite numbers about the game, Clarke was being a complete pain, whistling away to himself and carrying on in a most arrogant manner.

He and I are very much contemporaries. Having first met on a night out in Blackburn in the late 1990s when he was an overseas player in the Lancashire League, we then made our international debuts within the space of a month during the VB Triangular Series in 2002–3. And his aloof behaviour on this occasion seriously pissed me off.

I said as much to Damien Martyn, who I was sat chatting to at the time, and, looking down at my feet, added: 'See this pad here, I really want to wrap it around his head.'

'Do it,' Martyn replied, completely straight-faced.

Now while Martyn was notorious for being someone who did not mix particularly well with his own team-mates, and was not close to anyone, preferring to be something of a lone wolf, his bullish attitude nevertheless took me aback.

I looked at him again as if to ask: 'Are you sure?'

'Do it!' he repeated.

As I'd had a couple of beers, I didn't need a second invitation, so I picked this pad up and cuffed Clarke with it, making the biggest thud imaginable in the process, and causing everyone in the room to stop nattering. For a split second there was complete silence.

'What the fuck ya doing?' he snarled.

Naturally, the temperature in the room had risen and the sensible thing to do was to cool it by cutting the night short and leaving. For once that winter, we did the sensible thing.

It was not an episode I look back on with any pride but the theme of drowning our sorrows and seeking solace in beer was extended throughout the rest of the trip. It is fair to say that I was lacking direction both on and off the field at times.

Although I considered that scene with Clarke to be something and nothing, there was one incident during the one-day triangular tournament that followed which makes me cringe with embarrassment and regret. It came on the eve of the series when, typical of the drinking culture that had developed, a few of us really went for it one night. Not any night, mind: a night thirty-six hours before a one-day international.

Now we all make mistakes, and I've made my share during a ten-year international career, but this escapade in Melbourne broke all the rules. In a disciplined team you do not need curfews and clock-ins because common sense prevails and players self-police – but on this tour we lacked maturity.

There were no thoughts of anything heavy when Andrew

Flintoff, Ed Joyce, Chris Read and I headed out from our Hyatt hotel base for the evening. We were just popping out for dinner and a glass of wine. But one thing led to another, a late night developed into an early morning and we ended up staggering back at 6 a.m. We hadn't ventured very far – both the pub and the karaoke bar we frequented were within spitting distance – but the fact that I would even consider boozing in the early hours, other than after a landmark Test victory or series-sealing one-day win, during an international tour obviously doesn't reflect well on me.

We displayed complete disdain for the trust that had been placed in us, and such was our lack of self-respect that we sneaked into fast-food joint Hungry Jack's – Australia's Burger King – for breakfast before nabbing an hour's sleep. Hardly an ideal diet for an international sportsman, let alone one that was required on the bus for practice at nine o'clock that morning.

Stuff like that shows how bad things had got on that tour. It had worn us down to such an extent that all sense of professionalism had been eradicated. Nights out, guzzling, were our form of escapism, our release from reality.

Fred was pulled up by Duncan Fletcher after turning up for training in Perth smelling of alcohol, following a typically one-sided defeat against Australia on Australia Day a couple of days earlier. He was fined for his dishevelled state and threatened with removal of the captaincy. But he was one individual among many on a tour that turned into something of a booze cruise. The presence of New Zealand, probably the most sociable team in world cricket, as the third country in that VB Triangular Series hardly helped. Because there were always a few days between games, it meant you could generally hit it hard immediately after a match – the Kiwis were nearly always in town and hail from a nation that doesn't need asking twice when it comes to a night out – with the guarantee of a recovery kip the following afternoon.

The management were certainly not aware of our state of inebriation in the build-up to the MCG opener, and I must confess

I managed to wing it very well at practice that day. I am sure others did too on other occasions. The universal attitude seemed to be that as we couldn't do any worse preparing properly, we should try to have a bit of fun along the way, and see where that got us. There was a real mood of *c'est la vie* around the camp, and whenever you've got social animals like Fred in tow, and aren't discouraging them from drinking, things are bound to get messy.

So the seeds of excess were sown thousands of miles away, down the road from St Kilda, rather than in St Lucia, the place in which our shoddy behaviour was well and truly exposed. These things tend to snowball if you don't nip them in the bud immediately, and to add to the routine of getting blitzed immediately after one-day internationals, one or two crept out for a few quiet ones rather too often. Evidently, I was one of those transgressors. It was indicative of my state of mind at the time, and is behaviour I would not contemplate these days a week before a match let alone a few hours. At the time I was in my mid-twenties, one of a number of young players in the squad, and confidence was fragile as we switched from red- to white-ball cricket.

The job we are paid handsomely to do is win cricket matches for England but in many ways we are not so different from cricket clubs up and down the country. Team spirit plays a part at times and, perhaps because ours was in need of repair following the Ashes humiliation, the management team attempted to foster some with a 'fines' system. Hundreds of weekend club cricketers up and down the country will be familiar with this light-hearted concept, and will have their own rules and regulations for what constitutes fineable offences.

Now given the circumstances of our tour, there was certainly some logic in trying to develop a bit of camaraderie – laughter had been in short supply after all – so the system of a judge and jury trying players for dodgy haircuts, dress sense or shabby time-keeping was met with some enthusiasm. Particularly, you will not be surprised to hear, because these court sessions involved a few beers and a sing-song.

From the management's point of view, I suspect they saw this as an opportunity for players to let off steam in a controlled environment, and Dean Conway, our Welsh physio, was the man in charge of trying to protect team morale as best as possible in the face of these regular on-field hammerings. Dean would be in control of the charge sheet, and each week would call his court session in the team room at the hotel in which we were staying.

Because there was a distinctive pattern to the schedule – we generally played New Zealand on a Tuesday and Australia on a Friday – songs were developed for these meetings to be sung depending on who our next opponents were. We adapted the Boomtown Rats' 'I Don't Like Mondays' and 'Friday, I'm in Love' by The Cure, it was a bit of fun and everyone got involved.

The first fines doled out at these gatherings would be for anyone who had not adhered to the dress code Dean had randomly come up with for that particular meeting. Instructions would usually be sent by text stating what those in attendance had to wear. Generally, he would get us to sport some attire that would make our passages from the sixth floor to the team room, down the corridor or across the lobby, and potentially past other guests, as embarrassing as was possible. Typically, his summons would demand that all members of the touring party wear a dressing gown, one sock and some form of head gear.

This was all seen as a bit of fun, and Dean is a convivial kind of bloke, whose permanent deadpan expression while holding court for these fines meetings only added to the humour. Duncan Fletcher would also be among those gathered, although I am not sure he ever had the dressing gown–sock combo going on. I am guessing as the boss he was exempt.

Deano would have us in stitches as Judge Conway. In addition to the fines, forfeits would also be meted out as punishment, and on one occasion Chris Tremlett was handed a dog lead, which he was instructed to place around Chris Read's neck, so that he could take him for a walk around the room. They completed their lap to Robbie Williams's 'Me and My Monkey' blaring out of the stereo, and with Chris Read 5 ft 5 in and Tremlett 6 ft 8 in, it made for a pretty funny spectacle.

These in-house japes were certainly not harmful to anyone else, as they took place in the privacy of our own appointed room, and were designed to provide light relief away from the serious business of facing Australia.

Further respite came with a variation in opponents. After the nightmare trip we'd had, no one really wanted to be in Australia any longer, simply because every time we played a game of cricket we lost. So it was nice that the New Zealanders were around to provide us with some different opposition. Now if you were picking tough opposition to face at that time, New Zealand would have been up there, but, quite frankly, we would have taken anyone rather than the Aussies in the immediate aftermath of that Test series.

Our first neutral meeting in Hobart coincided with our first victory on the tour, in fact, some seventy-two days after we had landed. It was such a liberating feeling bowling to guys who weren't Matthew Hayden or Adam Gilchrist, and that probably shows what dark places some of our minds were in. We were still up against top-quality players but there was no mental hang-up against them, and with confidence coursing through our veins we restricted the Kiwis to 205 for 9 on a slow surface. My four-wicket haul included Brendon McCullum, Stephen Fleming and Ross Taylor – a pretty good trio of scalps.

After just five wickets in the Ashes, it certainly gave me a boost in self-belief and I actually bowled all right throughout that one-day series, even against the Aussies. We kept getting annihilated by them until the penultimate group match but success over New Zealand helped terminate that dominance at the business end of the tournament.

By that stage, I'd developed a recurrence of my back niggle, and, because there was soreness in exactly the same area where I had suffered my stress fracture, I was sent home. Although it was a mild concern that discomfort had returned, the positive aspect to it all was that the management's priority was to make sure I was fully fit for the World Cup.

Despite having played a fair bit of international cricket by this stage, I had yet to establish myself as a regular, and this was a move in a positive direction for me.

Little did I imagine when I returned home with Jon Lewis, who also succumbed to injury, that the side I was leaving behind would go on to win that Commonwealth Bank Series. It was one of the biggest injustices in the history of international cricket and occurred in spite of all the nonsense occurring off the field, thanks to the most inspired batting form of Paul Collingwood's life.

A hundred from Colly settled the last group game against New Zealand at the Gabba, which was effectively a semi-final, and another hundred and a seventy were match-winning contributions in the two finals against Australia. He more or less won that trio of games off his own bat.

That we were even in that position was courtesy of a dropped catch by Shaun Tait, from a dolly Ed Joyce offered to third man early on in an earlier match at the SCG. That came on 2 February, the day I left Australia; Ed went on to hit a hundred, and we beat the home team for the first time on the tour. It began a run of four consecutive wins that came about more as a result of luck than judgement, and ended in silverware. When I boarded that flight home, it looked for all the money that New Zealand were going to meet Australia in the final, and that the rest of the squad would be following me sooner rather than later.

It is probably why my abiding memory of that series was not one captured in person but one witnessed on TV from my front room, and involved Paul Nixon. There was Nicko, having been called up at the age of thirty-six, being tossed about in the crowd, loving every minute of it. It was a madcap end to that tour of Australia – and the fact that one of the heroes was a veteran wicketkeeper no one would have given a prayer of appearing again at international level summed up what a debacle of a trip it had been.

However, normal service was resumed that spring in the Caribbean when our lack of tactical nous found us wanting in a World Cup once again. While other countries always seem to have aggressive plans we were still tackling matches in the old-school English way: 'Let's lose no more than two wickets in the first twenty overs, and we'll take it from there.'

While we took the conservative route, New Zealand, also in our World Cup group, were proactive. They went hard with both bat and ball at the start of each innings, and secured crucial points against us by virtue of their approach. In that tournament, as with other recent ones, any points secured against opponents that made the second-round stage were retained, and so we would start the Super Eight stage with work to do.

While we plodded to 209 for 7, New Zealand kept their foot to the floor despite losing three wickets inside the opening five overs of the new ball. They won with nine overs to spare, and the difference in approach highlighted to me how far behind the best teams we were in the limited-overs game.

But it was not the performance at the Beausejour ground that drew most attention in the aftermath of our six-wicket defeat on Friday 16 March 2007. Within the next forty-eight hours, England cricketers, myself included, featured on the front pages of newspapers back home for an excessive night on the tiles.

We were in such a habit of going out after matches that we thought nothing of heading from our St Lucia hotel complex to the beach bars a few hundred yards down the strip. A few beers after play was a staple that winter, win, lose or draw, and, lads being lads, and fairly young lads at that, it often turned into something quite a bit bigger than just a few.

The teams in our group were all accommodated in a resort that was about three-quarters of a mile long, just off the beach, and so there were other players out, too, most notably the New Zealand lads. The difference was, of course, that they had just won, and had a few days off to look forward to. In contrast, what we did was inappropriate less than thirty-six hours before our next match, against Canada.

Not that our shenanigans were planned, nor were they particularly outrageous. We just wandered down to a place called Lime, a typical open-air Caribbean bar, which was packed full of revellers. It was a Friday night, and there were people from the cricket mingling with holiday-makers and locals. It was a decent atmosphere and it was perhaps the relaxed nature of the environment that made us drop our guard.

After a couple of hours there, with rum and Coke literally on tap, our thoughts became more adventurous and instead of calling it quits shortly after eleven o'clock, four or five of us decided to head around the corner to the Rumours nightclub. 'It can't do any harm,' we must have thought. How wrong we were.

To be truthful, I am not sure we were thinking straight at all that night. Our behaviour was heavily criticized afterwards, but, for all the words written about it subsequently, I would probably sum it all up in two – 'spontaneous' and 'foolhardy'. And how we came to regret it. Some suggested it was disrespectful to our Canadian opponents that we even considered drinking alcohol on Friday night when we were due to face them at 9.30 on Sunday morning. But I am not sure we gave that match, or anything else to do with the tournament, too much consideration.

We had spent a warm-up week in St Vincent, which is one of the quieter Caribbean islands, and were stuck out in a quiet resort away from the main town. Time had passed pretty slowly there, and there was little else to keep us occupied aside from the two practice matches against Bermuda and Australia. Tours like this can be painfully monotonous, and we had been on the road for pretty much four months solid.

So this Friday night in question actually provided the chance to get out, with a day off on the Saturday to recover. Back then, it all seemed so straightforward, yet only five years later acting like we did would be unheard of for any England cricketer. The culture has changed so much that you wouldn't even have a beer in the dressing room if you had a game just two days later. The more I've thought about it in the interim, the more ridiculous it has seemed that we did go out and drink that night. It was stupid in the extreme to be out as long as we were.

Little did we know it at the time but that night out would lead to a full-scale inquisition of the squad, and a national inquiry into our conduct back home. Because of his public profile, Andrew Flintoff bore the brunt of it all, but although our paths crossed during the evening, he was not part of the group I was out with. He was still in our hotel when we hit the bars, and it was not until an hour or two later that he turned up with Jeremy Snape, our team psychologist, and a group of journalists. He later popped into the nightclub but didn't stay long and slipped out pretty much unnoticed.

All sorts of reports about what happened once he left surfaced over the next forty-eight hours but, whatever the truth, it is fair to say that while we were getting sloshed in Rumours, he was out tasting an altogether different drink – the water in Rodney Bay. Some would have you believe he was halfway to the United States when rescued but what was certain was that, under the influence of copious amounts of booze, he had attempted to clamber on, and subsequently capsized, one of the little vessels lined up on the beach in front of our five-star accommodation.

Word about that incident and the fact that several England players were out late spread unbelievably quickly the following morning, and it led to disciplinary action being taken against half a dozen of the fifteen-man playing squad, the others being Ian Bell, Jon Lewis, Liam Plunkett and Paul Nixon.

For my part, I was blissfully unaware of developments at the team hotel that morning when I returned from the local hospital. Despite being out until the early hours, I was up at what felt like the crack of dawn to have the finger I broke at net practice on the eve of the New Zealand match reset in its temporary splint. The ball had caught me flush on the end of my little finger as I attempted a low catch, and I immediately thought it felt a bit sore, looked at it and recognized it was out of place. I presumed, as did our team doctor, Mark Witherspoon, that it was dislocated.

He spent ten minutes of that training session yanking it, trying to put it back into place. 'It's not going back in,' he finally concluded, and it was only an hour or so later when we got it X-rayed at the local hospital that we discovered the reason. There was no dislocation at all; there was actually a massive crack in the bone, and some had been chipped off the tip. Mark's face when he realized the agony he had put me through was a picture.

'Am I going home?' I asked.

'Yep, I'm afraid so,' he told me.

However, we spoke to a finger specialist at the hospital whose recommendation was to insert a rod through the finger, to ensure it straightened normally, and it was during the course of these discussions that an alternative solution was floated by Dean Conway. As soon as he suggested there might be another way, one that involved me staying rather than going home, I was up for it.

A splint would straighten the finger, and I would receive two painkilling injections before every game. The only downside to this proposal was that it might look a bit funny – still function properly, just look a tad crooked for the rest of my life. A damaged little finger keep me out of a World Cup? Not if I could help it. After all, you just don't know how many World Cups you are going to play in your career.

Thankfully, I didn't go as far as Jacob Oram, who during the same month had said – tongue bolted firmly to cheek – that he would have had his broken finger sawn off if it meant he could carry on. I bet he was glad the New Zealand team management didn't take him as literally as some of the reporters covering that competition – because his throwaway line soon became one of sport's most gallant statements, at least according to some publications around the globe.

One wag in our squad suggested that, being from Burnley, I could afford an amputation and still have five fingers left . . .

Which was not quite as funny as discovering that Stuart Broad, who has subsequently become a really good mate, had been called up as my replacement, booked on to a flight and had actually made his way to the airport as advised, only to receive a second call in the terminal to say that I was staying put. Having missed so much cricket over the previous couple of years through loss of form and the stress fracture of the back, I wanted to do everything possible to stay in the England team rather than sit out several more weeks.

It had been a no-brainer for me, and I had returned from my 9 a.m. appointment in relatively high spirits when I was greeted by the sight of the entire squad traipsing into the team room of the Royal Resort complex. Because I hadn't been around, I had no clue as to what was going on, but I could have had a long-shot guess by the looks on some of my colleagues' faces.

Once the door was closed, Duncan Fletcher made it explicitly clear that he had cottoned on to all that had passed the previous night, and that we would all have the chance to explain our conduct. We were all to go up to the front of the room, in batting order, and write on the whiteboard our names, the time we had rolled in, and an explanation as to why we had come in that late.

Nobody spoke as all this was going on but I was sitting next to Liam, and when Ian Bell went up, at number three, we gave each other a knowing look to acknowledge that we would put down whatever time he plumped for. Belly wrote down 2.30 a.m. – which was accurate enough, give or take a couple of hours – so we were compelled to copy it for consistency's sake.

It was pretty clear that those of us who had been out late were going to be reprimanded but that court martial led to a fracturing of any sense of team spirit. Let's just say that while we might have been a little economical with the truth regarding the time of our return, some were more truthful than others. People being disingenuous about the time they had left the conclave of bars caused some divisions within that squad. Whether some players had got wind of what was going to happen in that disciplinary meeting I cannot say for sure, but it appeared that Fletcher went in with the intention of punishing any player who had been out after midnight. Eyebrows were raised when one player wrote down 11.30 p.m. Everyone in that room knew he had been out later than that.

Now when the majority of those who have overstepped the mark are willing to acknowledge it and face the consequences, blokes putting down false times, having egged others on to back their claims up, as we later discovered, inevitably causes disharmony. Yes, a group of us had stepped out of line but at least we accepted the error of our ways and were willing to take our medicine. There was a feeling that some had wriggled off the hook, and their subsequent behaviour only served to make matters worse. Things were pretty awkward within the group from that weekend onwards.

Following that initial meeting, we were all seen individually by Fletcher later that weekend, issued with £1500 fines and subsequently received a written warning that any further indiscretions would result in the end of our international careers. That certainly put the wind up the younger players among us, although Fred offered a typically brilliant one-liner to Phil Neale, who was entrusted with handing out the letters. 'I'll file these with the rest of them!' he said. Good old Fred.

Because of the attention the affair got back home, opportunists tried to make a buck or two – and succeeded – by sending in photos of us taken with mobile phones in Rumours; some even had the audacity to taunt us from the boundary during play on the

Sunday with the information that they had done so, and, sure enough, they appeared in British newspapers the following morning. It was pretty ordinary behaviour from these late-night revellers, many of whom we had obliged by posing for snaps with them.

Things were still rumbling in the camp, too, after we had completed a fifty-one-run win over Canada minus the suspended Andrew Flintoff. Kevin Shine and Jeremy Snape, two of the coaching staff, were belatedly hit in the pocket after Fletcher had got wind of their presence.

I felt sorry for Shiney as he had been away all winter, had hardly had a drop of alcohol and was out having a few drinks with his brother, who he had not seen for some time. Less so for Snape, who'd been drafted in as team psychologist only a month earlier.

Although Fred had spoken up and apologized on our behalf, the rest of us had not apologized personally to Duncan and were unsure whether to do so, or to let the incident lie and concentrate on performing in the rest of the tournament. We deliberated among ourselves a fair bit on the Monday and Tuesday but we concluded that the next best course of action was to put things in the past, determine not to put another foot out of line and concentrate on the final group game against Kenya on the Saturday.

Going out at all, even for a meal, became taboo so we ended up staying in the team room the whole time, ordering takeaway pizzas and watching films. We'd made our own beds and now we had to lie in them, we knew that, but we dared not venture too far from the hotel complexes as a result. Doing so might jeopardize our futures, and contrary to what had occurred, none of us wanted that. We had shared similar dreams of becoming successful international cricketers from young ages and so we remained in a goldfish bowl environment for the next four weeks.

We paid a heavy price for our excesses, and not being able to have a beer without feeling under the most intense scrutiny was unpleasant. We felt like naughty schoolkids. However, while there was considerable fretting between those games against Canada and

Kenya it was not necessarily from me. I knew that we had received a stern warning but we had to keep it in perspective. A lot had gone on before, without admonishment, and it was inevitable we would be brought into line at some point over that winter. And there was even criticism of Fletcher in the aftermath, with some eminent scribes suggesting he should have nipped the gallivanting in the bud much earlier, in Australia.

I recall letting one or two of our batsmen have it the rest of that week in St Lucia, and, come to think of it, Liam and Fred steamed in, too. It was hardly a united team and the dynamic was awkward at that time anyway. Little cracks in its make-up had already appeared, under the weight of pressure we were under in Australia. We had some big personalities, some big opinions, and had gone through three captains within a six-month spell. We had been away from home a long time.

The atmosphere of the tournament was hardly a pick-me-up, either. This was meant to be a World Cup, the game's flagship limited-overs competition, but the purpose-built stadiums were uninspiring, posted in the middle of nowhere, rarely attracted crowds of note, and contained slow surfaces hardly conducive to attractive spectacles. Even those I spoke to from successful teams in that tournament didn't really enjoy it.

Cricket in the Caribbean should be a unique experience, to be enjoyed. The sport is ingrained in the culture over there, and the attitude is fun, but that simply didn't come across. It was pretty much a flop from start to finish – the opening ceremony was carried out late one afternoon in Montego Bay, Jamaica, or so we were told. We were there, of course, but could not see a thing positioned as we were directly in line with the setting sun.

It was a rather fitting image for our World Cup – we did not seem to have a vision of how we would win the tournament; we were just lurching along more in hope than expectation, and although we beat Ireland on a brief visit to Guyana, back-to-back defeats against Sri Lanka and Australia in Antigua sealed our fate.

They also sealed the fate of Duncan Fletcher, who announced his departure at the end of that World Cup, during a practice session on the police ground in Barbados. It was one of the strangest experiences of my professional career.

As captain, Michael Vaughan tried to say a few words in response on behalf of the team, but broke down in tears. There were others who got emotional, too. The majority of the management, particularly Dean Conway, who had worked with Fletch since their days together at Glamorgan, were visibly upset. But it was something of a surprise that Paul Nixon, given that he had only been with the England team two months, was similarly moved.

To provide a bizarre contrast at this low-key and inauspicious end to an era, at the other end of the gathered group, lads high-fived each other, champagne corks popping in their heads.

In political terms, as I think I've made clear, I was the personification of Switzerland, with splinters in my bum. In contrast to others who were vehemently against Fletcher, I had no real emotional pull one way or another, but from a practical perspective I felt like his departure hailed the dawning of an exciting new era.

Someone else would be coming in, with new ideas, and a clean slate, so I viewed such a change as a potentially revitalizing time for me. I had been in and out of the team under Fletch, my career had drifted along; others might have suggested it had stagnated, and, by my own admission, I had never done enough for it to be any different. I was honest enough to concede I had yet to set the world on fire, despite numerous chances, but I was excited by the challenge of trying to impress a new man in charge.

People always reckoned Fletcher had his favourites. We had seen it at the start of the Ashes, and it revealed itself once more at the start of that World Cup when Ed Joyce was dropped just a few matches after getting a hundred, to get Andrew Strauss back into the team. There were other examples, too. We had used around two dozen players in winning the one-day series in Australia, with people flitting in and out. Mal Loye had been opening the batting in Michael Vaughan's absence but didn't then make the World Cup squad.

In just a few short weeks we lost all sense of adventure and our pre-tournament master plan appeared to be light years behind our rivals's. Generally, when discussing tactics at team meetings you will break games down into sections and formulate ideas of how you would approach areas like Powerplays, both in terms of batting and bowling. But we were so unadventurous that our batting plan amounted to us not wanting to be any more than two wickets down once the fielding restrictions were lifted. Other teams would have been targeting a scoring rate in excess of seven runs per over but as we lacked batsmen at the top of the order who could smack it out of the ground, we took the option of allowing individuals to play their natural games.

But as far as I am aware scoring at four an over to conserve wickets, with the intention of catching up at the back end of the innings, is a formula that has never really worked. Paul Collingwood was actually quite good at smacking a few at the back end but we were off the pace too often, and from that planning meeting onwards the general mood was that there were so many more teams present who were so much better organized than us. At that point we didn't really know what our best XI was – what our batting order should be, or the make-up of our attack.

Forget the fact we had just beaten them 2-0 in the triangular final, Australia were incomparable, a ridiculous team. Or a ridiculously good team, ridiculously well prepared, I should say. They had such a well-orchestrated plan of how best to use their talents, knew exactly what they were doing and implemented it all perfectly in Caribbean conditions.

There is always a collective belief that you can win any tournament before a ball is bowled: it goes with the territory of being an international cricketer. However, it is only in more recent times, in my opinion, that that belief has had substance. There was certainly no substance to ours in 2007.

As with any competition you could look back at the small margins; had Ravi Bopara squeezed out a couple more runs, after he brought us back from the dead against Sri Lanka in Antigua, we would have won more Super Eight games than we lost. But in truth our tournament was as stop-start for us as Dilhara Fernando's final over of that two-run defeat. I managed eight wickets in nine appearances, and was at the crease at the end of Fletcher's final game in charge, a consolation one-wicket win over West Indies, after we chased down in excess of 300 in Barbados.

For many of us, however, it was something of a relief that this particular winter was over.

9

Resurrection

Almost from the moment Peter Moores took over as England coach, I felt a new lease of life as an international cricketer. During a four-year cycle under Duncan Fletcher, incorporating two World Cup campaigns, for every stride forward I had taken it was inevitably followed by at least one step backwards.

But I genuinely felt that the slate was clean at the start of the 2007 season, and although I didn't begin it in the England Test team, I was willing to be judged on my county performances for Lancashire. With a new man in charge there was no baggage for anybody, and those whose relationships with Fletcher had bordered on cosy at times would be judged afresh.

It did not quite happen overnight but by midsummer it became evident that selection under Moores would reward those who performed well in County Championship and one-day domestic cricket. Suddenly, players like Ryan Sidebottom, one of the best performers on the circuit, came in from the cold, Chris Tremlett was finally given a go in Test cricket, and Graeme Swann, like Sidebottom, was recalled after several years' absence.

Naturally shy, and lacking in confidence, I saw something of my younger self in Swann and decided to take him under my wing.

He found the transition of going from the relative calm of the county scene to the spotlight of international cricket incredibly difficult, and was fearful of putting himself forward socially when he first walked back into an England dressing room. And if you believe any of this, you'll believe anything . . .

Truth is, when he was recalled for the 2007–8 tours to Sri Lanka I knew Swanny but only in the 'I know him' kind of way that develops from a mutual respect when you are on the county circuit. I had obviously played against him a few times, and the basis of us being mates was actually that he'd said 'All right, Jimmy lad?' at a Professional Cricketers' Association end-of-season do a few years earlier. Our friendship was naturally sealed by me mumbling 'Er . . . all right . . . [Christ, what's his name?] . . . er . . . Swann-eee' as we passed outside the toilets.

Although that was pretty much the limit of my previous conversations with him, I knew his brother Alec very well as we had sat next to each other in the Lancashire dressing room for three seasons. During the 2004 season, when I wasn't going through a particularly fruitful spell performance-wise and had faced disappointment over losing my England place, which meant more county games for me, Alec was the perfect bloke to change next to.

His sense of humour – dry and sarcastic – is very similar to mine and we had quite a lot in common in terms of our personalities. His demeanour really is a lot quieter: perhaps because Graeme did all the talking in their household and he never got a word in edgeways? Yet he has that inherent sense of comedy that you would expect from a Swann, and made me laugh constantly, often without trying to be funny.

One year during the final game of the season, at Taunton, he strode off after getting out, dumped his bat in the bin as he walked up the steps and declared: 'I've had enough of that.'

In contrast to Graeme, none of his laughs were sought, it was all just natural. They are quite different characters, too, and I imagine the way their relationship works is very similar to how mine works with Graeme. Both Alec and I are a lot more straightforward than Graeme, and remain content even when a room is silent. And we are a hell of a lot less showy.

Graeme and I have become close to the extent that we actually holiday together with our families between tours, and he and Alastair Cook are godfathers to my eldest daughter Lola. Graeme and Alec are incredibly tight, too. I'm often in the car with Graeme on the way to matches and he will ring for a chat with Alec on the way. It just goes to show some people need their dour fix for the day – let's just say that of all the things that Alec and I had in common during those Lancashire days, the most prominent was our mutual grumpiness. As people close to me will tell you, being grumpy actually makes me happy.

Our wives, Daniella and Sarah, give us horrendous stick because they think Graeme and I act just like an old married couple. They also think it's odd that we often finish each other's sentences. We don't – that has just developed from the amount of time we've spent together both on and off the field.

Because we think the same way about a lot of stuff, we tend to tee each other up with stories whenever we are at social occasions or cricket dinners. Obviously we are capable of individual thought, despite accusations from our other halves that we share one brain.

And I am thankful for that independence because there are times when Swanny goes too far. While I have a little man who sits somewhere between my ears letting me know to nip what I intend to say in the bud because it is inappropriate – 'you are going to offend someone if you say that, so don't' – Swanny does not. If he ever had one, he emigrated long ago.

He will crack a sexist joke in a room full of women and think nothing of it, and I was with him at one event when he turned the conversation to shagging, oblivious to the fact that an 8-year-old was standing about three yards away. He just doesn't care, and in one way I admire him for that. It's quite a rock 'n' roll attitude to have, befitting the lead singer of a band, but not one I could adopt.

We clicked from the moment he arrived on that tour to Sri Lanka. He picked his seat on the bus, which happened to be just in front of mine, and a beautiful bromance blossomed. We talked a lot there, and I know this sounds really corny but although we had only met once, maybe twice, previously, we talked as though we had known each other for years. It is fair to say I collapsed under the weight of his man crush on me, and have since caught him trying to cultivate a monobrow in my honour.

When he first got recalled, I am not sure he had fathomed out when to stop being stupid and when to be serious. Or at least he didn't care enough to try. There's no doubt he's different now; he's even started to listen in team meetings. Well, ever since a very crude interruption of one of Andy Flower's team talks in Antigua in 2009, at any rate.

His interjection, as we sat on the outfield at the Sir Vivian Richards Stadium discussing how to improve on a horrendous first Test display, came not from his voice box but his bowels. It was one of the loudest farts you could ever imagine, and although he said sorry immediately, it was hardly his most sincere apology. Flower, not a man to cross lightly, stared at him, initially attempted to carry on with his point, but after brief consideration, stopped to administer a dressing down.

Since then he has been known to offer his own opinions on occasion. As he has played a lot of cricket, his experience has actually proved quite useful at times. And above all else he cares. As a senior player he realizes the role he has to play, showing the young lads how to go about things properly, which obviously means not taking the piss in team meetings. There is a time and a place for that – it's the dressing room – and Strauss, who remains keen to keep Swanny and me apart as much as possible, is a prime target.

Swanny loves being the centre of attention, although he doesn't tend to say too much on the field. Nevertheless, the fact that he is loud, crass and generally entertaining changed the dynamic of the England dressing room. We already had some quite dominant alpha males, and it got really interesting when Andrew Flintoff and Swanny were pitched together. You see, Swanny is loud and likes to take the mickey out of people. And Fred was always the loud one who took the mickey in the past. Now they were fighting for airtime. During this period of career crossover, my observation was that Fred felt a little bit threatened by Swanny's presence. All of a sudden, there was a new funny man around, and it could get quite icy at times.

As much as I love him, there is no mistaking Swanny has a big ego, too – he will admit his confidence borders on arrogance – and the same is true of both Fred and Kevin Pietersen. Arguably, we all have egos as international sportsmen but some hide them better than others, and when you have a number of that type contained in one environment, it makes for an interesting time. The thing about Fred was that he worked hard to deflect attention from his ego, by playing the public so brilliantly. The 'I'm just a lad from Preston' line was all part of his man-of-the-people image, and because he always had the punters on his side, he could get away with almost anything.

I was happier with my prospects as the Moores–Michael Vaughan era opened, for although I was not selected during the Test series against the West Indies, it felt as though England chances would come. Playing four-day games for Lancashire at this stage was actually beneficial to me because I was around experienced bowlers like Glen Chapple and Dominic Cork, and a good volume of overs allowed me to further groove my action, the original one I had reverted to the previous year. The week before my Test recall against India, I took five wickets in the first innings of a rain-affected Roses match, my best display of the 2007 season to date.

It proved to be a pleasing return personally but a frustrating one from a team perspective as the Indians somehow held on for a draw at Lord's, aided and abetted by dark clouds, rain and a slice of good fortune when it came to a crucial umpiring decision.

There were a number of landmarks for me in that first Test. I bagged my fiftieth Test wicket when Mahendra Singh Dhoni steered to fourth slip. Later, I found out that my five-wicket haul in India's 201 was also unique, as it was the first time the same bowler had dismissed Sachin Tendulkar, Rahul Dravid and Sourav Ganguly in the same innings.

Although we dominated the game, however, bad weather scuppered certain victory when, with India nine wickets down, requiring a further ninety-eight runs to win, bad light and rain intervened terminally in the penultimate session of the match. To add to the sense of injustice, we could see the menacing clouds coming towards us for the final half-hour we were on the field, a period which included Steve Bucknor turning down what was a stonewall lbw shout from Monty Panesar after trapping Sreesanth in front. Had the Decision Review System been around then – and India acquiesced to its use – we would have been celebrating being 1-0 up heading to Trent Bridge, as replays showed it hitting middle stump halfway up. It highlighted what small margins can sometimes exist at the highest level between winning and losing.

The change in personnel that summer led to an increase in responsibility for me on the field of play, and I considered my seniority within the bowling group to be a privilege with benefits. Ryan Sidebottom is older than me but quite a quiet guy, not the sort who would push himself forward in that environment, chiefly because he had only just returned to England level following a six-year absence. Chris Tremlett is a similarly undemonstrative character so, although I had been fairly withdrawn during my early years, I took on the role of communicator.

Being the bowling go-between meant discussing field placing and tactics with Siddy and Tremmers, what the ball was doing, whether it was swinging or not, what the pitch was doing, what lengths we should be bowling, and reporting back our conclusions to Michael Vaughan.

This was the first time I had been confronted with this role. Because of the number of established bowlers we'd previously had around, there had not been a need for me to do it, and some people were keener than others on sharing thoughts. To be fair to him, Matthew Hoggard was always pretty good at it. In contrast, Fred would never really talk to you, and Harmy did only a little bit. Even then, they would never really come to you to say something when you needed it; they would always wait for you to go to them. You would always need to ask the question to get something out of them. Now I saw for myself that there was a chance to start being proactive with stuff like that, and helping others.

As it was, we went 1-0 behind there in a match where most of the attention shifted from our under-par first innings total of 198 to the culprit in the jellybean incident that so incensed Zaheer Khan on the third evening. When he arrived in the middle to bat, he discovered one of the aforementioned beans on the crease, and took umbrage. A number of our players eat sweets during sessions in the field and one had clearly gone astray. Now if it was intentional, it would be best described as childish rather than malicious to drop one near the pitch, as far as I was concerned. Yet Matt Prior took considerable heat for it, even though it wasn't his doing. If you think about it, a bloke with big gloves on is not the most likely culprit to have sweets stashed in his pockets.

When it came to it, a combination of a flat Oval pitch and the depth and quality of India's batting line-up nullified our attempts to claw our way back level in the decider. Despite the toil, however, there was some reward for me. Four more first-innings wickets, and the eye-catching dismissal of Tendulkar, albeit a thick inside edge contributed to the uprooting of leg and middle stumps, among two in the second took my overall tally to fourteen, and earned me England's man-of-the-series award. Some people claimed that Tendulkar's eyes had gone but that was absolute nonsense. I wish my eyes would go if that was the case – he had scored thirty-seven Test hundreds at that stage and improved that by more than a third over the next four years.

But the main cheer for me, as I assessed things heading into the one-day series against the Indians, was that I was bowling well, and actually felt like the senior bowler for the first time in international cricket. Ryan Sidebottom had more experience than me at county level, and so, arguably, did Chris Tremlett, but in terms of the attack dynamics I viewed myself as the spearhead. Things had come quite a long way from twelve months earlier when I had yet to play a game following my lengthy injury lay-off, and little could I have envisaged how dramatically my standing would improve in the struggle through the Ashes.

The NatWest Series see-sawed over seven matches, but beating India 4-3 with a strong performance in the decider avenged the Test loss, provided Paul Collingwood with a first campaign win since succeeding Michael Vaughan as one-day captain, and showed signs that we could be competitive against the very best limited-overs teams. With fourteen I was leading wicket-taker for England once more, and this contributed to my call-up as a replacement for the World Twenty20 in South Africa, where I maintained my good form.

But it was actually the win in Sri Lanka the following month that I rate as highly as any one-day series success during my time as an England player. Most teams going around on the international circuit are extremely proficient in their home conditions, but arguably none are as proficient as Sri Lanka in Sri Lanka, which is why the 3-2 victory was all the more pleasing.

It was unusual in that it was a self-contained limited-overs tour separate from the Tests which were scheduled for later that winter, which meant complete focus on one-day stuff. There was none of the usual influx of specialist players as the series came to its conclusion, and it was a relaxed atmosphere.

Normally England's chances there would be as remote as some of the jungle in which Dambulla, the scene of the first three matches, is situated. None of our predecessors had managed to win a series on the island but there was a good energy about a new-look squad and despite losing heavily in the opening match, we managed to wrest control by restricting the Sri Lankan batsmen. Their conditions are normally punishing for our bowlers but on this occasion none of our attack conceded as many as five runs per over across the course of the five matches, which was a phenomenal effort.

We were obviously on a high after winning the fourth one, to take an unassailable 3-1 advantage, but life was about to receive a serious jolt for me on the eve of the fifth and final match on 13 October, when Daniella rang to give me the gravest news. She'd had a miscarriage.

In situations like these, when you are thousands of miles away and a loved one needs you, you feel pretty hopeless as a husband. All I wanted was to be with Daniella right there and then. We had been so full of excitement at the prospect of becoming parents for the first time.

'I'm coming straight home,' I told her down the phone.

But Daniella persuaded me that there was not a lot I could do, and that I should play the match as normal. Given the devastating blow we had just experienced that was easier said than done, but she was being incredibly strong, and I had to be, too. It was obviously a private matter and although I didn't want others to know, I had to inform Phil Neale and Peter Moores, and request a flight home as soon as was possible after playing the match.

I got through the game at the Premadasa Stadium but I didn't perform particularly well and Sri Lanka clawed the score back to 3-2. As hard as you try to block external events out when you are on the field of play there are some things that are too overwhelming and this was one of them. As well as an international sportsman, I am also a husband – something that can easily be overlooked in the modern world – with similar emotions to bricklayers, builders and bakers all across Britain. And to give those emotions a further jolt, a message was sent on to the field during the match informing Owais Shah he had just become a father for the first time. While the rest of the team congratulated him – myself included – I suffered in silence.

Owais and I flew home that evening, him so full of excitement that he barely paused for breath, me so full of angst that I wished away every minute of the ten-hour flight. However, as I did not begrudge him his good news, I gritted my teeth and listened. He felt awful when, deep into the flight, he asked: 'Hang on a minute, why are you going back early?' Naturally he felt awful but he wasn't to know, and I told him as much.

The reappearance of some of the more experienced players for the return to Sri Lanka knocked me back in the pecking order once more. We had played throughout the second half of the 2007 summer without Andrew Flintoff, Matthew Hoggard or Steve Harmison, who were all absent through injury, but while Fred's ankle problems persisted, the other two were in the Test squad.

All three of us played in the warm-up contest against a President's XI in Colombo, one of those in which the team is rotated to give all squad members some playing time, and although I experienced some soreness in my left ankle, which restricted me to only one over in the second innings, I felt I had done enough, and had enough credit from the summer to secure a place for the first Test in Kandy.

That is how it turned out when it came down to selection but just as in the Ashes the previous year I was asked to bowl first change, which I have never seen as my strength, with Hoggy and Ryan Sidebottom sharing the new ball. To be fair, Hoggy bowled well in that first innings, and we had control of the match when we dismissed the Sri Lankans for 188 but we did not back that up in securing a big enough lead – ninety-three was under par in the circumstances – and narrowly failed to hold on for a draw after being put under pressure on a very slow surface. This was the match in which Muttiah Muralitharan surpassed Shane Warne as Test cricket's most prolific wicket-taker.

Swanny and I found the song written in anticipation of his world record feat, and one blasted through the PA system from literally the moment he dismissed Paul Collingwood, his 709th victim, amusing in the extreme. The words were catchy, I will give it that, but it was completely out of tune, and Swanny and I spent numerous hours during the rest of the tour perfecting our own renditions, paying tribute to 'Muttiah Muralitharan, the greatest spin bowler the world had ever seen'.

I recorded an ignominious high – or low, depending how you viewed it – when Sanath Jayasuriya hit each ball of my fourth over of the second innings for four. To add to my frustration, one of them flew through the fingers of Ian Bell in the slips, and another also came from a flashing edge. But the scorebook still had my figures good for twenty-four as I claimed my cap and sloped off at the end of the over. 'You're not a proper bowler until that's happened,' chuntered Hoggy, shaking my hand. He had suffered the same fate at the hands of Chris Gayle at the Oval in 2004, so at least someone else knew how bad it felt. That in itself made it a teeny bit better.

There was plenty of downtime to kill after that first Test for me as I was dropped for the remaining games in Colombo and Galle, and during the final match I was rebuked alongside Swanny and Stuart Broad for larking about in playing hours. I know more than most how tedious it can get on an England tour when you are not in the first XI, and so we were passing the time while the lads were out in the field, singing along to various tunes blaring out of the iPod speakers in the dressing room.

We went through some classic Charlatans and Stone Roses, and tailored a couple for Broady's taste such as Rick Astley's 'Never Gonna Give You Up'. Mark Garaway, our team analyst, kept turning around, taking pictures of us on his mobile phone and laughing. For all the money we thought he was joining in with a little bit of fun, even singing along at times, but Mooresy got his hands on the pictures and gave us an absolute bollocking at the post-match debrief for doing a sub-standard job as twelfth, thirteenth and fourteenth men. It was because of us three, apparently, that England had just been dismissed for double figures and conceded a first-innings lead in excess of 400 in the process. But for a combination of Alastair Cook's match-saving vigil and the rain that blew in off the sea, I think he might have killed us.

Naturally, we didn't agree with the draconian reaction to us letting off a little steam in private but we were guilty of certain other levels of unprofessionalism in a quest to cure tour boredom. One of the tasks we set ourselves was to sabotage some of the medical research being done on the trip. At this time, the team was going through a phase of doing Osmo tests. Now if you're not familiar with them, basically you piss into a cup and your dehydration level is tested directly from your urine sample. In places like Sri Lanka where the humidity is so high, and cramping is prevalent, these tests are helpful in keeping eleven players on the field.

But we checked their accuracy levels by concentrating all our efforts on getting as high a reading as we possibly could. We drank copious amounts of coffee and Coke, and stopped eating for the day, just to see if we could knacker things up. This was clearly the first evidence of the influence of one G. P. Swann on me, and I have since devoted plenty of time to improving him as a citizen and colleague.

The next talking to I got from Mooresy was far more positive, however. It came in New Zealand on a tour that I had started on the periphery once more. Just as in Sri Lanka, changes were going to be made after we had lost the first Test, and this time, as one of those from the outside looking in, I was a beneficiary of that policy. And it was a fairly seismic decision in modern English cricket history: I was being called in for the middle match of a three-Test series, along with Broad, because Matthew Hoggard and Steve Harmison were being axed.

Sacrificing both was quite a big shift in personnel and surprised outsiders because they had been permanent fixtures in the team when fit for quite a while. Until a side strain in Sydney just over a year earlier, Hoggy had played forty consecutive Tests and with 248 wickets he was in the top ten England bowlers of all-time. Harmy had been dogged by injury a fair bit, had experienced some loss of form and had a habit of starting tours slowly because he was not renowned as the best at keeping himself fit while off-duty.

Here were two experienced fast bowlers but they were culled in clinical fashion for two significant drops: Hoggard in pace and Harmison in intensity. In their pomp they had been crucial cogs in the team that conquered all before them for eighteen months from early 2004 to the end of the 2005 Ashes-winning summer but international sport is such a harsh environment that there can be no let-up. There was certainly a feeling that both had lost a yard or two in that first Test defeat at Hamilton, and in Hoggard's case he was down below 80 mph, which is generally the low-water mark for new-ball operators at international level. Neither of the pair seemed overly keen on Moores's devotion to improved fitness either, so while externally it might have appeared a drastic decision, internally it was received as a pragmatic one by the majority.

Both those blokes had been such integral members of the team that had risen up the rankings under Duncan Fletcher so this was a watershed moment, and therefore no little pressure to perform would be placed on those selected to replace them. Mooresy took me to one side and told me that not only did he want me back in the XI but he wanted me to be the leader of the team's attack. It was a conversation that did me a power of good because, although I have never lacked belief in my own ability, I have always been someone who flourishes when being backed by others. I have always been the kind of bowler who has responded to the metaphorical arm around the shoulder rather than the boot up the arse, and I was determined to repay this renewed faith.

My chance came after Moores granted my request to go off and play first-class cricket for Auckland to search for some form after a disappointing end to the one-day series. Because of that dip, it was pretty evident that I would not start the Test campaign, but this was a much better option for me than sitting on the sidelines again. Ottis Gibson, our bowling coach, had been hatching a plan for one of our guys to play for Auckland after Kyle Mills and Chris Martin were called up for New Zealand, and Daryl Tuffey and Andre Adams went to the Indian Cricket League.

It was felt that such a deal could be mutually beneficial and I got wind of the fact that they intended to dispatch Chris Tremlett. But as I knew I would not be in the XI for the first Test, I persuaded them that it should be me, as I didn't want a repeat of the situation three years earlier when I was thrown in cold on tour in South Africa. It was agreed but it was not a move that pleased everyone, not least Justin Vaughan, the chief executive of New Zealand Cricket. 'We are not particularly enthusiastic about it but we can understand why Auckland want to do it,' Vaughan said. 'We would be happier if they gave a chance to a young New Zealand bowler because we can see a scenario where Anderson bowls himself into form and then helps England win the deciding final Test because of that.'

Those words came home to roost sooner than Vaughan anticipated and when I was recalled for the second Test at Wellington I was grateful for having some bowling under my belt. I went in match-sharp, and the extra responsibility of leading the attack definitely inspired me both in that match and in the longer term. Feeling like I was the senior man helped me think more about my bowling, rather than just running in, and think about others' bowling, too. It was the start of me offering more advice to the rest of the bowlers, which is why you will often see me appear at mid off for a chat.

No coach had previously spoken to me in the way Moores did on that tour, never put so much faith in me, but I thrived on the new experience. As a coach, he is constantly thinking about the game and constantly thinking about how he can improve the performance of the team he is in charge of. To do that he needs eleven players who are playing as well as they possibly can. Also, when he talks to people, he understands that the context of what he says can have an influence on how they perform. I've always found his communication skills excellent, and to me a good coach doesn't only get a response by spending time with players in the nets. Talking to them away from the practice sessions, about specific roles and sharing plans has its benefits.

The talk had its desired effect on this occasion and if he was looking for an immediate dividend, he certainly got one, because I took career-best figures on a surface that you had to remain patient on. The ball went past the bat quite a bit but I finished with a five-wicket haul in my first innings back, and thanks to Tim Ambrose's first England hundred, we secured a 144-run first-innings lead, an advantage that proved crucial to the result.

My involvement had actually been jeopardized after an incident on the first evening, shortly after I had walked off the field with Monty Panesar with us nine wickets down at the close. We were going through a stage of doing a team fitness activity in the evening on batting days in that series, designed for us all to get a sweat on, but mainly for the guys who had been sitting around doing nothing.

As was often the case, this meant a game of football, during which I attempted a run-of-the-mill Johan Cruyff turn and went over heavily on my ankle, in exactly the same manner I had done in Sri Lanka four years earlier. Carried into the dressing room, I later left the ground on crutches, coming face to face with Angus Fraser, who was cricket correspondent of the *Independent* at that time, behind the pavilion.

'What the hell have you done?' he asked.

'Oh, it's nothing, really,' I said. 'Only a minor twist, these things are precautionary.'

As I was speaking to a journalist I had to play it down, as we didn't really want word getting out that it was anything to the contrary. The ankle remained on ice all through the night, to flush out the bruising, and although it was still absolute agony when I returned to the ground the next morning, the medical team checked to make sure the damage was nothing drastic with their ultra-sound machine before strapping me up, filling me full of painkillers and shoving me back into the middle.

The best thing for ankles sometimes is to try to run through the pain, and although mine went black that week it was worth it. A distinct hobble was noticeable in my initial approaches to the crease, but things certainly got easier as the match went on, and winning is usually a good cure for aches and pains.

Ryan Sidebottom then bowled brilliantly with 7 for 47 in the first innings in Napier to set up a victory despite us being 4 for 3 in the opening quarter of an hour. His performance with the ball allied to hundreds from Kevin Pietersen, Andrew Strauss – who, like me, had benefited from playing domestic cricket over there in the build-up – and Ian Bell contributed to a fine comeback series victory.

Preoccupied with my own delight at being in the team, I didn't spare much thought for Hoggy's plight as we returned from that tour but in the greater scheme of things it was a huge deal. He had been so consistent for such a long time, developed into a really skilful bowler, and was just two shy of the 250-wicket mark in Tests, but there was undoubtedly a clash of both personality and attitude with Peter Moores, an advocate of a hard-work ethic. We would not see Hoggy in an England shirt again.

Harmy notoriously started poorly on tours because if he'd had any period of time at home in the build-up, he probably wouldn't be in the gym as much as he should have been, and it would take him two or three weeks of a tour to get bowling fit. On this occasion that backfired because it was pretty obvious that he wasn't up to speed by that first Test. Modern cricket doesn't really allow for the old-school approach of getting yourself into shape with a sustained period of netting or matches for your county. It had worked for him during summers when commitments with Durham kept him ticking over but in the winter he would wait until he got on the plane to start his regime.

Both Hoggy and Steve Harmison were at stages in their careers where they didn't feel the need to bowl a lot in the nets. It was pretty evident to them what they could do from a few years at the very top, and when you have played a fair bit of international cricket you genuinely get to know your games inside out. Nor were either of them gym bunnies by any stretch of the imagination, so they dropped another notch in Moores's estimation during this tour. He tends to take to people who look to push themselves both physically and in terms of skill acquisition. Ultimately, however, the decision was based on performances in the first Test rather than on personalities and the changes proved to be an inspired move given the scoreline.

There was obviously a feeling of satisfaction within the camp at our achievement but there remained a disharmonious backdrop throughout that tour because of the work ethic and devotion to fitness Peter Moores was trying to instil. And those irked by it extended beyond Hoggard and Harmison.

Marques Church, our Kiwi fitness trainer on that tour, tried to get us to buy into what appeared on the outside to be a rather unusual concept. He took pictures of us at the start of the trip, and told us that he would take the same shots at two-weekly intervals throughout our time away. 'You'll see the physical change,' he said, enthusiastically, upon announcing his plan.

We did buy into that a little bit, or at least a group of us did, but thankfully we never did get to pose for pictures two, three and four. The whole fitness issue got a bit out of hand in the first half of the tour in Napier when we played a game that ended as a tie. New Zealand had chased down our 340 in searing heat, and it got all the way down to the last ball with any result possible.

We had just walked off the field, felt absolutely knackered, having gone through the emotional swings as well as the physical exertion of a game like that, and were given a choice of doing the fitness there and then or at seven o'clock the following morning before we travelled. We opted to get it out of the way, although it was really no choice at all given the circumstances. So here we were doing running drills – sprint the straight, jog the corner – completely goosed. Siddy started cramping up, and even those not averse to a bit of extra fitness work were inclined to ask: 'What the heck are we doing?' It was just ridiculous. It didn't help that we could see the New Zealand lads laughing at us from their dressing room. It was absolute madness. There was such a devotion to doing fitness every day after a game that there was no room for compromise but compromise was needed in that situation. There is keeping fit and there is common sense, and this was a time when it wasn't applied.

The way the itinerary worked out, people might have been sick of watching us play New Zealand but I quite enjoyed having another crack at them in home conditions during 2008.

They pushed us really hard in that series, in fact, and it took a big turnaround at Old Trafford to force victory. The biggest damage I did during that match took place in New Zealand batsman Daniel Flynn's mouth rather than in the wickets column. One just climbed on him, and I didn't initially realize the extent of the mess he was in as I turned back towards my mark.

You clatter grilles of helmets occasionally as a fast bowler, and I believed I had scored a point in our duel, no more. It wasn't until I saw their physio had come out that I went back to discover one tooth on the pitch, and blood everywhere. Later it was revealed that a couple of teeth around his new gap were also weakened by the impact, and had to be removed, and I have since heard he is quite happy with the work he got done by the plastic surgeon. Apparently, his pearly whites weren't so pearly or so white before that day, so I actually did him a bit of a favour. It probably explains why, having not been previously included, I suddenly appeared on his Christmas card list.

At least that blow was within the etiquette of the game. The one that was dealt to Grant Elliott by Ryan Sidebottom in the one-day international at the Oval a few weeks later was more open to question and it was a poor decision on our part to uphold it. Poor on Sid's part because he should have declared it unfair from the start when he floored him in running across his path to field the ball; poor on Paul Collingwood's part for allowing his competitive juices to influence his decision because the buck stops with the captain in that situation; and poor from the rest of us for not displaying greater sportsmanship. There weren't many dissenting voices, and I certainly told Colly to uphold his dismissal, so we were all culpable.

Sometimes, in the heat of the moment, when all you want is to win the game, that becomes your primary focus and anything goes. But in hindsight we were grateful for Swanny's overthrow off the final ball of the game. You never want to lose a match, of course, but good old Swanny helped us avoid an even more sensitive diplomatic incident. We've always got on well with the New Zealanders, they're a good set of blokes, but they turned their backs on us that night as we went to shake hands afterwards. They are also a very talented team, particularly in one-day cricket, competitive virtually every time we play them, and it was no real shock that they responded in kind to our Test series victory with one-day success.

That match was also notable for one of Monty Panesar's best ever spells in an England shirt. We were staring defeat in the face after giving up a 179-run deficit on first innings, and New Zealand had moved to 50 for 1 before Monty took advantage of the turn and bounce on offer from the Old Trafford pitch with a six-wicket haul in double-quick time. We were still required to knock off 294 runs and it is certainly one of the most impressive wins I have been involved in.

Immediately after one of the best team performances, I returned my own career-best to date, with 7 for 43 to set up an innings victory and claim the man-of-the-match award at Trent Bridge. It is a ground that I have done very well at, mainly due to the fact that the ball swings there, and this occasion was no exception. When the ball swings late at pace as I got it to in New Zealand's first innings, you always know you are in the game, and when it does it from a middle stump or middle-and-off line it can have pretty spectacular results. Turning batsmen around to knock out off stump as I did to Aaron Redmond and Brendon McCullum that day is the ultimate kind of dismissal for me.

Controversially, with Ryan Sidebottom injured, I was given a new new-ball partner for the second Test against South Africa later that summer. Michael Vaughan was keen to have another bowler who could swing the ball in Sid's absence, particularly as we had three hit-the-deck bowlers in Stuart Broad, Chris Tremlett and Andrew Flintoff, returning from injury, in our squad. With Matthew Hoggard jettisoned, the little-known Darren Pattinson, of Nottinghamshire, was called up.

British-born but Australian-raised, few of us had even seen him play before let alone spoken to him, and as he had been called up at literally the very last minute there was little opportunity to do so, but we tried to make him feel as welcome as possible. As a fellow bowler, I tried to encourage him whenever I could, and after a few overs had gone by in the match, as we passed on the field I asked him: 'Hey, mate, you got it swinging?'

'Dunno, I don't really swing it,' he replied.

Unfortunately, it turned out that he was just a seamer who hits the pitch as hard as possible and nips it around a little bit, and after we posted an under-par 203 first up, we needed to create some chances. However, although we took a few early wickets, Ashwell Prince and AB de Villiers dug in for big hundreds, and we ended up getting hammered.

With Sid not around, nightwatchman duties in that match fell upon my shoulders, and I began the third morning attempting to prolong the match as long as possible alongside Alastair Cook. I managed the first hour and three-quarters of play, which I considered a pretty good effort, as I sat covered in ice packs in the dressing room to reflect upon it. My innings of thirty-four represented my best in Test cricket but it came at a price as I had been hit on the wrist, and clunked on the back of the head, from consecutive Dale Steyn deliveries. He is one of the most difficult bowlers to face in the world game, and although I was in something of a purple patch as an international batsman, getting hit on the head was a little bit unnerving. There have been other times when I have struggled to pick the length up properly and ducked into ones that are not short enough, and at Steyn's speed you are in trouble.

He is a ridiculously consistent bowler, someone who has been a prolific wicket-taker throughout his career, and someone who I have trailed in second place in the world Test bowling rankings, not that I have ever got particularly close to him. You have to admire the volume of wickets he takes and the fact that he takes them on all surfaces in all conditions around the globe, and that is why he's always been way ahead of me on points.

Being recognized as one of the best bowlers in the world is obviously a source of pride but doesn't do as much for me as being a contributor to winning matches. There is obviously a correlation between your standing in the world rankings and what you are contributing to your team, and we have seen that with a number of England batsmen over the past couple of years as they have churned out hundreds so prolifically. But statistics only truly mean something if there is a W in the result column. For example, I once again finished as leading wicket-taker in a home series against South Africa, but just as five years earlier it had not come in a series win.

After defeat at Edgbaston, a game which was in the balance until Graeme Smith and Mark Boucher shared an unbroken century stand for the sixth wicket, came something of a shock: Michael Vaughan's resignation as captain.

Now I am pretty useless in these situations because I rarely see events like this coming, and this was no exception. We were beaten in Birmingham on Saturday night, and by the Sunday lunchtime it was announced via a tearful press conference in Loughborough that we were looking for another captain. A matter of hours later and Paul Collingwood's tenure as limited-overs captain was a thing of the past, too.

It resulted in the appointment of Kevin Pietersen, uniting the England captaincy across all formats once more, and a decision in that regard that made sense. Nor was there any real opposition at that time. Although Andrew Strauss would have been my choice for the Ashes when the captaincy issue raised its head two years earlier, at this time he was no longer guaranteed a place in the side, having only just got back in after being dropped for the previous winter's tour of Sri Lanka. Colly wanted to concentrate on sustaining his Test place but I am not sure he ever enjoyed leadership that much anyway, and it was too soon after Fred's infamous winter disciplining for him to be a realistic candidate, even if he had wanted to be considered once more. So, 2-0 down, we turned to Kev. Everyone is always excited by a change in captaincy, and it is natural to want to help a new guy out, so there was a genuinely good feel around the camp when we won the dead rubber at the Oval, where Harmy was recalled and Kev got a hundred, and then triumphed 4-0 in the NatWest Series. Little did we know what was to follow.

10

Testing Times

I have to confess to possessing a guilty conscience when it comes to the ill-fated Stanford Super Series in Antigua in the autumn of 2008. And I am not talking about feeling bad for being a part of it, as sorry as I am for those who lost life savings at the hands of that crooked cricket financier Allen Stanford.

No, as England cricketers, all you can do is to prepare properly and go out to perform to the best of your ability wherever your employers tell you to. I was selected as one of fifteen to go and represent England that week, and, like any other series I am picked for, I went. However, my attitude towards this landmark $20 million match on 1 November stunk, and it was an attitude unfortunately shared by some of my team-mates. One thing you should never do as an international player is disrespect your opponents, yet I and the majority of our squad dismissed the West Indies as being crap from the moment the fixture was announced.

'We're going to win a million' was the common thought in our dressing room. Everyone believed this venture was easy money. KER-CHING!

Now confidence is a crucial ingredient to any successful team but this was overconfidence in the extreme. You want to be positive before any big match, and encourage it in your team-mates, too, but our assumption pre-departure that we would win was based not on recent evidence – although we had displayed good one-day form in the 4-0 win against South Africa – but on the fact we had defeated West Indies regularly over recent years.

Cue an almighty shock when we got there. Far from being the pushovers we anticipated, this team of Stanford Superstars, as they were called, played like, well ... er, superstars. They looked mega-professional, fit as fleas, and were fresh from an intensive month-long training camp designed to sharpen their twenty-over skills. Our attitude was 'we've beat 'em before, and we'll beat 'em again'. But they rolled out some players we'd never heard of, who had been good in their domestic Twenty20 competition, and we did not give them enough credit.

Some people suggested the concept of playing one match for so much money was wrong, even insensitive, at a time when the British economy was in freefall and jobs were being culled. Yet nobody ever challenged the annual million-dollar Sun City golf challenge for its riches, purses for heavyweight boxing matches or the prize money in Formula One.

Competing would not have been a problem for me. I was excited by the very prospect but unfortunately everyone including myself was already spending the money (in our heads at least) in advance. The squad was awash with talk of fancy cars, flash watches and how much would be slashed off mortgages. In one way it was perfectly natural. Whatever walk of life you're from, it is an exciting prospect when someone informs you that for doing just one day's work well your reward will be a cool million. Especially when that day's work is no different from any other day's.

Our families were in tow and despite the opulence of the occasion we were shoved into a shocking hotel – some all-inclusive resort – on the east side of the island. People were falling sick on a daily basis: Stuart Broad and Luke Wright both succumbed to food poisoning. Samit Patel got so bad that he was confined to the complex one day, and all he managed to keep down was Bounty bars. Or, at least that's what he told us when we got back that evening and caught him with a carrier bag full of them on the way back to his room.

Stanford's ground at Coolidge, across the road from the international airport, was smart enough but we soon discovered in two warm-up games against Middlesex and Trinidad & Tobago that the outfield was too long and the pitch too slow to produce the kind of batsman-dominated Twenty20 games we were used to in English conditions. Nor did the ball seem to be going very far off these horrendous black bats we'd had specially made for us by our sponsors. Come on, if there was a reason not to take the tournament seriously this was it. Instead of the ball speeding off them, it just seemed to stop dead on impact. It felt like we were preparing for a night at a fairground rather than an international cricket match.

Given these conditions, and the evidence of how difficult it was to score when pace was taken off the ball, Kevin Pietersen and Peter Moores, who controlled selection as captain and coach, believed it was essential to play two spinners. Consequently, I was surplus to requirements, and therefore one of the four told they would not be playing at our team announcement two days before the big match. Forget any of the peripheral stuff: what I thought of the concept, the money on offer, or the increasingly annoying behaviour of our Texan host. This was an England international, and, as with any England international, I was extremely disappointed to be left out.

Andrew Flintoff, being a big mate at that time, came up to me to console me as soon as that meeting was over.

'You're not going to get the cash, are you?' he said, before adding an afterthought: 'If we win . . .'

It was clearly me Fred was looking out for when he called a meeting of the players later that day, at which he proposed a restructuring of how we would split the cash beyond how it was paid to us through official channels in the event of us winning. As things stood, each playing member of the winning team would pick up a cheque for $1 million, with a further $1 million shared between the four non-playing members of the squad and the England and Wales Cricket Board and West Indies Cricket Board halving the remaining $7 million. The losers were to get nowt.

Further to this, however, Fred announced a proposal that each of the named XI would put a tenth of their million into a pot to be divided out among the four guys who had not been selected. Effectively, that meant our $250,000 cheques would be doubled. His argument was that we had gone out there as a group of fifteen and to be paid so disproportionately when we had no control over selection was not right. Under the terms of his suggestion, myself, Ravi Bopara, Alastair Cook and Ryan Sidebottom would be better remunerated and those in the team would still get $900,000 each.

A big debate ensued and some of the tighter lads in the camp immediately dismissed the proposal. Others suggested it was fine, although the expressions on some faces belied the fact they were 100 per cent comfortable with it. There was no doubt that this prize money split was divisive because of its all-or-nothing nature, and although it was an issue that had been fairly well documented in advance, when you are part of any squad your competitive nature means you always anticipate playing. Not a great deal of thought had gone into the finer details but the fact that we were discussing it at all suggested we were being too presumptuous.

Any notion that we would walk the game was blown away along with our batting and the Stanford openers hurtled to their 100-run target at breakneck speed. Afterwards, I actually considered it a good thing that we lost because I am not sure how it would have affected certain individuals in our team. I have an idea that it would have been bad.

In the grander scheme of things it was obviously better that we lost given Stanford's subsequent conviction for a multi-billion dollar fraud. Can you imagine the ignominy of having to hand back dirty money?

As it turned out the Stanford saga was only one leg of a fractious winter itinerary. The limited-overs section of the tour to India was a shemozzle, and became increasingly frustrating with every passing day, momentum seemingly careering the hosts towards a 7-0 whitewash. Everything we tried that series, India had an answer to, and then some. It was typical England in one-day cricket away from home, as once again we failed to get our heads around how to win a game in Asian conditions. India away is always a huge challenge and you have to be on top of everything even to stand a chance.

From a personal perspective, I travelled out there in the belief that we might get some joy bowling short at Virender Sehwag and Yuvraj Singh, rather than allow them to exploit their favourite trick of setting themselves on the front foot on these slow sub-continent pitches, and hitting through the line of the ball. It was a tactic I had experienced some joy with on the previous tour of 2005–6, and it was something we discussed as a squad in team meetings upon arrival.

This time, however, we got little joy out of it and, after Yuvraj blasted back-to-back hundreds to start the series, wicketless I lost my place in the side to Steve Harmison for the fifth match in Cuttack.

Tactically we had tried numerous things by this stage, without success, and so Andrew Flintoff took it upon himself to try a different tack, producing a rousing, theatrical speech in the dressing room pre-match, in a bid to instil some extra passion into our display. He spoke about the lions on our England shirts, the pride we should feel sporting them and completely went off on one, shouting and screaming.

'Come on then, who's with me?' he bellowed, in a dramatic finale, and stormed out of the room. Unfortunately, although he'd had the best intentions, the impact was lost as there were still fifteen minutes before the start of play, and some of the guys, who had stopped what they were doing to listen to him, still didn't have their boots on. It was one of the more awkward dressing-room moments I have experienced, and it got slightly worse when the other guys finally traipsed out to find him sitting outside alone, waiting.

However, our struggles, personal and collective, on the pitch paled into insignificance with what we were to find out on the hour-long bus trip to Bhubaneswar that evening of Wednesday 26 November 2008. News spread around the bus that the Taj Mahal Hotel in Mumbai – a place we had stayed at earlier in the tour, on previous tours, the location of some of our kitbags, and indeed where we were due to be staying the following month for a Test match – had come under attack.

What was uncertain as we surfed news on our smartphones was the exact detail of what had happened. Who had been attacked? And why? Questions were being asked as we arrived back at the team hotel, which already appeared to be ringed by tighter security. Once inside we headed to the bar and witnessed the scenes being beamed to the nation on television. It soon became clear that some of those innocent people who had been murdered, and some of those taken hostage, in familiar Mumbai tourist spots were westerners, and that this was no coincidence. Reports suggested they had been targeted. The images on Indian TV, of dead bodies, people being shot, were unbelievably graphic and not something we would have been subjected to in England.

Naturally, most of the lads began phoning home at this point, and there was concern given the proximity of the trouble. I don't think there was much doubt in any of our minds even at that stage that this tour was over for us. Naturally, too, some of our family members back home began to panic when they heard what had happened – they would not necessarily have known how far away from it all we were, and some may have lost track of exactly where we were anyway. But what they did know, in the age of world news travelling around the globe at breakneck speed, was that one of India's most famous cities had come under attack. So it didn't take long for the lads to start phoning home to reassure loved ones we were okay.

One subject that the lads chatted about in the bar was whether or not this was the start of something, and whether there was more to come. The most unnerving thing, though, was that I was among those who had stayed at the Taj Mahal Hotel several times before. Some of the staff who had served us, some of those who may have carried our bags and equipment into storage facilities, had been killed in cold blood. A security guard familiar to some of the longer-serving members of our touring party was caught up in the mayhem and led an escape from a restaurant. It was inevitable that we started to consider what would have happened if we had been in town.

Next morning at breakfast it was not really a question of if but when we were flying back to Britain. It didn't seem possible that, at a time when India was under terrorist attack, normal life as we knew it would continue. The series, in our minds at least, was over. Both Peter Moores and Kevin Pietersen, in their roles as coach and captain, spent a good deal of that morning in phone conversations with our top brass back at Lord's. Within a few hours, at a team meeting, it was confirmed that the two remaining one-day internationals had been cancelled.

But there was a motion to delay any decision on the two-Test series for a few days while the authorities and the two cricket boards took stock. And it became evident very early in our meeting that the ECB wanted to fulfil that part of the itinerary as a show of solidarity to their counterparts at the Board of Control for Cricket in India (BCCI), as if staying and playing the matches at rearranged venues would show the terrorists that they had not won.

Other sides to the argument for staying were presented to us that Thursday lunchtime, and one of them was disturbingly familiar.

We were informed about the financial implications of not fulfilling our obligations for any reason other than an instruction directly from government to return home – the ICC imposed hefty fines for doing so, to cover losses by home boards – and how this could impact on both the county and recreational game. The knock-on of shelling out would be a cut to county budgets, and that might lead to a colleague losing his livelihood, or a local club being over-looked for grass-roots funding.

This had an all-too-familiar feel to a small number of us who had faced similar pressure over the Zimbabwe issue at the 2003 World Cup. But while we accepted that the funds available to our ECB bosses were important, and that we had a duty to listen to them as our employers, we were being asked to commit to staying in a country which was dealing with one of the worst terrorist attacks in history. More than 150 innocent lives had been lost just hours earlier, and the first thoughts were not of our safety, or the feelings of our concerned families back home, but of the financial knock-on.

The desire of the ECB to improve relations with the BCCI, the richest organization in world cricket following the success of the Indian Premier League, had been well documented, and although it was never confirmed publicly, a group of us could not help but feel that they were acting to appease their counterparts rather than prioritize our return home.

Our entire squad were keen to get back in any way possible, as soon as possible, following that first meeting in our Bhubaneswar hotel but we knew the one problem at the time would be, because of the increased security at airports and the cancellation of some flights, the availability to block-book to get us to the UK. Alternative plans were being investigated to send us in little groups when a counter-proposal was made at another meeting convened after lunch. It was suggested that instead of flying back to the UK, we travel to a halfway house such as the United Arab Emirates, where we would have access to good cricket facilities.

It was at this point that Andrew Flintoff and Steve Harmison, two of those who, like me, had experienced the Zimbabwe affair, spoke out against such an idea. They told our management that if we were leaving India, we wanted to get home and that any further discussion could take place there. A good number of us felt the same way on this – we wanted to put our families, who already had to cope with us being away from home for two-thirds of every year, first for a change.

By the time we had a third meeting of the day, they were dealing with a disgruntled team, a good percentage of whom were not willing to be shepherded into further meetings over a number of days in another completely unconnected country. Once we found sufficient space on an aircraft to house the entire twenty-eight-strong touring party, we headed to Bangalore, one of only two international airports in India allowing flights out of the country, under high-security escort. By the evening of Saturday 30 November, we were back on British soil.

Although our wish to return home had been granted, it soon became clear that the ECB intended to dispatch an England team back to the subcontinent at the earliest opportunity, whether it was the first-choice one or not. In transit back from Bangalore we joined the England performance programme players who had been based there in a training camp. They were briefed in much the same way as we were and would effectively be given the choice of whether they wanted to go back to India to feature in the Test series in the event of any of the original squad pulling out.

Before we left, one final meeting was called, this time by us, the players themselves, to discuss the situation. It soon became clear that half of the sixteen-man squad were against returning and I detected uncertainty in the voices of a couple of those who said they were willing to acquiesce on the basis of security being at optimum level. Safety on overseas tours was becoming more of an issue at this time, and the fact that westerners were being targeted inevitably led to trepidation.

England cricketers are high-profile figures in Asia – probably, because of the popularity of the sport, the only continent in the world where we would be at least as recognizable as some Premier League footballers – making us pretty viable targets. Daniella was seven and a half months pregnant, and arguably the eve of fatherhood made me think about things more deeply. Perhaps if the scenario had developed a year or two earlier, I would have just gone along with the recommendations of my superiors.

However, danger now lurked menacingly in places on the international circuit. Only a few months earlier, a handful of international teams had opted not to travel to Pakistan for the Champions Trophy following independent security advice. That same September in which the tournament was scheduled, a huge bomb blast decimated the Marriott Hotel in Islamabad. A matter of a few months later, the Sri Lanka cricket team came under horrific attack by terrorists as they made the early-morning bus journey on the day of a Test match in Lahore.

Even though we felt vulnerable, in truth we probably did not realize just how grave a position an international cricket team would get into that winter. Ultimately, we also acknowledged that we would be fenced with a ring of steel if we agreed to the wishes of both the Indian and England boards and resumed the tour. Although they could not guarantee 100 per cent that we would be safe, they would put everything in place to get as near as damn it.

Just two days after walking back through my front door, I received a phone call from Hugh Morris of the ECB inquiring as to what my position was with regard to the tour and which of several hypothetical scenarios I was comfortable with. One of those was for the original party to depart for an Abu Dhabi holding camp while Hugh, his namesake Sean Morris, then chief executive of the Professional Cricketers' Association, and Reg Dickason, the England team's Australian security adviser, flew back to India to inspect proposed security arrangements for two new Test venues – Mumbai was now off the agenda for obvious reasons, while Ahmedabad's volatile recent past made it another no-go location.

The plan was that we would train at the Sheikh Zayed Stadium so that we would be as prepared as possible for a Test match in the event that the security report presented by the Indian authorities was deemed satisfactory by Reg, Hugh and Sean. As a centrally contracted cricketer, there was no reason for me to decline the offer to be part of a training camp in the United Arab Emirates, so, despite having reservations about returning to India, I agreed.

Although everyone followed suit on this, there was still a strong feeling among us that we should not be in this particular position. The squad was bolstered by a number of performance programme players whose presence served a dual purpose. In the first instance, an expanded group would ensure top-quality net bowlers and batsmen at our practice sessions. Furthermore, those guys would be up to speed and feel part of the squad should any of the senior players pull out.

We arrived in the UAE on the night of Thursday 4 December 2008, and had training sessions planned for Friday and Saturday. Talk on the situation, it was agreed, should be saved for later, because Peter Moores's job as England coach was to prepare as if we were playing a Test match against India a week later. When we were not practising, however, talk inevitably turned to the question of whether we should be going back and who would say yes, and who would say no, when it came to the crunch.

The situation was being debated by various media outlets back home – and we were already getting praise for our attitudes before we had opted definitively to return. Of course, some, including captain Kevin Pietersen, had resolved that they were in the yes camp before decision day, which became Sunday 7 December. But there was a group of us who had stuck together since we left Bhubaneswar for our international flight from Bangalore the previous week.

Word had got out that Andrew Flintoff and Steve Harmison were not keen on the plan to go back – and Moores confirmed their feelings to the press on Saturday lunchtime when he was quizzed about who had reservations – but there were five others of us who shared the same views. Myself, Alastair Cook, Matt Prior, Graeme Swann and Ian Bell all believed we were being too hasty.

A week earlier we had vowed to stand together on our principles. It was not just fear that ruled our stance; we discussed the pros and cons of the situation and just did not think an immediate return was the appropriate course of action.

One argument doing the rounds was that getting on with the show would send a message to the terrorists that their attempts to disrupt everyday life had failed – that because cricket was so inherent in the lives of the Indian people playing these matches would help normality return to a traumatized country. I am not sure these gun-toting murderers, with such little regard for life, either their own or others, were taking scores.

Another was that if the scenario was flipped and the attacks had happened on British soil, we would be reassuring the touring team that their protection was a primary concern, but that ultimately we should not disrupt the schedule.

Nasser Hussain, who was captain of an England team that travelled to India in 2001 two months after 9/11 minus Robert Croft and Andrew Caddick, wrote in the *Daily Mail*: 'Eventually, the game has to go on, just as people in London had to get back on tubes and buses after the 2005 bomb attacks. As long as the security people say it is as safe as it can be to return and as long as the Indian people want the tour to continue, England can make a statement by going back.'

But the thing about our rebel group was that we were not saying we did not want to go back to India, just that we did not want to rush back so soon. Lest we forget, more than 150 people had been slaughtered, hundreds of others were maimed, parts of the city of Mumbai had been decimated, rubble and blood lingered on the streets, and it was all just a bit too raw. We were very much in favour of the tour being rescheduled for a more appropriate time rather than carrying on as if nothing had happened.

We were advised that our welfare was their primary concern, and with that in mind, there would be armed personnel for our security both at the ground and our hotel. The dressing room would be surrounded by machine-gun wielding guards. Over the past few days in India, Reg had made several demands, on our accommodation, transit routes, the employment of army commandos rather than ordinary police and been in dialogue with several of the world's leading security agencies as well as local experts and India's Counter-Terrorist Unit. In terms of protection, the ECB were undoubtedly committed to reducing the risk level to the England team to as low as was possible. But that only served to emphasize our major point of contention. Should a cricket match – any cricket match let alone a Test match – be played against such a backdrop? This would be nothing like the environment we were accustomed to in international cricket. It certainly didn't feel right to be playing in a match which featured armed guards protecting the dressing room. So why were we forcing it? Why not wait and rearrange the matches for the following year?

The counter-argument we offered was that rushing back to play these matches under such circumstances was more than a tad insensitive to the families who had experienced such horrific loss of life, and were still coming to terms with it. We were putting two cricket matches, which were trivial in comparison, ahead of more important issues.

Crunch time came on the Sunday evening when Hugh, Sean and Reg arrived back from their fact-finding mission in India. As journalists milled around the lobby and television cameramen and photographers jumped into action you might have been lulled into the impression that a decision was imminent.

But our group remained fairly entrenched in our views as Hugh and Reg began their reports on what we could expect in terms of security if we travelled to Chennai, the new venue for the first Test, the following morning. They spoke about the procedures in place, the volume of soldiers and commandos committed to our care and attention, and how the police escorts would be of a level similar to those given to heads of state.

To recap, it was not just about safety for us. We also took into account whether or not playing these matches really was morally the right thing to do, and whether an international cricket match should be played inside a circle of thousands of militia.

Over the course of that week, some individuals' minds had wandered to different places, and Graeme Swann's was among them. Although he initially held a fairly deep-rooted view that we should not go back, Swanny's viewpoint altered when he considered his career prospects: he had waited seven long years to get back into an England squad, following his maiden tour in 1999–2000, and here he was as second spinner on a tour where the second spinner was all but guaranteed to play. He was approaching thirty, and a Test debut was in touching distance. From a personal perspective, having been snubbed for so long, he was on the cusp of fulfilling a dream he thought had fizzled out. Selection implications for those not wanting to return were discussed at these meetings and the ECB advised us that pulling out would not affect an individual's chances of a call-up in future. But for Swanny the equation was a simple one: if the tour went ahead and he committed to it, he would earn his first England cap. If it did and he didn't, someone else would be offered the chance, and if they impressed he might never return to the front of the queue.

Earlier in my career, I might have felt the force of such an emotional pull and, although I would not say my place was secure, the fact I had been a feature of England teams over the past couple of years in all forms of the game allowed me to make an informed decision on whether it was ethically right or wrong to return rather than worry about its effect on my future international prospects. Swanny was honest enough to inform us of his thinking well before the final presentations were made, and earned our respect for that. His easy-going nature sometimes masks the fact that he is a ruthlessly ambitious cricketer, and once pledges were made to keep us as safe as was possible, his final decision was made.

So when, following an hour or two of presentation and two-way discussion, those who were content to travel were asked to leave the room whenever they wanted, it was no surprise that Swanny was one of those to do so. Those of us that were left remained at an impasse. We were being pressed for a definitive answer and given an hour to consider our positions. All of the performance programme players, who were also in on the meeting, had left and so it was obvious a full complement of England cricketers would be jetting to Tamil Nadu the next morning. Now it was a question of confirming their identity.

So we were asked to report back within an hour to inform them of our final decisions. We chatted among ourselves, and headed to our rooms to have further chats with our loved ones at home. I am not sure Daniella wanted me to go back but she has always supported me 100 per cent throughout my career and understands my total commitment as a team player. And it was that that ultimately led to the five of us who were still wavering to accept boarding cards for the flight.

You see, regardless of how others had reached their decisions, our small group went back not because we thought it was the right thing to do but because we thought we should do the right thing by our team-mates. When you are part of a collective there are times when things don't go the way you might have envisaged, so you have to allow majority rule, and if the majority were going, there was an onus on me to show loyalty to them, and stick together as a team.

All of us said as much to Hugh and Sean when we confirmed

our places. Ultimately, it was the camaraderie and respect you develop for your colleagues, and for the values of the team, that had influenced us. All for one, and one for all, and all that.

Even then I remained uneasy about the motives for returning and – keen to air them to a neutral – texted one of the press blokes I trusted, asking him to meet a few of us in the hotel's Irish bar. By this stage it was getting late but I was keen to discuss the situation with a third party, someone not directly involved in the whole process, to reaffirm the validity of our argument, and to provide a form of closure on the whole episode. Within half an hour, the majority of the squad were at the bar, chatting among themselves, and to a number of other journalists who had meandered in for a late-night beer. Within a few hours, we were buckling our seat belts bound for southern India.

11

A New Dawn

Although I don't tend to get too sentimental about stuff that happens on the field, even the hardest of souls would have found it difficult not to appreciate what Sachin Tendulkar's match-winning hundred in that first Test at the Chepauk Stadium meant to everyone around India in the aftermath of the most horrific terrorist attack on their soil.

Sure, at the end of the day this was a Test match, England were there to win and the disappointment of losing is never any different, but it was outstanding on his part to play an innings like that at a time like that. He has to live daily with the pressure of being a national icon and, given the fervour with which the Indian people worship him, he has become accustomed to having to deliver in tense situations. But this was something different. This was Mumbai's most famous son delivering victory in his home city's hour of despair. It was as if it had been scripted.

They say cricket unites people in India, and they certainly got behind Tendulkar and Yuvraj Singh as they pushed for an unlikely victory in that fourth innings. The whole atmosphere as they got closer to their 387-run target was incredible. And it was no mean feat to get home by six wickets, having been faced with the

challenge of scoring the highest total to win a Test on the subcontinent.

Virender Sehwag hurtled them out of the blocks and Sachin
showed touches of genius to guide them home. It was all a very
different atmosphere from the one we'd experienced when we
arrived back in southern India just a few days earlier. There was a
lot of security around and despite having great faith that our security adviser Reg Dickason would not condone sending us
somewhere dangerous, we remained somewhat on edge. However,
the one thing in our favour was that, because of the lack of turnaround time, we were focused on cricket from the outset. There
were just a couple of days' net practice ahead of that first Test,
although, as we had acclimatized during the limited-overs series,
lack of preparation was not so much of an issue.

That much was evident when we began the two-match series so
well. Having opened up a 75-run lead in the first innings, Andrew
Strauss's second hundred of the contest set up the chance of a
second consecutive Test win on Indian soil but the home batsmen
mastered the dry pitch to secure what was effectively an impregnable series lead.

Impregnable because there was never going to be the time to
force a result up in Mohali, scene of the second Test after it had
been switched from its original venue, Mumbai. Daylight is at a
premium in the north of India during December and we knew
hours would potentially be lost from both ends of the day. So it
transpired. On game days, we would set off at ridiculous o'clock
from our hotel in Chandigarh and during that hour-long trek we
would not be able to see ten yards in front of our faces, it was that
foggy. And the evenings came in quickly, too.

The start was delayed due to the poor visibility and the cricket
that was played over those five days was fairly flat. However, the
atmosphere within the dressing room was anything but, because it
was during this Test that the first signs that something was wrong
between the captain and the coach emerged. Or certainly it was

the first time that negative vibes between Kevin Pietersen and Peter Moores were transmitted to the rest of the team. Others might have been taken into confidences privately but certain goings-on were like a beacon warning that all was not right.

For example, when Steve Harmison was told he wasn't playing at practice the day before the game, he ordered a taxi and went back to the hotel there and then. That behaviour, and the fact he was not reprimanded, racked everyone off. Because of who he was he managed to get away with that kind of thing, but if it had been someone else, and not a Steve Harmison, particularly a younger player, he would have been dragged over the coals.

That incident alone meant it was a little bit frosty around the dressing room in the build-up to the match. It is not the kind of conduct you would expect to find in a united, contented team, and inevitably it sparked whisperings around the squad that something wasn't right. What was noticeable during the course of that match was that a few of the senior players had begun to whinge publicly about Mooresy. Or shall we say they were less discreet about their feelings towards him because, if it had been going on for any prolonged period of time, I certainly hadn't been party to it.

It had become clear before we headed home for Christmas that there was a core of people who didn't enjoy him being in charge. Some individuals had developed a personal dislike of him, and opted to make it more obvious that was the case. Almost overnight it became a subject everyone was talking about in the ground and in the team hotel, and when that kind of subject is being talked about on a match day it is a bad place for a team to be in.

However, although none of us could have anticipated what was to happen next, it was acknowledged by some of us during that match that things couldn't go on as they were. It had to be one or the other. I just don't think anyone considered it would come to a head so soon.

When it did, following KP's disparaging assessment of Mooresy's credentials and the bombshell that he could no longer work as captain under him, there appeared to be an inevitability that the ECB would side with the player rather than the coach. After all, Kevin had been one of our biggest players for the previous four years, and had the potential to be one of our biggest players for the following half a dozen years, too. One was dispensable, the other wasn't.

But with Daniella thirty-eight weeks pregnant and preparing to drop, I had other things to think about when I arrived home for Christmas. And as it was a situation that was played out in the media, I followed the story in much the same way as other people did, by catching bits of it on the TV news as it developed. I remember one day turning on to see KP walking through an airport in South Africa somewhere, before he flew back from holiday to meet with officials from the ECB. But in terms of what was being said, and what would happen, I knew nothing more than those fans who had bought tickets to watch us out in the West Indies in the upcoming weeks.

Early in the new year, I received a phone call from the ECB, as the majority of the established players seemed to, during the course of which I was asked my opinions on Kev as a captain, on the atmosphere in the dressing room and how I felt about the situation that had developed.

Giving the best impression of a politician I could manage, I tried to be as honest as I could without saying too much because I didn't want to be seen to be taking sides. This kind of scenario is always a difficult one to be forced into as a player because you don't know how things are going to unravel from that point, and no matter what anyone says there is always an element of self-preservation about it. I considered that if I took sides with one or the other it might affect my future opportunities as an England player, but I also knew it was my duty to give an honest opinion about Peter Moores. I stressed to Hugh that I liked him as a coach – it was only natural for me to do so because he had been great for my game.

The end for Mooresy was rather unjust but it would have been hard for him, nigh-on impossible perhaps, after his relationship breakdown with KP, to stay on as coach. It was not as though switching captain was a feasible option, and, in the circumstances, removing them both from office was the logical conclusion to the saga.

Unfortunately, despite the fact I got on well with him, others did not, and sadly a lot of the ill feeling stemmed from Mooresy's desire to improve us as a team in every possible aspect. People did not take to his drive for improved fitness, and he didn't help himself sometimes, most notably perhaps on that occasion in Napier that I have already mentioned. Yes, that was downright stupid – but when you detach yourself and view it from Moores' perspective, all he was trying to do was make us fitter as a squad.

He has a heart of gold and a total dedication to improve both his team and his set of players. In hindsight, he will no doubt reflect on that Napier incident as a mistake. We all make mistakes, however, and it was never Peter's intention to rub anyone up the wrong way. That's just not his style. His goal is to improve individuals as cricketers, and get them playing to the best of their ability.

One of the accusations levelled at him as England coach was that he was a bit too intense; he didn't know when to switch off. Some players didn't enjoy his full-on, energetic approach. But having been around him with Lancashire since, I have seen the benefits, and it's something that the lads at Old Trafford quite like. The County Championship season is a long haul and you need the odd nudge at times, more forceful pushes at others. His enthusiasm is extraordinary.

I know for a fact that guys in the England team had less respect for him because he had not played international cricket. Unfortunately, that goes through some minds whenever a coach emerges who has developed exclusively via the county route. I find it difficult to understand, and we have seen quite a few coaches come into the international fold since his departure who were of the same ilk, but there was a bit of a black mark against him from the start. Some might even have had it against him because he was not Duncan Fletcher.

Perhaps he was a little heavy-handed in trying to change the culture of a squad that had become a bit too comfortable. Put simply, those who didn't mind structure and could cope with being pushed in new directions enjoyed Moores as coach. The guys who knew how they wanted to prepare, and were stuck in their way of doing things, didn't.

The senior player grumbling 'another gym session, I can't be doing with this' became all too familiar as his short tenure ticked by – and responses of 'actually, I quite like the extra sessions' only served to antagonize them. Peter Moores wanted his England team to be fitter than previous ones, and there were a few barricades up from the start. Neither did the appointment of the Kiwi fitness instructor Marques Church help, as he didn't seem to grasp the machinations of a team environment even though he had come from a rugby background.

Not only did he lack understanding of humour in the dressing room, he also failed to grasp that there are times and places for things. To be fair, there are a lot of strength and conditioning guys like that out there. All they know is how to teach people to lift weights, to build strength and improve individual fitness. They fail to get to know you as individuals or understand that there are certain times when it is just not appropriate to schedule a gym session.

These days we are lucky to have Huw Bevan, a former professional rugby union player, who has the nous to leave players alone at certain times. Huw would never consider approaching a batsman immediately after he's been dismissed; an hour later he might sidle up and suggest an activity. Most people initially need space when they are out but will then be looking for things to occupy them for the rest of the day, and getting some of your fitness in for the week is ideal. In contrast to Marques, who was always full-on, Huw has a friendly way of pushing you in the gym, and I for one respond better to that personable style. We are certainly a fit side now, and the key to it, to Andy Flower and his staff's credit, is that the change has been implemented with a degree of subtlety. Unfortunately, under Mooresy it was shoved at us unceremoniously, and not everyone bought into it.

Lest it be forgotten, though, one of the things that Peter Moores did during his time as team coach was to bring Flower on board as batting coach. That was obviously a significant appointment for English cricket and I am sure Andy has a lot to thank Mooresy for. They both believe in the importance of statistics in coaching, as converts of American sports studies like *Moneyball*, and I do see some of how Mooresy operates when Andy is going through tactical planning or assessing certain stats.

Post-Ashes whitewash, post-2007 World Cup, was a very tough time to inherit the job. There was a great deal of rebuilding to be done after such a winter of discontent, and Peter would have got that time to rebuild, I believe, under normal circumstances – and done a good job. Unfortunately, the situation didn't develop normally.

It meant that we headed to the Caribbean in mid-January 2009 with Flower as interim coach. Meanwhile, Andrew Strauss, chosen to succeed Pietersen as captain, was keen to begin his tenure with a greater emphasis on setting our own standards.

We had a meeting at Gatwick Airport before we flew, which Strauss headed, and in which he asked us to take greater responsibility as players and no longer leave it to coaches to pull us into line. We were to discipline ourselves and make sure we were all working as hard as each other, as hard as we should do. We knew the standards expected of international players, and this was all about reclaiming control of our own careers and the direction in which the team was heading.

There had been speculation on whether KP would be a member of the touring party to the Caribbean but typically, being the sort of character he is, he didn't want to show anyone that losing the captaincy had affected him. Privately, of course, it would have done, but to his credit he got on with things as a player and slipped straight back into the ranks.

However, it was not long before some more straight talking from Strauss was to knock me out of kilter. My previous Test appearance in Mohali had been a case of labour without commensurate reward, but I hoped they would look past the figures and remember the performance when they considered the team for the first Test in Jamaica. Whenever a new regime takes over, everyone naturally has an extra spring in their step at net sessions in their bid to impress, and any new captain–coach combination inevitably develops certain preferences when it comes to selection. My case was not helped when we ran into Lendl Simmons on a batting paradise in a warm-up match against West Indies A in St Kitts. When someone scores 282 in the manner he did, all the bowlers suffer, and it tells you something about the true nature of the surface. But once again I considered that I had bowled better than figures of 2 for 92 suggested.

'We've had to pick what we feel is our strongest attack at this current time, and I am afraid you are not in it,' Strauss explained to me, after paying a visit to my hotel room, on the eve of the contest.

There was a bit of a 'here we go again feel' to all of this, and it was not a great start for me to hear his assessment. I had toured the West Indies before as a spectator and if the new think tank had plumped for Ryan Sidebottom, Andrew Flintoff, Steve Harmison and Stuart Broad as their pace attack at the start of the series they would, all things being equal, have to show them some loyalty in the short term at least. All of a sudden this fresh start had a disturbingly familiar look.

With another spell on the sidelines looming I did what came

naturally in a situation like that and headed to get a few drinks down me.

Little could I have imagined as I stood at the hotel bar that night contemplating my fate that I would, courtesy of a humiliating first Test defeat, be back in favour so soon. The focal point of the innings' loss was one of England's biggest collapses of all time but aside from the fifty-one all out, we had also allowed West Indies to make 392 on the same surface, and changes across the XI were almost deemed compulsory.

There were a lot of hard yards to be done on the surfaces served up to us during that four-match series, and although I didn't think I bowled particularly impressively in Antigua during the rescheduled match at the Rec, following the Test match in the sandpit that never was, I was really pleased with how I did at Barbados, on the flattest pitch I think I have ever bowled on. My figures might have read 37-9-125-3 but they were thirty-seven of the best overs I have ever sent down. It was a series made for batsmen, and with West Indies able to go on the defensive with their 1-0 advantage, we had to work hard for openings.

In the end we came agonizingly near to closing it, narrowly running out of time in the final Test in Trinidad. We had played well to manufacture a situation that left us around sixty overs to dismiss West Indies for a second time on another typically comatose pitch, entering the final session of the series requiring seven wickets to take a share of it, and I managed to get the ball reverse swinging dangerously as the clock ticked down.

Momentum was with us, in fact, and with regular wickets we felt on a roll towards victory. Personally, I felt in such good rhythm that despite the heat I didn't want to come off. I would have kept going all day, and to be fair Strauss kept me on for quite a long spell in the afternoon as Graeme Swann and Monty Panesar rotated at the other end. But every time Strauss needed a breakthrough he turned back to me, and that was encouraging. I obliged a couple of times with the ball tailing in nicely, and as a bowler you want to be in that position where you can win games for your country.

Ultimately, the match ended with me on my haunches in disappointment but with figures of 3 for 24 from sixteen overs, and some complimentary write-ups of my display. Certainly, the series end offered a distinct contrast to its start. In the space of three matches I had gone from being on the periphery of Strauss's thoughts to the bloke he was now turning to as his match-winner. It was a huge turning point for my career. Truth is I've always wanted to be *that* guy.

For the following three years I felt every inch that guy, too, although he naturally turned to Graeme Swann if the pitch was spinning. Conditions and surfaces vary from game to game, of course, but it was me more often than not that he threw the ball to when he wanted a wicket and if you want to be considered a top-class bowler it is important to have a few different strings to your bow.

Reverse swing has always been a weapon for me when the ball becomes older, and to bowl with that amount of control was very pleasing. It took me back to learning my trade at Old Trafford, where the pitches and squares were hard, and exponents of the art were always in the game. As with any skill it is something you master over time with practice, and generally, if you can swing the ball you can learn to reverse swing it pretty quickly.

One of the pitfalls of it is getting greedy, just like bowlers do with the new ball, when they try to send deliveries down that pitch on leg stump and hit the top of off. Similarly, one of the traps with the reverse-swinging ball is that people bowl it too full.

And you are always more dangerous if you can get the old ball to duck both ways. A lot of people can tail it in but not necessarily out, yet for it to be at its most effective you try to set people up in the same way as with conventional swing. You might bowl a succession of in-swingers and then try to outfox them with an away swinger or vice versa.

You also have to vary your line of attack depending on where you are playing in the world. For example, if you are using reverse swing on pitches on the subcontinent, you might look to bowl more balls that will go on to hit the stumps. In England, you might bowl more balls outside off that swing away in the hope of locating the edge. These differences are just part of the knowledge you acquire through bowling in different conditions.

Buoyed by that performance in Port of Spain I maintained good form throughout the 3-2 win in the one-day series that followed. Containing any team with Chris Gayle, Ramnaresh Sarwan and Shivnarine Chanderpaul in prime form is no mean feat, and we generally did that well as a team aside from one Gayle explosion in pursuit of a small score in Barbados.

That limited-overs section of the tour opened with a token Twenty20 match but we played with a very different team from the one we used in both the World Twenty20 held in England that summer and the subsequent tournament held in the Caribbean the following year.

The 2009 World T20 opened with a seismic shock against the Netherlands, and finished somewhat unjustly with defeat in a weather-shortened match against West Indies at the Oval. Generally, we hate games in these tournaments against teams that we are supposed to beat, and for good reason. We tend to slip up. You only have to look at how difficult we make games against Ireland when we are warming up for the NatWest Series. We don't tend to enjoy those, and we always seem more susceptible to mistakes when we are playing opposition we are expected to beat. It's a head-scratcher as to why this happens and, of course, if we knew why we wouldn't do it.

But it was not a case of us underestimating the Netherlands – we treat all opponents with the same level of respect – more that we failed to deal with the pressure. We were expected to kill them off throughout their pursuit of 163 but never did, and they just kept coming at us.

Our potential in the format was highlighted back at Lord's with victory over India a couple of days later, and a win against Pakistan at the Oval – two twenty-over world champions in their own rights. Keeping the Indians quiet – you don't tend to get that kind of aggressively vocal atmosphere at Lord's very often, and being abused was something of a shock to us as we warmed up – both in the stands and in the middle was pleasing, and by virtue of defeating Pakistan we showed glimpses of tournament-winning potential. But the rain was as decisive as any of West Indies' play in a must-win final group encounter and an adjusted target of eighty in nine overs was arguably too generous. One thing was for sure: it was unusual in my experience to have anyone other than ourselves to blame for being ousted from a major competition before the final stages, but this was an exception.

12

Ashes Regained

You dream of being cheered off the field in an Ashes Test but probably not in the circumstances I experienced in my first such match on home soil.

The celebration in the stands at the SWALEC Stadium as I traipsed off alongside Monty Panesar on the evening of Sunday 12 July 2009 will live long in the memory. The 16,000 packed house roared with approval, and we were the heroes of the hour. Heroes, I must add, for securing a draw.

Not any old draw, though. One that came against all odds, and courtesy of efforts greater than just those of myself and Monty during an epic finale. Sure, the 2009 Australian tourists were a different proposition because many of their old guard had gone but it still took some monumental resistance, most notably from Paul Collingwood, to allow us our hour in the sun.

Not many would have given us a prayer of survival even then. Earlier in the match, Andrew Flintoff had such confidence in my ability with the bat that he felt safe to have a wager with me that I could not get to thirty on the second morning, having gone in the previous evening as nightwatchman. My reward for doing so, had I not holed out going for the four that would have taken me to the target, would have been a case of Cloudy Bay Sauvignon Blanc. The initial offer was for a half-century but as everyone else thought that was a tad unrealistic, and lacking in generosity, it got readjusted.

By the time I walked to the crease, at 5.30 on that Sunday evening, it had been downgraded once more. Survive the next eighty minutes and I would be the proud owner of some very decent tipple. Of course, I am still waiting for delivery, and as I am pretty sure Fred knows where I live, it must have slipped his mind. If you've got this far, Fred . . .

Perhaps he'd felt safe in dangling that kind of carrot. Let's face it, heading into the fifth and final day, we acknowledged it was going to be extremely tough to rescue the situation. Beginning from a position of 20 for 2, with a minimum ninety-eight overs to negotiate, I am not sure there was overwhelming belief that we could do it.

But Colly played a great innings, and others supported for extended periods of time, including Graeme Swann, who started slogging even though we were trying to save the game, scoring half the sixty-two runs they shared for the eighth wicket. Peppered by Peter Siddle's short stuff – three times in one over he was struck – his response was to lash out. As it turned out, it was vital that he did.

Those runs proved crucial, as they allowed us to get ahead of the Australians, and bought us extra time. Because once in front, we knew that Australia would lose ten minutes for a change of innings, so it effectively brought our target that little bit closer.

So much so that when I began batting with Colly, we discussed not only saving the game but also, because we were close to making them bat again, the importance of hitting the ball, if it was there to be hit. Any runs scored then because we were so close to parity represented a double whammy.

I managed to put a gift from Mitchell Johnson away for four, and was soon into double figures but then, shortly after that final hour was signalled, and just six runs away from making Australia bat again, Colly got out to one of the most innocuous balls he had received throughout his five-and-three-quarter-hour stay, dangling his bat out to provide a catch to gully.

Now in the real world it is not possible for me and Monty to bat for such a long period together against an Australian quality bowling attack. But something extraordinary unfolded in the Welsh capital on that July evening.

I felt a responsibility not only to see it out from my end as long as was possible but also to keep Monty in a state of mind to get through too. He is a fairly unpredictable character and that is reflected in him as a batsman. He has got a really good technique, and every shot in the book, but he sometimes struggles to match the right shot with the right delivery. And he can also act quite frantically at times, especially when he has a bat in hand. My advice to him was fairly simple: watch the ball.

With those wide eyes staring at you, you feel as though that should not be a problem, and sometimes he is looking so intently it appears he needs to be calmed down. But he is only like that because he is so desperately keen to do well.

I don't know whether I was a help but we just kept talking after every over, took our time with things and got to the stage where we might possibly just deny them. We were congratulating each other on getting through every over and in that situation you really do try to break it down to ball by ball.

Then, if we weren't chatting after these individual deliveries, I would be shouting down to him at the other end every time he played a good shot or left one well outside off stump. As the senior partner I took the lead but Monty was chatty, and we both knew what we had to do. Everyone did. Our remit remained fairly simple: WHATEVER HAPPENS, DO NOT GET OUT!

Early in our partnership, I was concentrating so hard on two things: keeping the ball out, and remembering to take as long as possible between deliveries, a ploy both to compose myself and run down the clock. This took the form of me idling towards square leg far enough without taking the Michael, or gardening the pitch just for the sake of it.

Having something to do all the time can keep you focused on the immediate job in hand and not the stuff that is going on around you – the opposition chat, the scoreboard, the noise from the crowd. It was a case of ticking a ball off, having a wander and ignoring the situation of the game for a few seconds. Of course, shutting out the atmosphere became harder with every run we scored, and, once ahead, with every ball survived. Quite simply, the buzz got louder and louder, and it was pandemonium towards the end.

There were moments when Monty would set off for a run, which would have been a really quick single, and we both had to hurriedly return to our creases. Just a few deliveries after getting into credit via the first of my two consecutive fours off Peter Siddle I had to send Monty back, then we bumped into each other as we ran a single. In that situation the equation is always in the bowling team's favour because they only need one ball to go their way. On the other hand, we needed to negotiate lots.

The Australians kept pretty calm, playing the situation expertly as there was really no need to chase things. They just kept plugging away, having been in this position so often before, and Ricky Ponting mixed up his bowling options a little bit. Rotating your attack is always a good idea in that situation as it does not allow batsmen to get set but it was nevertheless a big surprise for me when he brought Marcus North on to bowl.

Fair enough, I understood the logic: he was an off-spinner bowling to two left-handers, and, taking the ball away from the bat, might entice an edge. But the light wasn't bad, and Nathan Hauritz was on at the other end. With them bowling in tandem it all got a little bit samey. We were able to get into the same rhythm at each end, rather than having to change pace, and that simplified things for two tail-enders. Peter Siddle, Ben Hilfenhaus and Mitchell Johnson were bowling well and in comparison we were

relatively comfortable against the spinners. The only other possible reason for doing so was to maximize the number of balls sent
down before 6.40 p.m. – the cut-off time for Australia to start any
potential innings.

The exact location of our finishing line only became clear after
our twelfth man, Bilal Shafayat, had answered my call to bring out
new gloves and a drink. To be brutally honest, I had done it
because Monty and I had found communicating with umpire
Aleem Dar problematic. We weren't getting a clear answer from
him as to what time the bails could be removed, and a draw
agreed. Every over we asked him how long was left and he simply
kept replying: 'Nearly there, nearly there.'

That lack of a definitive answer was frustrating but in order to
keep calm and focused we'd agreed to target ten minutes to seven
as a cut-off. Any earlier would be a bonus.

Bilal's presence on the field clearly irritated the Australians, particularly Ponting, but I felt compelled to know definitively when
that final hour would end, and how the loss of overs on the fourth
day to rain might affect things. Would you believe it? As we discussed things on the square, I managed to spill some water on the
new pair of gloves I'd been given. How clumsy of me!

There was only one thing for it – Bilal would have to come
back with a fresh pair. Only my signal was misinterpreted on our
dressing-room balcony for me having an injured wrist, so next
thing both Bilal and our physio Steve McCaig ventured out.

As you can imagine it's difficult to grip a bat handle with gloves
that are wetter than an otter's pocket, but the appearance of Steve
only served to stir Ponting's ire. I had told Steve politely that he
was not required. Ponting, however, was not so polite.

'Fuck off, you fat prick,' he roared.

Hardly the words you want to hear from a bloke you grew up
idolizing. Steve is an Aussie, you see, and had just discovered in
the crudest possible way that there is truth in the old maxim that
you should never meet your heroes.

Of course, there was more than a smidgeon of gamesmanship in my actions but in the same situation Australia would have done exactly the same thing. There isn't a team in the world that wouldn't. And the most important thing to Monty and me was walking off that field with our partnership unbroken.

It had been far from plain sailing. There were a couple of close calls – an appeal for caught behind, and an appeal for lbw from a ball that I left, but that goes with the territory for a number ten attempting to negotiate his way to the close. You expect some shouts from the opposition and some harum-scarum moments.

We'd only been in tandem for forty-odd minutes but our smiles told of our pride. Mission accomplished, we congratulated each other, but didn't say much else as we returned to the dressing room, adrenalin pumping. Before we could reach our team-mates, indeed before we had reached the boundary edge, we were grabbed to do television and radio interviews. The crowd were raucous, but the most satisfying part of the immediate aftermath was getting back to the dressing room where the atmosphere was incredible. We were engulfed by hugs and high fives, team-mates were punching the air and although we had drawn this undoubtedly felt like a win. Anyone who witnessed these celebrations would have recognized that.

Momentum was with us, we felt, as we reflected on the game and we were given an extra spur when we discovered that the wives of the Australian players had ordered the champagne to their hospitality box when we were nine down. How sporting of them to raise a glass to our achievement. Cheers!

As has been customary in Ashes summers, all the focus in the build-up had not been on the here and now but the five Tests against Australia. Even during the comfortable 2-0 win over West Indies, we were made aware that the countdown to the first ball had dropped below fifty days, and now the wait was over, things were full-on. There were just three days between the first Test at

Cardiff and the second at Lord's, and we didn't want the effort we had put in on the final day to be for nothing.

No sooner had we arrived in the capital, however, than attention turned to Andrew Flintoff. Troubled by his knee, he spent Monday in consultation with his surgeon, and underwent cortisone injections in his bid to be fit for the second match. He had also made the decision to retire from Test cricket, and a few of us knew of his intention to do so before he sat down and told the team officially on the Tuesday before practice. The *Sun* newspaper had splashed the news that morning. Having fought back from injury so many times over the past three years, he had vowed to get through four more games before calling it a day.

But why had he chosen this moment to go public? That was a question asked by myself and others within the England camp. Why was he choosing the eve of a massive match for us? Why not wait until the end of the series? Whether he thought it would gee us up, or whether he thought by announcing it he would gee himself up, I am not sure. We appreciated that he was struggling, and had done all he could to get physically prepared for back-to-back Test matches. But why, we wondered, did he need to do it in the middle of a series? The biggest Test series England were involved in. The consensus was that he should have left it until later, as we didn't need any distractions from the task in hand.

Not that the way in which he told us allowed much time for sentiment. In his words, he told us that he was letting us know so we would know what to say if it came up later in press conferences. Fred's fitness, along with that of Kevin Pietersen, who was struggling with an Achilles injury, had become a side issue, but although Steve Harmison was called up as cover, he was passed fit, and we went into the Lord's game without Monty. My partner in crime from the Cardiff heist was replaced by Graham Onions in an otherwise unchanged XI.

Back-to-back Tests can be a good thing if you are on the front foot in a series. We were, and, having finished in the ascendancy a matter of days earlier, there was a feeling in our camp that winning the toss and asking the Australian attack to get back out there and bowl again would deliver another psychological blow. It was only seventy-two hours since they had failed to dismiss us and secure an expected 1-0 lead, and to do so would be both demoralizing and physically demanding given the minimal recuperation time. To add to the mix, this attack had little if any experience of the Lord's slope. Some people find it particularly tricky adapting to it, and it soon became obvious that the Aussies, and Mitchell Johnson in particular, were struggling to do so.

It was nice to get the feet up and watch on that first morning after Strauss won the toss. There is always a sense of occasion about a Test match at Lord's, and those who had featured in the corresponding fixture four years earlier spoke about the wave of noise that crashed around the Long Room when the England batsmen passed through on their way to the middle. Stoked by curiosity, the rest of us naturally called for hush in the dressing room so we could experience the posh cheering as Strauss and Cook emerged through the throng, on to the pavilion steps and onwards on to the turf.

Cookie later told me he was determined not to fail after that because the reception when he trudged back would be too much of a contrast to bear.

He latched on to the loose stuff on offer, as did Strauss, and for bowlers there is no better feeling than sitting watching your opening batsmen negotiate an entire session. It means that you can enjoy your lunch, and plenty of it, pretty safe in the knowledge that you are not going to be bowling any time soon. Not that I didn't have sympathy for their fast bowlers that morning. They were struggling big time, especially Johnson, and I can empathize with anyone who has to go through that kind of experience. Whereas our middle order were revelling in Johnson's misfortune – 'wa-hey, he's completely lost it' – I think all of our bowlers, me included, thought: 'Yeah . . . but . . .'

For months Johnson had been the spearhead of their attack, and suddenly his form had dropped off. That kind of rapid regression can happen to anyone – it's a fast bowler's lot – so you are just glad it's not you when you are sitting watching one of your opponents going through it. I recalled my nightmare performance at the Wanderers back in 2004–5 when I suffered such a crisis of confidence that I had no bloody idea where the ball was going or what I was trying to do with it. I was bowling so badly that even when I took a wicket I was slightly embarrassed, and so I did feel a connection with the mental anguish he must have been suffering as Cook and Strauss kept smashing him to the rope. They hit twenty-two boundaries between them during that morning session, taking full advantage of the alien feeling bowling at Lord's gives to bowlers.

The slope on the ground is very tricky to negotiate when you are running in at pace. You have got to get used to feeling a little off balance when you plant your feet in delivery stride and that can be hard when you are so used to the feel you get from landing on the crease repeatedly in practice sessions. When bowling from the Pavilion End, you are pushed into the stumps through your own momentum. It's not obvious to the naked eye of the spectator but when you get past the umpire's shoulder you feel a lot tighter in than you ideally want to be. The opposite applies from the Nursery End, and it certainly takes a little time to start feeling comfortable with it.

Australia's bowlers clawed it back later in the day, however, and the nature of the innings began to change when Strauss was out to the second ball of the second morning. When Swanny and Stuart Broad followed in the next two overs, it meant that despite having been 196 for 0 just twenty-two hours earlier, Graham Onions and I came together at 378 for 9. My exploits with the bat in Cardiff had given me confidence, though, so I backed myself to be positive and hit anything in a scoring area. Twice I crashed Johnson through the off side for four, and suffice to say he was less than impressed. He wasn't shy in letting me know either, directing his frustration and anger at me in rather unpleasant terms. Never one to retreat from a verbal joust, I started giving it back.

Although I am generally placid off the pitch, I've always had a short fuse, and combined with my competitive nature, it tends to be a relatively short time before I snap under provocation. At other times the challenge of the contest gets me going; it has always been the same on a sports field for me, and I know sometimes when I am bowling I look like I am constantly having a go at people just for the sake of it. So here's half an apology. Yes, there are times when I cross the line, but I have tried to rein in the aggression, and keep things hostile but within the spirit of the game, since things got physical with the late Runako Morton in a one-day international against West Indies at Edgbaston in 2007, when our shoulders kissed quite passionately. Nevertheless, I hope people can accept that operating close to the line is the way I've always played sport.

Thankfully, I have never barged anyone on the golf course – but I've been known to lose it even in that game of great decorum following a bad shot. It usually ends up with me lobbing my club into the nearest trees, and I did almost decapitate Graeme Swann once in that manner. I have to have an angry swing of retribution after every shanked or sliced drive and on the occasion in question the club slipped from my grasp and flew straight at him, thudding into his chest.

I enjoyed myself with the bat and I guess we were feeling rather upbeat again as a team after that late flurry of forty-seven runs for the tenth wicket. So to nip a couple out served only to enhance our dominant position. At that stage of my career, people still tended to dismiss me as a threat unless the ball was swinging but the two early successes here were nothing to do with movement through the air. The first was fortuitous, to be honest – Phil Hughes strangled down the leg side – but the ball that got Ponting was just one that nipped in off the seam if anything. The plan had been to drag him across his stumps by bowling outside off, effectively setting him up for the straight one, and it worked.

The ball beat his defensive prod, crashed into pad and flew to Strauss at slip. I immediately thought he was plumb lbw, and that the only thing that could have saved him was an edge. However, as he had been caught low down, he was out either way in our book. For a few seconds nothing happened as Rudi Koertzen weighed things up. However, as soon as he consulted with his fellow umpire Billy Doctrove at square leg to check whether the ball had carried, we knew Ponting was on his way. In checking with television umpire Nigel Llong whether the catch had been taken cleanly, it confirmed that Koertzen was of the opinion that Ponting's bat had connected with ball.

The ball was coming out nicely during that opening spell for me and when you are on top of the batsmen, beating the edge, and generally looking like taking wickets, you feel a real wave of energy. The fielders tend to sense something could happen any moment, too, and there was a real buzz created at the start of that innings. Following the procession of Australian hundreds at Cardiff, it was the first time we had been on top in the series, and we had gone from thinking 'how the hell are we going to get these guys out?' to believing it would happen if we remained patient and kept asking questions of them.

As a team we always talk about how creating pressure can lead to chances, and when you are playing the lead role in that, it feels huge. Sure, when thrown the ball, it's part and parcel of a fast bowler's job to take wickets but it doesn't always work out as you want – opponents are allowed to play well, too – so when the captain asks 'are you okay to give me another one?' in contrast to him telling you it's time for a blow, it breeds confidence.

It was not until my next spell that I would add to my tally but I always felt threatening in that first innings. They got to three figures without further losses but, as so often happens, once the third-wicket pair of Simon Katich and Michael Hussey was separated, wickets fell in clumps. We thought Michael Clarke was vulnerable clipping off his pads early in his innings, and so it proved when he picked out a specially positioned short midwicket. Then, 111 for 5 became 139 for 6 when Marcus North became my fourth victim half a dozen overs later, bowled attempting to pull.

Our only other concern of note during Australia's first innings was whether to enforce the follow-on. We discussed it overnight with the Australians some way short of the mark at 156 for 8, and Andrew Strauss remained unconvinced as to the best course of action until the next morning when their lower order got to within eleven runs of making his deliberation futile. The sun was out, and he opted to make use of the good batting weather.

It was the start of the fourth morning when I was eventually thrown the new ball again, and Australia had been set a world-record target 522 in six sessions. But we were confident as a bowling unit as we began the push for victory. We didn't necessarily have better plans for the Australian batsmen during that series, in comparison to previous ones; we just executed them very well. One of the most obvious examples of this resulted in the early departure of Simon Katich.

Ottis Gibson, our bowling coach, had been encouraging Andrew Flintoff to bowl around the wicket at the left-handed Katich, to make him play more. When facing right-arm-over-the-wicket bowlers, Katich was content to allow the ball to carry on with the angle down the slope past his off stump, but from round he would have to play at a greater proportion of deliveries. It worked when he was caught at slip feeling for ball on bat, and Fred acknowledged the tip with a wave to Gibbo on the balcony.

Australia's second innings followed the same pattern as the first and we were halfway to our target of ten wickets when they had only 128 on the board. Yet, the sixth-wicket stand between Michael Clarke and Brad Haddin meant we headed into the final day considering that victory was far from a dead cert.

'What do you reckon? They can't do it, can they?' Swanny had said to me that evening on the drive from the ground to the Landmark Hotel.

'Nah,' I said, unable to mask my uncertainty.

We both started giggling but with the equation down to 209 runs with two batsmen set it was nervous laughter, and we knew we had to be on it from the start the following morning. I began with a maiden, which was pleasing, but it was from the other end that all the action happened as Fred bowled brilliantly, charging in with the pavilion behind him, getting the ball to nip back down off the slope.

He just kept pounding in that morning. It was a morning that was all about him. As if he had written himself a script, and was acting it out – it was the last time he would play in a Test at Lord's, and he was determined to milk every moment. Even the celebrations, when he started getting among the wickets, were performed with choreographed precision.

Australia hadn't added to their overnight 313 for 5 when Haddin edged the tenth ball of the morning into the slips. Yet Fred only got to wheel out the most symbolic celebration of the lot – the down-on-one-knee-look-at-me pose – after persuading Strauss to let him have one more over, and overstepping to give himself one last delivery. None of us could begrudge him his five-wicket haul after all the miles he had got through in his Test career for so few such returns, and this, his third, put us into a position from which we knew we could win back the little urn.

The end to the 2005 Edgbaston Ashes Test meant the next one held there always had the potential to be a damp squib. It certainly started that way, damper if anything, and my abiding memory of the opening day was Sir Ian Botham sitting on one of the ground-staff's water hogs as they mopped up.

Play did not get under way until the evening session, in fact, and when it did Australia confirmed a change at the top of their order. While some considered the dropping of Phil Hughes for

Shane Watson a moral victory for us, as Watson was not known as an opener, the fact was that Hughes had not been getting any runs against us, and we knew exactly how to bowl at him to be confident of extending that sequence. When you have had success against a player you want him to stay in the team while, in contrast, we acknowledged Watson was a good batsman. So as far as we were concerned their move had been a positive one.

Perhaps we got a little thrown by the presence of Watson at the top of the order, having in our heads that he was a number seven, because we just didn't bowl well at him when the rain finally abated. You sometimes con yourself into bowling differently at players when they appear in unusual positions – take nightwatchmen as an extreme example – although generally speaking that thirty-over session was one in which we couldn't get the ball to behave how we wanted, and our sole success came from Swanny's off-spin.

There was a little bit of niggle in the game. Let's be honest, you are never going to get through an Ashes series without tension developing between the teams, as you've all grown up dreaming of playing in one and give your all from start to finish.

But I've always felt a bit sorry for the Australians because they have this thing about their nation being really aggressive and getting in your face when the simple fact is they're not very good at it.

Now I've always advocated that if you're not good at something you shouldn't do it. But that hasn't ever appeared to put them off sledging, unfortunately, and that in turn can have a detrimental effect. Naturally, we wanted to give Watson a warm welcome but his retaliation was to blow a massive raspberry. As this was his best, nay, only, comeback, it merely encouraged us to chirp a bit more.

It became pretty obvious in Birmingham that Mitchell Johnson had been told to dish out more of the verbal stuff – but again his execution of it let him down. Glenn McGrath was good at it, in the sense that his bowling allowed him to say what he liked. It was not necessarily genius but he would use these exchanges to get himself fired up and into aggressive mode, whereas someone like Mitchell was never consistent enough to make it work in the same way. If you are going to sledge you've got to make sure you can back it up with your actions. McGrath had the skill to do it, but Johnson did not in that series.

Some bowlers feed off that conflict, and from my point of view I feel my performances improve when there is a bit of a battle with the batsman, when the contest becomes full-on, if you like. Part of it is actually self-perpetuating. If I mouth off and then don't bowl well I know I am going to look like an idiot, so it actually helps me to focus on the job in hand if I get into a verbal ruck. Rather than distract me like some people might suggest it does, it actually helps me concentrate on what I am doing.

Watson undoubtedly gave Australia a different dimension up front because his natural game is quite aggressive. But we didn't worry ourselves that he was the sort of guy who could go on and get a big hundred. He has since improved dramatically as an opening batsman but in those days he was always liable to give you chances.

Andrew Strauss threw something of a surprise the following morning by revealing that Graham Onions was going to bowl the first over – and he couldn't have started any better. His first ball skidded on to trap Watson deep in his crease, and the very next one took out Michael Hussey's off stump. Talk about the perfect start.

Bunny rushed Ricky Ponting with a bouncer for a third success within the first hour, and as soon as I got on to bowl I found that the ball was hooping around corners. It is for days like this that you put in all your practice as a swing bowler, and the rewards were spectacular. Matt Prior produced a stunning one-handed grab to his left to provide me with my first wicket, from an edge by Marcus North, and after sending back Johnson, who shouldered arms, next ball, I pulled off the classic dismissal for the conditions on the stroke of lunch.

Delivered from wide on the crease, the ball angled in and just left the debutant Graham Manou enough to snake past the out-side edge and crash into off stump. Strauss reckoned it was as good a ball as you'll ever see, and who was I to argue?

Australia, very much in the ascendancy at the start of the session, closed it on 203 for 8, on what was – despite the helpful overhead conditions – a very true pitch. An outside edge from Peter Siddle after lunch gave me a five-for in what was otherwise one of the most forgettable matches in modern Ashes history.

Edgbaston Tests tend to have a great atmosphere, particularly at the weekends, but heavy rain on the Saturday denied the Birmingham support the chance to roar us on in their usual manner, and totally washed things out. With so many overs lost it was going to be hard to manufacture anything from a position of 116 for 2 heading into the final six sessions, and although we were well placed to exert some pressure with a 113-run lead on first innings, it would have needed something special to happen for us, and Marcus North and Michael Clarke both batted well to hold out comfortably for a draw.

So my maiden five-wicket haul in an Ashes series didn't really mean anything to me. Don't get me wrong, as a bowler it's always nice to finish up with five wickets, but I have always been some-one who relishes individual performances that contribute to collective success. Give me five wickets that help secure a win, and I remember them all the more fondly, but if the team doesn't get the result, it doesn't feel anywhere near as special.

Despite Australian resistance in that third Test, we remained in confident mood as the series moved further north but things turned into a bit of a circus at Headingley.

It started with Andrew Flintoff's fitness, and he literally hobbled into the nets on the Thursday afternoon in a bid to prove his fitness for the following morning. He was trying to tell people that his knee was fine but it was obvious it wasn't, so the management took it upon themselves to rest him and concentrate on getting him fit for the last Test.

Not that the rest of us knew what was going on, and on the Friday morning in question, when I saw his kitbag in the corner, I texted him to tell him to hurry down to the ground, thinking he had overslept. As it was, he didn't turn up until after the game started, and it is fair to say he was not best pleased to have been omitted. From his point of his view, as this was going to be his last series, he wanted to be a part of every minute of it. Of course, as a fellow player I could understand that, and it probably played on his mind that a win at Leeds meant series victory.

Such thoughts were natural to someone about to bow out of the Test scene – you treasure being part of the big moments and really don't want others to decide you can't be – but it was a similar thought that infected the rest of the team to devastating effect. Undoubtedly one of the reasons we slipped up at Headingley was that we knew we were so close to claiming back that little urn.

Victory would have provided us with an unassailable 2-0 lead but we shouldn't have been thinking about that, we should have been thinking, as we had in the recent past, of all the little things that, when chained together, result in wins. Our blueprint had always been to do the simple things right session by session, rather than think too big or too far ahead.

Confidence is one thing but optimism became a little bit too feverish in the build-up, with the national newspapers full of talk about how the Ashes could be won with a match to spare. Everyone anticipated us finishing off what we had started three weeks earlier with success at Lord's. A big sign in front of the building work at the Kirkstall Lane end of the ground simply read: Roar for England.

However, there was not much to roar about in the most fraught start to a Test match I have experienced. The fire alarm going off at the team hotel in the early hours of the morning, which forced us on to the drizzly streets of central Leeds, was not ideal and it started what felt like a domino effect. We were informed that Steve Harmison would be playing instead of Fred before we headed out for our pre-match warm-up routines, and towards the back of this another change to the XI looked eminently possible when Matt Prior went down with a back spasm.

The toss was delayed – thankfully we had some credit in the bank after Brad Haddin was injured in similar circumstances at Edgbaston – as the medical staff worked on Matt, and contingency plans were discussed. Although he was declared fit before Andrew Strauss walked out to the middle, it simply added to the complications when considering what to do after Ricky Ponting's wrong call in the middle. The pitch seemed drier than usual, which would have encouraged batting, but there was early-morning damp to help the bowlers, and overhead conditions which can be so influential at the ground were difficult to judge. As it was, Strauss plumped for batting, we were all over the place on that opening day, and by the end of it the match was almost gone.

The frantic preparation was not ideal for a Test match but it could be no excuse for not playing well. There was no doubt that we batted incredibly poorly, to be dismissed for 102 shortly after lunch, and unfortunately we bowled poorly, too. It's not that we were trying to bowl short at Australia's top order, we just did. Perhaps because we were defending such a low total, we thought we had to get them out cheaply, too, and therefore instead of doing our usual thing we went a bit too gung-ho and paid the price.

By the end of that first day Australia led by ninety-four runs, with six wickets in hand, and they had almost completed their task by the end of the second. I was at the crease as nightwatchman when, having conceded a whopping 343-run deficit, we left the field 82 for 5 second time around.

It is when you are down that people tend to put the boot in, and it was overnight that a dossier compiled by former Australian batsman and then Somerset captain Justin Langer emerged. The deconstruction of our team, penned by Langer and handed to

Australian squad members before the first Test in Cardiff, had been leaked to and published by the *Sunday Telegraph*.

In it English cricketers were derided for not being up for the fight. 'As soon as it gets a bit hard you just have to watch their body language and see how flat and lazy they get.'

Of me, he added: 'He is hugely improved but can be a bit of a pussy if worn down.'

Of course, this wasn't great timing, coming as it did in the middle of a game, but because it caused such a stir that Sunday morning we were all aware of it. I don't think there were any of our guys who hadn't read it but we dismissed it for what it was – no more than someone's opinion, and from a bloke who wasn't held in the greatest regard in our dressing room anyway.

Bizarrely, later that week I got a text message from Langer – or someone claiming to be him, as, unsurprisingly, I do not keep his number in my phone – which amounted to a half-arsed apology, reiterating that it was just his personal opinion.

'I'm sure you'll prove me wrong!' he concluded. I would like to think I did in the series that began 15 months later.

This kind of thing is expected during Ashes series, it adds some extra spice and is typical of the fact that matches between England and Australia are fought both on and off the field. Imagine if we had done a dossier on their 2010–11 team; that would be fairly derogatory as well, but usually disparaging comments made away from the middle only serve to drive their targets on. When I look back on this episode it reminds me of those remarks made by Andrew Gale about Lancashire on Sky Sports News during the 2011 season, shortly before a Roses match, when he revealed surprise at how well we were doing because he'd marked us down as relegation candidates. Anyone recall what happened next?

The only positive aspect of what transpired over the two and a half days of the Headlingley defeat was the performance of Stuart Broad. There had been a lot of debate after the third Test about the prospect of him being dropped, and I knew he was aware of that. It is hard not to be aware of what the media are saying even if you don't read the papers and turn on the sports channels on TV because family and friends tend to get back to you on it. But he believes in himself and is a serious talent. He showed that with a return to form with the ball and the way he played with the bat in the second innings when he and Graeme Swann made merry.

Otherwise, the whole Headingley experience came and went as a bit of a blur. Although one thing that stuck in our minds, thankfully, was the post-mortem meeting called by Andy Flower. In normal circumstances, debriefs of performances are carried out after there has been time for the dust to settle but on this occasion we were made to stay in Leeds to discuss what had gone wrong and how we intended to put it right. There was no throwing of tea cups – a bollocking was hardly necessary, as it was so blatantly obvious that we hadn't played well – it was a civilized meeting about how to move forward, during which everyone was allowed their input.

We had also collapsed in Jamaica earlier in the year but had experienced some very positive stuff in the six months in between – fifty-one all out was immediately followed by declarations of 566, 600 and 546 in our next three first innings in Tests, so we knew we had the potential to come back strongly from losses and poor performances. Therefore, despite the disappointing nature of events of the previous seventy-two hours, there was latent confidence in that room that we could turn it around. We all agreed how our focus was wrong, that we thought about winning the series rather than thinking about the nuts and bolts of how to win the game. We got caught up in the prospect of making history rather than concentrating on the contest in the middle.

As coach, Andy is meticulous about the little processes we have to go through to win games, and we left Leeds determined to revert to type. It was all fairly simplistic stuff but we knew that if we were to come back in the fifth match we would have to concentrate on performing in the first half-hour, then the next, and start piecing those little passages together again. Having lost sight of them temporarily, the small bits were given a lot more care and attention, and we vowed to stick together and not lose sight of the fact that the Ashes were still up for grabs. Neutrals would have reckoned Australia to be in the box seat heading into the final Test at the Oval, entering it off the back of such a resounding innings win at 1-1, and now only needing a draw, they had one hand on the urn already.

There were other changes as we gathered underneath those famous gasometers for our first practice session nine days later. Jonathan Trott, who had been in the squad for the Headingley contest, came in for Ravi Bopara, and Fred was back after advice from the knee specialist that, with the right management, he would get through the rigours of a full-on Test match. Of course, it was known by that stage that surgery at the end of the series was necessary, but he so desperately wanted the chance to depart on a high, and given his ability to produce his best against Australia, his selection ahead of Graham Onions was inevitable.

I became something of a doubt myself after incurring a problem in my left hamstring while running between the wickets at Headingley. From the moment I did it, I spent long periods stretching it out, a process that continued for numerous days after a scan had provided the news I hoped for: no tear. Our long-serving physio at Lancashire, Dave 'Rooster' Roberts, wanted to err on the side of caution, so that meant daily manipulation, massage treatment and running exercise to put it under pressure.

Obstacles in my path were the last thing I wanted. In 2005, my presence in the deciding Test match was a fleeting one, but my mood could not have provided a starker contrast. This time, I was desperate not to miss out. Then, we had only to avoid defeat, but now with an Ashes series all square heading into the final game for the first time in forty-three years, only victory would be good enough to complete our mission, and I wanted to be one of the contributors.

From a personal perspective, my batting lost its notoriety during our 332 all out, when Ben Hilfenhaus did for me lbw. At fifty-four innings, it thus ended the longest stretch without a duck by anyone at the start of their Test career. The wider debate, however, concentrated on whether our team total was enough.

It did not look it when Australia manoeuvred to seventy-three without loss, a position from which they would have fancied securing a lead on first innings, but one from which Stuart Broad conjured a brilliant spell just when we needed it most. I hadn't been able to secure a breakthrough despite feeling in good nick, nor had Fred or Harmy, so Strauss turned to Broad as third change, to bowl in tandem with Graeme Swann.

If a player is not performing there is always someone somewhere crawling out of the woodwork to suggest they shouldn't be in the team. It goes with the territory when you are playing for England, and everyone gets a dose of it now and again. Whenever you experience a bad run of form that kind of speculation hangs around you like a bad smell but there is nothing you can do about it other than continue to strive for wickets. So I was pleased for Broady when his spell of four wickets in six overs decimated Australia's top order, although I always would prefer it to be me in the wickets and runs.

His height made the most of the variable bounce on offer from the Vauxhall End even at that stage of the match, and in one session, delayed by a lunchtime shower, Australia had slumped to 133 for 8.

Despite such a healthy advantage, early losses at the start of our second innings gave Australia a chink of light before Trott showed us the kind of innings we were to become accustomed to from him. At the time it was a surprise to me but once you get to know him, and what sort of character he is, his 119 was not surprising at all. He loves nothing more than batting, has an insatiable appetite for being out there in the middle, and that very fact meant he was able to perform under the combined pressure of it being his debut and the fact that it was a decisive Test against Australia.

Talk about taking your opportunity. The series was on a knife edge when he walked in to join Andrew Strauss on that Friday evening but in his favour was the fact that he wouldn't have been distracted by the bigger picture at all. He had not been involved in it for a start, and there would have been enough individual pressure for him to worry about. The way he performed in such a high-profile match was incredible, and he made himself undroppable overnight.

Trott is very good at what he does, and has sustained an extremely high level of consistency over his first few years as an international player, promoting him as exactly the sort of person you need at number three. I was at the other end when he became the eighteenth England batsman to make a hundred on Test debut. Few of those would have been as crucial.

Because the pitch, despite taking turn, was getting slower as time wore on and batsmen were able to adjust when the bounce was not true. In fact, despite being set 546 for victory, Australia were looking quite comfortable on the fourth afternoon until Fred produced a game-changing piece of fielding. Typically of him, it was almost as if the move was choreographed when he swooped on a Michael Hussey drive to mid on and hurled the stumps down at the batsman's end with a nonchalant flick of his wrist. Ricky Ponting, as the TV replays confirmed, was short of his ground.

There had been nothing doing with Australia 217 for 2 in mid-afternoon. Three hours had passed without a sniff of a wicket, and so we were grateful for Fred's inherent ability to make something happen out of nothing on a cricket field. In respect of his retirement we allowed him to milk the moment with his celebration, and it was not until a couple of years later when Swanny took a five-wicket haul at the same ground that any of us tried to mimic it. Fred was always quite a difficult person to take the mickey out of in his playing days because you always knew he would come back at you twice as hard, so people generally didn't do it. It was undoubtedly easier once he was not around!

Just as with Broad in the first innings, I enjoyed the fact that Swanny was among the wickets, and for him to complete victory with the final one, Hussey caught at short leg, was a nice touch. It was manic when Alastair Cook clutched that ball, and scarpered with it in his pocket! The rest of us chased each other around the square, Swanny went down on his knees and the crowd noise was truly amazing. The feeling of exultation was overwhelming. Those next few moments on the field were as special as it gets. Ultimately, that is where you share your success, but we were also mindful of getting back into the dressing room to toast it with our coaching staff and management.

The celebrations went on long after we returned to acknowledge all corners of the Oval, with our wives and children coming onto to the field with us when the crowds had dispersed. Later, we cracked on in a private room at the City Grange hotel in east London. Although a small number of us had been around in 2005, this was a major achievement for what I considered to be a new team. Daniella, ever present during the series, and my mum and dad, whose presence was limited to weekends, joined the throng and it was nice to celebrate that kind of success with families who put up with so much.

My phone had run out of juice so – keen not to miss the text informing us what time the open-top bus was picking us up the next morning! – I left it to charge in the corner of the room. Unfortunately, when I went to retrieve it at the end of the night, both the charger and phone had gone. So if you did send me a congratulatory text, here's an apology for not saying thanks.

There wasn't much time to dwell on our heavy heads the following morning, either, because we had to get ourselves up to

Manchester to fly over to Belfast. Now playing the Irish in a one-day international just a couple of days after the biggest series for an England cricketer to participate in was not a popular decision among the squad. Nor was the fact that while Strauss got a captain's rest, myself and Stuart Broad were instructed to travel and then told we would be sitting it out upon arrival. Perhaps they thought we would bunk off with prior knowledge.

Our trip became a two-night celebration on the Guinness as a result. We were annoyed not to be told sooner because it had been a long summer, and we would have welcomed a couple of nights back in our own beds. Five Tests over seven weeks doesn't give you chance to get home much, and here we were away doing nothing.

There is little doubt in my mind that the Ireland fixture was scheduled to stop us going overboard with the celebrations, as had happened in 2005. Nobody said that to us but it appeared pretty obvious that, after the stir at 10 Downing Street, they were going to keep us on a tight leash this time. What better way to cool things than playing in sub-zero temperatures at Stormont? Getting trolleyed has serious repercussions, too – it takes a couple of weeks to recover from something like that, and there was no let-up in our schedule.

13

Plotting a Route to the Top

Actively resting players was just not cricket, at least not English cricket, prior to 2009, but was something Andy Flower introduced at the end of the home summer. Australia, our opponents in the seven-match NatWest Series, had been long-term advocates of giving their star names time off to recuperate during certain periods, particularly during home limited-overs campaigns.

Suddenly, we started following suit and I was one of the first guinea pigs, along with Paul Collingwood and Graeme Swann. All three of us had played for England across all three formats that summer, and so we all got scheduled time to put the feet up. I missed a couple of games in mid-series, and so did Colly, but we had all returned by the final match up at Chester-le-Street, where we were thankfully able to avert an Australian whitewash.

Being rested is a strange situation because you want to play as much as you can and my personal circumstances made it a bit of a double-edged sword. Having been in and out of the team for a number of years, I wanted to play every game now I was a regular but on the other hand the fact they wanted to protect me from injury through fatigue told me that I was vitally important to longer-term plans.

It was a policy that raised a few eyebrows as England's custom, traditionally and historically, had been to pick their best XI – a team best equipped to win the game in the particular conditions. If you were fit for selection, you were picked until you were not. September therefore represented something of a watershed, and proved a forerunner to the following spring. As coach, Flower is meticulous, and because the winter schedule was ridiculously heavy, Andrew Strauss and I had already been pencilled in to miss the Test tour to Bangladesh, not that I was aware of this at the time, mind. The captain being rested from an overseas assignment was unheard of, but everything under this England regime is done for a reason, and this was all about succession planning – providing Alastair Cook with his first taste of Test leadership – and prioritizing assignments.

No one truly likes being rested because you have always got that inherent fear as an international cricketer of someone else coming along and altering your place in the pecking order. But the coach, in conjunction with the medical team, has the final say in trying to serve the best interests of both individuals and the team.

For my part, I want to play as many games, come what may. Whenever I am in the team I want to make the most of it, as I don't know how long I'll have left, and being omitted is a frustration. The theory behind it is that being rested here and there can help me extend my Test career but you cannot help wanting to play all forms of the game. We are competitive beasts by nature, and if there are fixtures scheduled you want to play in them all despite the fact that the saturated international itinerary makes it almost impossible to do so.

Despite losing 6-1 to Australia, and playing our first game in Johannesburg on 25 September, just five days after our final NatWest fixture, the Champions Trophy – at least in comparison with other recent global events – proved a rip-roaring success.

Credit the Australians for going on to win this tournament and the two previous World Cups because, just like us, they have faced heading into World Cups immediately after Ashes series down under. It doesn't get any more physically or emotionally draining than that, and we had certainly been flogged throughout a gruelling home summer in 2009. The pattern is a recurring one and a major reason why the ECB negotiated a change in the cycle of Ashes series from 2013 onwards. It has been that way throughout my England career, and our performances in both South Africa in 2003 and the Caribbean in 2007 reflected that. If we are going to have any chance of winning a World Cup we need to be as fresh as is possible.

Despite facing Sri Lanka after such a short turnaround, we discovered rather welcoming conditions in Johannesburg, and took some early wickets on a helpful pitch. It nipped about early, Sri Lanka never recovered from 17 for 4 and we secured an opening six-wicket win.

With games so closely packed together, there is an opportunity to get on a roll at a tournament like the Champions Trophy, and we used the momentum developed at the Wanderers to secure an impressive victory over the hosts at Centurion. Having taken three wickets in the first game, I doubled my tally, with a display that pleased me, not least because of the fact that I was able to restrict the powerful South African left-handers during the batting Powerplay. Having picked up Herschelle Gibbs and Mark Boucher in my previous spells, I managed to tuck Albie Morkel up, which is no mean feat, and then dismiss Roelof van der Merwe, another of their dangerous hitters, for a duck.

My success came from mixing up cutters that were sticking in the pitch with yorkers, and whenever you finish with figures of 10-0-42-3 in a game when both teams score in excess of 300 you are understandably pleased. Bowlers can be on a hiding to nothing in limited-overs matches, as it has always been a batsman's game. But just as in Twenty20, where a similar pattern emerged and bowlers turned up only to be smacked out of the ground, the ethos has changed and it has encouraged people to tighten up their skills, and increase their threat. These days if you can't bowl a yorker or a decent slower ball, you are going to get smacked, and that's not an experience you want to go through too often. It happens to you occasionally, of course, so you need these weapons to help you fight back.

A fast bowler's lot has evolved quite a bit over the past five years, with the introduction and subsequent tinkering of Powerplays. It has been quite hard to settle into a specific role because you are never quite sure when you are coming back into the attack. All you do know is that when the batting side call for their five overs of making merry, the pressure is on. Stuart Broad and I discussed tactics on how to deal with the Powerplay when it was more often than not taken around the forty-first over by teams, before the restrictions preventing it being taken after the thirty-sixth over were imposed. That meant a block of ten overs, including the death, when things were completely in favour of the batsmen, and as us two went through a phase of bowling two in one set of five overs and three in the other, we had to lower our pain threshold. In those circumstances, if you went for under sixty runs you were delighted.

Conversely, bowling during these periods when batsmen are increasingly taking risks does improve your chance of taking wickets, and one of the things you are always aiming for is for your strike rate to be as low as possible. Unfortunately, it also means that economy rates are now very different from what they once were. In my first five years of ODIs I went at 4.8 runs per over but since then the number has jumped above five, and there is no doubt I am an infinitely better bowler. It just highlights the need for you to embrace the change, and it is certainly a very different game from the one played pre-2000 when guys could aim for economy rates of four or under.

Such is the disparity that batsmen think they can get away with anything at times, and so Graeme Smith was more than a little agitated when the umpires refused him a runner, for cramp, at the end of my first over of a final spell. He had struck a typically fine hundred against us but Broady dismissed him in the next over to give him the chance to put his feet up.

Back-to-back victories meant that we were through to the semi-finals with a game to spare but we were never really in the dead rubber against New Zealand, were never going to defend a score of 146, and only a rescue effort of eighty by Tim Bresnan gave us any sort of respectability against Australia on another good Centurion surface.

Nevertheless, we had shown some good signs with the ball in these conditions and were to make history of sorts by becoming only the second country after Australia to win a bilateral one-day series in South Africa when we returned in November. Although it was weather assisted, with the first and final games of five washed out, it did provide us with another of our one-day false dawns. Unfortunately, we habitually fail to kick on because of our inconsistency.

It is always nice to pick up wickets early on any tour and three on my return to Centurion in the opening win was followed by the man-of-the-match award and figures of 5 for 23 as we went 2-1 up in Port Elizabeth. It was a decent pitch but we bowled with great discipline to dismiss the South Africans for 119.

It was a desire to contribute to an increasingly successful England team that was behind me pulling out of the Indian Premier League auction list days after arriving back in South Africa. English cricketers' profiles had been raised by the Ashes victory in August and although the IPL is always tempting for any international player, I had my reasons. My main one was the same as that of Stuart Broad, who pulled out on the same day – it would help me to stay as fresh as possible for the following year, which would conclude with the Ashes defence. It would have been pretty foolish to go out there and increase the chances of injury by adding to our workloads. Spending extra time away from home was also a big factor for me, while Broady, being a few years younger, considered that his chance would come again in the future.

In terms of my career, it was way down the list of priorities. I want to play Test cricket for as long as I possibly can, so that remains top; I also have to factor in family as the greater the amount of time I can spend at home to see Lola and Ruby grow up the better; and I would truly rather be resting for international series than screaming around India to play twenty-over cricket.

Not that I would not fancy a short stint in the IPL – far from it. In fact, I have put my name forward every year since the third edition in 2010. A spell over there would have helped further my Twenty20 skills, and, although I would always put England first, I had an extra incentive this year as I viewed it as a potential benefit in my attempt to secure a place for the 2012 World Twenty20. We don't get much exposure to Twenty20 as centrally contracted England players because our scheduling prevents us playing much domestically, so being able to play in the IPL for a few weeks would have been a great help in increasing my exposure to the world's best players, as well as providing an ideal opportunity to show that I can be successful at the format. There have been such big gaps in between my Twenty20 appearances – between the end of the 2009 season and the start of 2012 I played just three matches for Lancashire – it is easy to forget how to bowl in it.

We headed into the Test series with South Africa with new focus, not least because after securing the Ashes there was a need to target another goal. We had begun the year as a mid-ranking team without a captain or coach but Andy Flower quickly went about setting targets of achievement. On face value talk of us getting to the number one ranking in Test cricket might have seemed madness but we were provided with method for it during a meeting with Nathan Leamon, our team analyst, a man the lads know by the moniker Numbers.

He explained the points system behind the world Test rankings in detail – something we hadn't known the ins and outs of – and produced some projections on his whiteboard in which he had laid out all our possible future series results and all the potential points we would claim for different scorelines.

It was only theoretical, of course, being charted on a graph, but for the first time we saw how we could get to the summit of Test cricket. For example, if we won key series – South Africa 2-1 away, India 2-1 at home, drew the Ashes in Australia, he was trying to keep the results as realistic as possible – we could potentially be number one before 2013. He made it clear that we could get there sooner if our results were better and it would naturally take longer if results weren't quite up to the mark but he was just trying to give us a flavour of where we were at by laying things out for us.

It was interesting to know that this was all eminently achievable, without us necessarily playing out of our skins, and I am sure that exercise provided us with direction. Although there were a lot of results to chain together, Nathan made it look challenging rather than daunting. Of course, on the back of an unprecedented set of results, we actually surpassed even the most optimistic forecast and got there in double-quick time.

Cricket is a very statistics-orientated sport, what with run rates and things like Duckworth–Lewis (half decent on the former, clueless on the latter). Before every match we touch upon what average scores are at the particular ground in question as a guide, so that if we get into a position where we are on course for 220 in a one-day game, a total that seems on the low side in terms of ODIs these days, and the average score is approximately that it averts panic. Peter Moores was always really into that kind of thing – average scores, differences between first and second innings totals in Test matches, biggest chases on certain grounds – for guidance.

This kind of information has always been a part of the game at the highest level but Nathan's numerical breakdown provided extra incentive, if any were needed, to climb the Test table. Its competitive nature is the reason why Test cricket is revered as the ultimate form of the game, and our standing was improved in South Africa by virtue of two battling draws in two of the best matches I have experienced. On both occasions, just like Cardiff five months earlier, we held on nine wickets down, yet I look upon the achievement fondly. That is what makes Test cricket unique in its appeal. You play for five days, and although one team can dominate, it is not necessarily reflected in the result. When you are on the right side of results like that – i.e. games that you've saved when the opposition looked as if they were going to win – they feel special, and can help you in tight series.

The start of the four-match series was something of a watershed moment for this England team for one other reason – the absence of Andrew Flintoff. He had missed lengthy periods through injury since the 2005 Ashes, of course, but his permanent departure forced a different dynamic upon the team. Post-Fred, there was debate about how best to balance the team, and without an all-rounder of desired quality, the preferred option, switching from a five-man to four-man attack, placed extra pressure on us all. Just as with the increased seniority, I thrived on the additional expectation.

The opening match of the series at Centurion was memorable as the first of the two matches salvaged by the narrowest of margins, and also for an unexpected first for me. Because it was during the first innings, after coming together with Graeme Swann at 242 for 8, that I hit my first ever six. His memory of events is that I cost him his maiden Test century by getting out to end our England record ninth-wicket stand against South Africa of 106. Not that he's harped on about it ever since, of course.

And the funny thing about that monstrous blow is that I didn't even intend it. I could not recall hitting a six in junior cricket (everything is given as four until you're thirteen anyway because the boundaries are so short) and I am pretty certain there weren't any in my senior outings with Burnley. I've hardly been known for my attacking instincts as a batsman either but Swanny and I were having a real giggle in the middle, he played his usual natural game and I just caught the mood. The stroke in question was a slog-sweep off Paul Harris which I intended to hit hard along the floor, but which went aerial albeit with flat trajectory. Balls tend to carry further up on the Highveld because of the altitude and this one went a lot further than expected.

This merely added to the fun. There was a moment when Swanny nearly got cleaned up trying to hook a bouncer, so when he came down the pitch to discuss things between overs, he told me: 'I'm not doing that again, it's too dangerous. I might get hit or I might get out.'

Two balls later he did the same thing and top-edged it for another boundary. Cue cheesy smile.

All the way through my career, I have noticed that guys who are good mates generally bat well together. Matt Prior and Stuart Broad have had some good partnerships, I went through a phase of some good ones with Alastair Cook, and this one with Swanny was my best yet. As a tail-ender, you feel like you're trying to help out your mate.

From a team perspective, those late runs got us closer to parity on first innings, and how we needed that given the course of events thereafter. Hashim Amla was in good form, so much so that he became a prime scalp, but it was the pitch, getting lower and lower, that really did for him when I got him out for an even hundred with one that went along the floor and hit off stump, with the second new ball. The fact the pitch was deteriorating so blatantly was rather unnerving for us as we went in last, with South Africa out of sight thanks to their 363-run advantage.

Having gone in as nightwatchman, I succumbed early on the final morning when I gloved one down the leg side off Friedel de Wet. But just as he did at Cardiff, Paul Collingwood showed his value in a scrap. Not that I saw Colly's finale alongside Graham Onions. Cricketers are superstitious beings, and so I was in the shower area for a final hour made tense by a ridiculous run-out when we were cruising towards an early handshake. During the last rites of the Ashes draw, Cookie had been out the back throwing a rugby ball around, so when we started losing wickets he wanted to do the same thing again. We could hear the odd cheer emanating from the stands but we could never tell if it was a home cheer or an away cheer so we kept our heads down while our hands relayed the ball back and forth.

The pressure they put us under in that match showed us the challenge we would face, and how competitively matched we were as opponents. South Africa had a pretty settled top six, in Morne Morkel and Dale Steyn a couple of excellent new-ball bowlers, and an under-rated spinner in Harris. All in all they had most bases covered.

Once again, however, we got full value for avoiding defeat in the first Test of a series, and hanging in gave us the chance to snatch the lead in Durban when, with South Africa 160 for 2 and the game not really going anywhere, we seized the initiative. Swanny got Kallis caught at slip and we went on to dismiss them for 343, which was an under-par score for the Kingsmead surface.

It's an easy game when the batsmen put big scores on the board and the bowlers back it up with wickets, and this was one of those games when everyone did their job perfectly. We had managed only two hundreds in the 2009 Ashes but this match began a period in which people began to turn in three-figure scores regularly, with Cookie and Ian Bell the main contributors. This had a real knock-on effect, and there were a number of occasions over the next eighteen months in which two or three England batsmen all scored hundreds in the same innings.

On the bowling front, this tour posed quite a challenge for us and one of the questions we were being asked was whether we could be effective with a Kookaburra ball. But the fact that we got it reverse swinging so quickly in South Africa's second innings answered that emphatically. Stuart Broad simply tore them apart, and we romped to victory by an innings.

There are certain grounds in the world at which you really enjoy turning up, and Newlands is one of mine. It is such a beautiful setting, with Table Mountain as the backdrop, that it is enjoyable arriving every morning, and there are few grounds like that around the world. I am not sure if it helps when bowling but it certainly puts you in a good frame of mind, and I have a decent record there.

My five first-innings wickets included Graeme Smith first ball after lunch on the opening day. I have had my struggles against Smith throughout my career, from the first time I ever came across him back in 2003. His physical attributes make him a very difficult oponent to bowl at: a bit like a goalkeeper who seems to fill the whole net. Someone like Neville Southall was like that and I imagine the feeling strikers got bearing down on him or lining up a penalty is the same kind you get when you are running up to bowl at Smith. He's so big he seems to cover the entire stumps, and because of his size they can seem like matchsticks at times. That is extremely off-putting, and then, in addition to that, you bowl balls that normal batsmen would defend just outside the off stump and he actually hits them through midwicket for four.

When he's in form, it's very difficult to bowl at him, and our team struggles against him have been catalogued over a decade: he got two double hundreds against us on his first tour to England, won them the series with a superb innings in a fourth-innings run chase at Edgbaston in 2008, and in this contest at Newlands he proved a thorn in our side once more.

Although we bowled well in the first innings, dismissing South Africa for 291, we did not bat well and Smith capitalized on our failure and their eighteen-run advantage with one of his trademark big hundreds. His 183 was the cornerstone of an unassailable lead and they pushed hard for victory once they had that kind of advantage. And this time, Cookie and I found a soundproof room down in the basement of the Newlands pavilion to spin our oval object back and forth as Onions and Swann blocked out.

Although this was the second occasion we had repelled the
South Africans, it was only so long before the dam burst, and we
were unable to contain them at the Wanderers, in a match marred
by high-profile glitches with the recently introduced Decision
Review System. They say luck evens itself out over time but it was
hard not to feel it was completely against us in this final Test when
it came to the implementing of technology.

Referrals were meant to eliminate human error from umpiring
decisions but an incident in South Africa's first innings when
Graeme Smith was on fifteen blew that theory out of the water.
Ryan Sidebottom induced a nick, the close fielders went up in
unison, only for Tony Hill to turn the appeal down. Naturally, we
expected this would be overturned when the decision was sent to
third umpire Daryl Harper for clarification. Rather than reverse
the decision, however, Harper upheld Hill's call, having been
unable to turn the volume up on the stump microphone. Had he
done so, the nick would have been clearly audible.

Andy Flower went berserk in response. And who could blame
him? When one of the pieces of technology being used to eradicate howlers is the stump mic, not having the volume at
maximum was pretty dumb. Excuses were made but we were left
fuming, and our mood hardly improved when AB de Villiers was
reprieved with South Africa sixty-two runs ahead with five wickets down, after reviewing a delivery from Swann that took a couple
of deflections on its way to me at leg slip. This time, Harper
reversed the decision. So incensed was Andy regarding our treatment that he officially appealed the loss of our Smith review. To no
avail.

From experience, it is a really weird feeling as a bowler when
you get someone out, you've celebrated the fact and then the decision gets reversed. It's pretty dispiriting to get back to your mark
and bowl at the same batter again but I try to treat it the same as
when someone drops a catch. You know you shouldn't be bowling
at the same guy, and you're furious about the ball being put down

when you've created a chance. But it is important to control that anger and bowl the next ball as if nothing has happened.

Of course, that is easier said than done because even at international level you can get distracted by this kind of thing. It's no different from playing club cricket at the weekend, or someone working in an office. There are always distractions – things going on at home, someone in the crowd shouting – and it's only really experience that helps you deal with them.

These teething problems caused us serious discomfort in Johannesburg but there has been improvement on all sides in the meantime. You can see from the expressions of disbelief on their faces when they have to cross their arms and overturn a decision, that umpires can be surprised by their errors of judgement and they undoubtedly feel more pressure in their decision-making process. But the better ones have accepted they are not going to be right 100 per cent of the time, and adapted fairly quickly.

And we have gotten better at implementing reviews, too. Andrew Strauss has become a lot more calculating as time has gone by and pretty much listens to Matt Prior and the bowlers before making a decision. All the bowlers, apart from Swanny that is, as he realizes nothing he says can be taken at face value. You see, Swann's standard response is: 'That's definitely out, review it.'

At the start it was like a new toy and we didn't use it as well as we could have done but, having learned from our own mistakes, we have become more skilled. Particularly with umpire's call factored in, which provides benefit of the doubt to the on-field call in borderline decisions, we have to be convinced it is smashing into the stumps flush for us to want to challenge lbw shouts that have been turned down. Rather than just go for a review in hope, Matt will now recommend things like: 'It might be umpire's call on height. Don't think we should risk it.'

Tactically as well there is a theory that keeping reviews in the bag will serve you better later in innings when it could be more crucial, so there is no point in wasting one you are not 100 per cent confident about. If you can keep them in the bank it can be an advantage, even when numbers nine, ten and eleven are in, and this is where Strauss has become really clever. Some captains get sucked into going for reviews for the sake of it towards the end of innings, and I've witnessed some ridiculous ones when balls are veering so far down the leg side they wouldn't be hitting another two stumps.

Defeat at the Wanderers, by an innings, proved to be my last international action of the winter as I was invited to put my feet up for the trip to Bangladesh. Missing a trip like that was the equivalent of a vote of confidence, as it was clear the management wanted me to have plenty in the tank when it came around to the 2010–11 Ashes when there would be no respite for five months.

However, a second omission before the home international summer – from the successful World Twenty20 team – felt like a hammer blow. I had played the World Twenty20 in England and a few twenty-over games after that, including the back-to-back matches in South Africa, when I had returned respectable figures of 4-0-28-1 despite us conceding 241 as a team, so I didn't really have any inkling that I wouldn't make the final XI.

Therefore when it was decided to go with Ryan Sidebottom, Stuart Broad and Tim Bresnan at the start of the tournament in the Caribbean it was a shock. We were practising in Guyana, the day before our opening Group D game against hosts West Indies when, during six-hitting practice on the square, Paul Colling-wood, the captain, came up to me and in front of everyone else declared: 'You're not playing tomorrow, mate.'

No further explanation; as far as all were concerned I had been told my fate but the manner in which it was done really annoyed me. As a senior player to be informed in front of everyone else, on the field, was pretty disrespectful, and quite frankly humiliating. What generally happens when someone is being left out is that they are taken to one side and given an explanation of the selection process, the reasons why a particular team has been picked, the reasons why you are not playing, and the things you need to try to do to get back in favour.

The least I would have expected is a bit of encouragement, a bit of a window of opportunity left open for me. Sadly that didn't happen, and, if I am honest, I reacted in completely the wrong way too. One of my self-criticisms is that I don't tend to handle things like that very well – although I have possibly learned to be a little more mature from episodes like this one – acting in a way I later regret. This was no time to discuss the situation in my newspaper column, which is the course of action that I took. Goodness knows why.

Then, before the third game against Pakistan, David Saker, our bowling coach, sauntered up to me at a training session at the University ground in Barbados to instruct me to switch my focus as if I was going to play. Siddy had had a bad time of things in the rain-affected defeat to West Indies, with his one over, the first of the innings costing fifteen, and more wet weather had restricted him to nine balls against Ireland. Sakes appeared to anticipate a change.

Because I was bowling really well at that particular practice, and had done so throughout our trip, it made me think there was a genuine chance. But it didn't happen, we kept on winning, Sid bowled really well for the rest of the tournament, as did the others, and I never got a sniff.

That fortnight became one long sulk for me and although I bowled with the same intensity in practice, and didn't allow my frustration to manifest itself at those times, outside of cricket and the ground, I didn't want to talk to anyone within the camp.

I was just so desperate to be in that team, to be part of its success, and to be the best possible cricketer I can be. That is how I've always been. And when I am not achieving anger takes over.

It was not really the point, and it shouldn't have had any bearing on the situation, but I considered Colly to be a mate, and therefore felt let down. I certainly expected something a bit better than the treatment I received at the Providence Stadium that day. Although I didn't go out of my way to ignore him, I generally kept my head down and out of his general vicinity after that.

I had been on tours for years as a non-playing member, and being in teams that win when you are not playing is a really strange position to be in. This was a déjà vu I despised. To the extent that when we beat Australia in the final, while all the other squad members ran on to the pitch, I didn't move. I was naturally delighted that England were Twenty20 world champions, genuinely delighted for my mates that they had won such a huge tournament but I hadn't contributed a bean, just didn't feel a part of it, so I couldn't drag myself on to the field.

To be fair, the lads in possession of the shirts didn't give me a chance because of their perfect execution of their individual plans. There was quite a focus in the media on us bowling full and wide of the off stump, thus negating leg-side strokes, but this was not necessarily a team plan. Sidebottom's natural angle of attack from left-arm over sent the ball that way but Stuart Broad had worked out his own method from around the wicket. Far from being instructed to do it, he just considered it to be the best way for him to bowl to keep opponents from scoring. It was something he first tried during the previous Twenty20 World Cup in England. Others had a go at it, and it was an option for everyone, but in that situation you have to come up with whatever plans you feel comfortable with, and those you can follow through, in a bid to stop runs. Broad chose that option while Bresnan went yorker-length straight.

My request to fly back from the Caribbean on the night of the final, to get back to England in advance of Lancashire's County Championship match against Warwickshire at Edgbaston, was turned down and I was instructed to stay and celebrate properly with the team at that famous cricket watering hole Harbour Lights.

This was not a fit of pique. Painful experience has taught me there is nothing worse than bowling in the nets, without a game visible on the horizon, and I just wanted to get back into some competitive action. With the Ashes coming up six months down the line, I simply wanted to keep bowling and remain in good nick, and so joining that game in Birmingham straight from the flight back to Heathrow, as I subsequently did, offered me a chance to play alongside long-standing friends, be invigorated by a change of scenery, and submerge myself in cricket once more. It definitely helped.

14

The Highest of Highs to the Lowest of Lows

Within a week of our return from the World Twenty20 began what was an unbelievably productive international summer for me personally but a sordid one ultimately for the sport.

It opened with a Test victory over Bangladesh at Lord's, and took in another more comprehensive one against the same opponents at Old Trafford. Our bowling as a unit was a little low key in that series but it got better and better as the summer developed.

Pakistan were expected to provide a much sterner examination of our credentials, having drawn their 'home' series against Australia on English soil 1-1. But the tone was set in the first Test at Trent Bridge, where I recorded career-best match figures of 11 for 71. That summer was a real spell of ball dominating bat on both sides, as a combination of conditions and circumstances created a bowler's paradise. It was not as if the pitches were particularly green, or that we were playing on damp seamers; the bowlers were just in good form and sending down some high-quality stuff, and the batters struggled for answers – thankfully theirs more than ours.

It just seemed to swing all summer, and at some grounds it was going around corners. Trent Bridge obviously sticks out for that, and is a ground where I have consistently made the most of the atmospheric aid on offer. And it was the same for both sides as Mohammad Asif and Mohammad Amir gave our batsmen a torrid time. There weren't many big scores going around in the main Test series of the 2010 season.

One of the anomalies of first-class cricket is that batches of balls can vary year on year, and some batches prove more helpful to bowlers one year than those in the past and subsequent years. This is particularly true with regard to those made by Duke. They are all handmade but for some reason you get drastic differences from one year to the next, not in their quality, but in how they behave, and we made best use of this helpful batch.

Amir and Asif bowled like the ball was on a string at times that summer, and were so competitive that none of us could have anticipated what would happen at the end of the series. It was a real shock when we turned up on the fourth morning at Lord's, on the cusp of a 3-1 series victory, having spent breakfast reading the revelationsin the *News of the World* that they had deliberately bowled no-balls . To suggest it was a surreal session of play as we wrapped up the game would be an understatement.

Pakistan resumed on 41 for 4, having followed on 372 runs behind, and it was only a matter of time before we completed the job. One of the things that went through my mind was whether or not the individuals I was bowling at had been implicated in the spot-fixing revelations. Running in to the crease I felt a little hollow.

Graeme Swann ended up getting five wickets, which included a beauty to get rid of Amir, but the game was played out in a deathly hush. We didn't celebrate the wickets properly, which was really strange for a team that genuinely does enjoy each others' success. Normally a big deal is made when someone gets five-for but no one really acknowledged Swanny and that was uncomfortable. It was far from an empty ground that morning, just a very muted one. Word had spread around the stands quickly, and everyone appeared to share the same opinion: they would rather not be there in those circumstances. Arguably, the lack of reaction from the crowd when the Pakistan batsmen got out impacted on our behaviour on the field. At times like these, when you are uncertain how to respond, you take your lead from the supporters.

There was no pleasure in any of it and it took the shine off what was a really good win. I especially felt sorry for Stuart Broad and Jonathan Trott because they got seriously big runs in our first innings to dig us out of deep trouble at 102 for 7 and helped post an imposing 446 all out. Yet it was all overshadowed by the allegations that Asif and Amir had been coerced into overstepping in delivery at certain scheduled points in the contest under instruction from Pakistan captain Salman Butt, and his agent Mazhar Majeed. They had messed with small parts of the game for personal gain.

Rather like people doubting the genuine nature of the contest, I would hate to think there were any doubts that Stuart Broad, a player whose Test batting average hovers around the thirty mark, was capable of scoring 169 in one visit to the crease. Broad has the ability to score Test hundreds, and will score more in the future, so it is a shame that anyone would question this one because of some disingenuous behaviour by a limited number of individuals on the cadge. The overriding emotion in our dressing room was sadness.

Pakistan are actually a super-competitive outfit and although we bowled them out cheaply a number of times, including for 72 in the first innings at Edgbaston on our way to a 2-0 lead, when they did get it right at the Oval they proved good enough to get back into the series. We were in good form that summer, and playing well as a team, and they were able to beat us, which showed what a talented group they were.

Pakistan traditionally have highly skilled individuals but when they complement each other and work as a team they are as dangerous as any going around on the world scene. I can see comparisons to us, certainly to us as a one-day side because on any given day, on any kind of surface, they can be the best team in the world but the next they will be the most average. Those drastic swings are obviously something you want to avoid but there is no doubt that they are like that.

Once you start querying the authenticity of certain parts of series you are in dangerous territory, and doing the honest competitors on both sides a disservice. A message to anyone who doubts the authenticity of my eleven-wicket display in Nottingham: have a look at the replays because some of those deliveries were absolute beauties. If you start questioning that match, or any other in the series, then it is inevitable that you would question every match you've ever played in. Every game in the history of international cricket would then come into doubt. There are probably games in the past where fixing of some sort has occurred that has gone under the radar and will never be unearthed but you have to believe in the honour and integrity of the sport as a whole.

For all the frustration being involved in a series like that delivers, you have to trust, as an international player, that the ICC have the right processes in place to eradicate it. It is certainly a foreign subject to me because I genuinely do not know anyone who has been approached in any shape or form. I promise you that is true, and I've played international cricket for ten years, so I've been around a bit.

These facts only strengthen my belief that the people who do get approached are actually scouted, based on whether they appear to be viable candidates. From what we have seen, I'm presuming that they target guys who are vulnerable, young and naive, and not as handsomely paid by their employers as we are by the England and Wales Cricket Board.

The only whisperings I have heard on match fixing around

dressing rooms have been the tongue-in-cheek comments. Occasionally, when a good team collapses people will say, 'Aye, aye, they're on the take.' But they never truly mean it. Things happening out of the ordinary is just part of cricket. Sure, you would never expect teams with great batting strength to be bowled out for next to nothing but anyone who has played the game knows it can happen.

Ironically, we went through the same thing when Amir overstepped so blatantly in his delivery to Trott, Paul Collingwood joking about it being done deliberately. He was that far over, Colly suggested he must be on the fiddle. Little did he, or we, know.

The post-match presentation, usually held on the outfield in front of the public, was relocated and held in near silence in the Long Room, to conclude the end of a sorry morning. Instead of smiles there were grimaces as we received our series winners' medals and cheques because an episode not of our doing had sullied one of the moments we treasure as a team. There were even whispers that the records from that game would be expunged such was the uncertainty about the extent of the skulduggery at that stage.

The next few weeks, as talks went on behind the scenes and the accused players were left out of the NatWest Series as the International Cricket Council launched an inquiry into their conduct, proved pretty uncomfortable. And things became even more so when Pakistan Cricket Board chairman Ijaz Butt made his inflammatory and defamatory claim that England players had accepted money to perform badly in a one-day international at the Oval.

Those comments on the morning of 19 September led to us spending hours in meetings at the Landmark Hotel, the day before the scheduled fourth ODI of the series at Lord's. We ummed and aahed about whether we should actually play that game after Butt's baseless allegations – cheating and betraying the game's integrity goes against all I stand for as a competitor, and the rest of the squad were equally disgusted by the insinuation.

These unsubstantiated claims triggered an emotional response from our squad, a good number of whom agreed our next course action should be to boycott the match unless a full retraction and apology were forthcoming. Meetings with Andy Flower, meetings with Andrew Strauss, and a meeting with ECB chairman Giles Clarke carried on all the way through the evening and did not conclude until between two or three o'clock in the morning. Obviously that is not ideal preparation for a one-day international. But it was indicative of just how abhorrent these ludicrous allegations were that the majority of our team did not want to play in that game, or the final one of the series in Southampton.

Their adamance that the game should not go ahead was not shared by me. My feeling was that if a strongly worded statement from the ECB went out rubbishing the comments from the Pakistan chairman, and we played the game, everything would settle back down. My fear was if we pulled out of the game that some people, even if it were the smallest minority, might see guilt in our actions. From my point of view, I was also concerned it might kick up a massive storm and cause us more problems for the sport than were necessary. In a decade as an England player I have experienced politics hurting the game more than is healthy.

That in turn, unfortunately, has meant I've been involved in too many of these kinds of meetings. This time I was in agreement with the ECB that the show had to go on but my reasoning was very different from theirs. Giles Clarke spoke to us about the monetary aspect, what would be lost in terms of television revenue, sponsorship and ticket sales for just two games. International matches, particularly those at Lord's are a profitable business and in the longer term if we had pulled out it would have put future fixtures with Pakistan in doubt.

On the morning of the Lord's fixture, we released a statement as a team expressing our disgust at Butt's comments while our bosses handed out a simple ultimatum: a full retraction or face legal action.

Under captain Andrew Strauss's name appeared the following:

We would like to express our surprise, dismay and outrage at the comments made by Mr Butt yesterday. We are deeply concerned and disappointed that our integrity as cricketers has been brought into question. We refute these allegations completely and will be working closely with the ECB to explore all legal options open to us. We do, however, recognise our responsibilities to the game of cricket, and in particular to the cricket-loving public in the country, and will therefore endeavour to fulfil these fixtures to the best of our ability.

On 29 September, Butt withdrew his comments in a statement in which he said he never intended to question the behaviour and integrity of the players or the ECB.

Tiredness might have been used as an excuse for defeat in that Lord's match – not that we would ever offer such excuses – which made the final match of five a series decider at the Rose Bowl. After everything that had gone on, it was particularly pleasing to complete a 3-2 success in a comprehensive manner.

These soured relations with Pakistan actually kept the issue of spot-fixing and match-fixing rumbling on when all we as cricketers wanted to do was deflect it with some good performances. It is sad for me that the more cases of spot-fixing that are unearthed, the more people will expect it plays a prevalent part in our sport.

The reality is that anyone who has played to any level will know of the possibility of dropping a dolly catch, missing a full toss or taking a wicket from a no-ball. That's just cricket. Teams can collapse in perfect batting conditions, a bowler can bowl three wides in a row whether he is James Anderson, opening bowler for Burnley Under-13s, or James Anderson, England player. The beauty of sport is that we are all fallible, and mistakes are commonplace whenever you are involved in a competitive game. Unfortunately, that very fact has allowed some individuals to exploit it for financial gain.

My personal opinion is that if you get involved in anything like spot-fixing you should be banned for life. Concern has been expressed as to whether Amir will get to play again, how if he does not it will be a career wasted, but the odds are heavily stacked in his favour that he will. He is certainly good enough and young enough to be able to come back and if they were selecting on ability alone Pakistan would welcome him back into their team at the drop of a hat. Whether that would be morally correct, and how the Pakistan authorities feel about his return, is another issue.

The International Cricket Council decide on sanctions for guilty parties further to their custodial sentences, and whether the five- and ten-year bans meted out were commensurate with their actions, I am not sure. To my mind, we need to deter people from doing this and a life ban would surely do that. Perhaps I am a little draconian but I steadfastly believe there is no place for any of it, and would therefore suggest that if you are implicated for underperforming, whether it is for overstepping, bowling wides or full tosses, or affecting the course of a match in any shape or form it is wrong and you should be weeded out of the sport.

It is a real shame that, in the case of Amir, cricket has been shorn of one of its really promising global talents. It is natural to want to play against the very best players, and he showed the signs that he was developing into one of those by terrorizing our top six regularly. Few others have done that in the past five years. It is exciting when you play against someone with such raw talent. He was a very intelligent bowler for his age, who had great control when swinging the ball, a skill that I appreciate. When I first saw him running through Australia earlier that summer – naturally I enjoyed watching that – his pace struck me. To be able to hoop the ball at that speed increases a fast bowler's threat considerably. How frustrating that he has disappeared when he had such a great career ahead of him, although if he comes back in his mid-twenties he still has the potential to enjoy one.

Amir was a polite lad off the field, someone not shy of saying a few words on it and an aggressive new-ball bowler. Having seen him at close quarters, I didn't buy all that innocence bullshit regarding his age. When I recall my own early days on the international circuit, even at twenty I knew exactly what I was doing. Playing international sport makes you grow up quickly. You know what is right and wrong, what you are allowed to do and what you are not allowed to do in the game. So I don't have any sympathy. He was old enough to know what he was getting into; it was not as if he was a kid, he was a young man of nineteen and we have regular meetings with the ICC in which they tell us what to do in certain situations. I cannot believe he was not party to the same.

The ICC's anti-corruption team educate us in how we are to report things if we are ever approached. So you are aware from the moment you play international cricket – whether that is at the age of nineteen or twenty-nine – of the dangers that lurk around the game, and what to do if you're ever confronted by them. The only sympathy I would ever have for anyone in his situation is if any of the rumours about exactly how deep this goes have foundation. Suggestions that people are emotionally blackmailed with threats against their families turn my stomach.

It is unlikely we will see Asif in a Pakistan shirt again but he left a different legacy during that series. Because I can reveal it was from watching him that I developed the wobble-seam stuff that was to serve me so well in the future. Everything I've learned about bowling since playing for England has come from watching my contemporaries and copying their best bits. For example, watching the way India's Zaheer Khan hid the ball when he was bowling reverse swing. I've never really talked to him about that, just studied him and tried to copy it. Similarly, wobble-seam was mastered from me watching Asif.

It is important never to stand still as a bowler and adding bits to your armoury as you develop can only serve to improve you. There was no doubt my reputation as an international cricketer had improved in the previous twelve months, a fact recognized by me being named in the ICC's World Test XI during that series.

It was around this time that I also had to give my off-field image some thought, following an approach from gay magazine *Attitude* to do a naked photo shoot. Initially I was sceptical but when I chatted it through with Daniella, she countered that it was a good idea. It was a very respectable magazine, she said, and I must admit the fact there were only three sportsmen who had done such a shoot previously – the prestigious trio of David Beckham, Freddie Ljungberg and Gareth Thomas – was an attraction. In the end, I thought: 'Why not?'

The boyfriend of *Attitude*'s editor is a big cricket fan and was very keen to get a cricketer on the front cover. Unsurprisingly, my breaking of the ice caused a bit of a stir, and at the time there were no openly gay cricketers. In general I have never seen cricket as homophobic and believe that any gay player should have the courage to come out. It was ironic, I suppose, that at the time I agreed to do the photo shoot wicketkeeper Steven Davies had the same agent as me. It was a brave move for him to reveal his sexuality later that winter but when I did the shoot for the issue published in September 2010, I genuinely had no idea he was gay.

Cricket's image needs to be inclusive, and I hope and believe that it is. For me it is the sport that unites a myriad of different backgrounds, races and beliefs. There's a perception that cricket is full of old men wearing blazers and sitting on committees but I feel the game is moving with the times. From the magazine's point of view, they just wanted to show that cricketers could be comfortable with gay fans.

Personally, it was also a chance to show more of myself – excuse the pun – which is something I have been actively working on as my profile has risen. The more successful you are as a sportsman the more in demand you become, but whenever I get approached for commercial ventures I weigh up carefully whether or not to commit. Doing something like that was quite liberating and conversely developed my confidence away from the field.

Of course, there are other ways to communicate with cricket fans these days, and social sites like Twitter provide an opportunity to show our personalities, and the things that make us tick as individuals. And I have seen how this works from the other side of the fence, too, because as an all-round sports fan I am interested in following others and discovering what kind of characters they are, and gauging how they come across to the public. People at opposite ends of the spectrum like Rory McIlroy and Joey Barton. From afar you have an opinion of someone just by seeing him play golf or football, and by being interviewed, and the same process will take place when people assess me.

But for someone who found the formal interview process quite intimidating early in my career, and has taken a number of years to become comfortable with it, you might not have got the real me. The actual 'you' tends to hide behind a persona with a microphone up your nose or TV camera in your face, and there is always something artificial about those situations. But I am very different to how I act in those instances and when I play the game to the real me. I get a game face on, if you like, and it stays on while I am doing my job. But I am keen to take that off, and, as keen as I am to get to know other people, I want people to find out what I am like behind the mask.

When a businessman has his suit on, he tends to be engaged in serious business and I am no different when I put the whites on – I won't ever let anything detract from me playing cricket because that is what I get paid to do all year round, and I want to be the best cricketer I possibly can be, and the team I play for to be as good as it can be. That is the primary focus for all of England's centrally contracted players, in fact, something that has been reinforced by the new rules Andy Flower brought in when he became coach. To ensure we got our priorities in the right order, any sponsor-led or commercial activities taking place within forty-eight hours of the toss were kiboshed. The focus has to be on the game 100 per cent.

Dismissing Aaron Redmond, the first wicket of my career-best Test figures to date – seven for 43 against New Zealand at Trent Bridge, June 2008.

Philip Brown

The second, Brendon McCullum . . .

and third, Ross Taylor . . .

number four, Daniel Flynn . . .

the fifth, Jamie How . . .

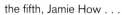

the sixth, Jacob Oram . . .

. . . and being clapped off after
the seventh, Gareth Hopkins.

We had begun 2009 as a mid-ranking team in all formats of the game, and without a captain or coach. But Andy Flower quickly went about setting targets of achievement.

With Monty Panesar, the final day of the first Ashes Test, 12 July 2009. The capacity 16,000 crowd roared with approval, and we were the heroes of the hour. Heroes, I must add, for securing a draw.

With Graeme Swann at the Landmark Hotel, between the first and second Ashes Tests, July 2009. He is one of my best mates in the game.

Appealing successfully for the wicket of Ricky Ponting, second Ashes Test, Lord's, July 2009.

Celebrating after dismissing Australian Mitchell Johnson in the third Test at Edgbaston, July 2009.

With Swanny and Alastair Cook, acquainting ourselves with the little urn, the Oval, August 2009. The feeling of exultation was overwhelming. This truly is as special as it gets.

England v South Africa, first Test, December 2009. The pressure they put us under showed us the challenge we would face to get to the top of the world rankings, and how competitively matched we were as direct opponents.

England v Pakistan at Lord's, August 2010. This is a match I look back on with little fondness given that it will forever be remembered for spot-fixing.

The dismissal of Ricky Ponting on the second day of the first Ashes Test, Brisbane, November 2010. It was one of only two wickets for me in the match but the statistics did not tell the whole story. I have rarely bowled better in my life.

Some light relief in the nets at the WACA, Perth, with Swanny and Tim Bresnan, ahead of the third Ashes Test, December 2010.

Such joviality was lacking on the field, however, as Australia levelled the series 1-1. Michael Hussey, next to me here, had become Australia's most reliable source of runs, and his second-innings hundred proved decisive.

Doing the sprinkler dance to celebrate retaining the Ashes, the MCG, December 2010. A collector's item this: Graeme Swann hogging the limelight.

Celebrating the 3-1 series victory, January 2011. There was a desire, driven by captain Andrew Strauss, to win the Ashes outright rather than simply retain them.

Disappointingly, there were only the briefest glimpses of my best form at the World Cup in March 2011, and this spell against South Africa in Chennai, when I got the ball reverse-swinging and bowled AB De Villiers and JP Duminy (pictured) in quick succession, was undoubtedly one.

West Indies batsman Marlon Samuels didn't miss the opportunity to have a joke at my expense during his hundred at Trent Bridge. I relished the battle against him in the summer of 2012. It was obvious he had worked really hard at his Test game and deserved his rewards.

Ten years after my first full county season, I was back to my original bowling action. Regrettably, there was plenty of tinkering in between.

15

Two Dozen Reasons to be Happy

I didn't need Shane Warne to tell me that I had a 'horrible' record in Australia on the eve of the 2010–11 Ashes. Five wickets at 82.6 runs apiece from three previous Test appearances is nowhere near the kind of statistical standard I want to be known for. But as Ottis Gibson used to say: 'Don't get bitter, get better.'

That is exactly what I had been trying to do during the 2010 summer, and by the end of it I felt ready to deconstruct the pre-series notion that I would lack threat in their conditions. That I totally relied on swing, that I could not bowl with the Kookaburra ball and that my past record in Australia would weigh me down.

Warne, writing in his *Daily Telegraph* column, had reminded the British public that conventional swing becomes extinct after the first ten overs of an innings down under. He certainly made some valid predictions – none more accurate than the fact that Graeme Swann would swagger around like David Hasselhoff and thrive on being the main man – on what would happen in our defence of the urn. It was nice that Warne thought England would rely on myself and Swanny a lot. But I was braced for what the Aussies had to say in the pre-series sparring.

Everyone who weighed into the debate came to the same conclusion. As Shane Watson put it: 'There's no doubt he'll have some
mental scars from the last series he played out here. But he'll be
trying to find a way to be more successful.'

Now this particular Shane was right. I was trying to unearth
ways of being successful, and was quietly confident I had. The
proof of the pudding is always in the eating, though. The reason for
my optimism, over and above the fact that my twenty-three wickets
against Pakistan had come at a cost of less than fourteen runs apiece
only a matter of weeks earlier, was that I had bowled pretty well in
South Africa the previous winter with the Kookaburra ball.
Although I did factor in that in Australia it would not swing as
much or for as long as it did in South African conditions.

Yes, I did have memories – however painful – of our previous
Ashes tour but stored alongside them were observations of what
the Australians had done well against us to take twenty wickets in
matches with such regularity. Stuart Clark had been really successful, as had the metronomic master Glenn McGrath, just by
hitting the seam. Naturally, I had been thinking ahead to the
Ashes throughout our series with Pakistan, and how I could prosper down under. And in Mohammad Asif I had someone on the
opposition who was a fine exponent of wobble-seam. It was at this
juncture that I began working on my own version in the nets. It
was a delivery that I began to bowl regularly at England practice
sessions throughout the season, and introduced it into a game for
the Lord's Test against Pakistan, although it was not something
necessarily picked up on from anyone outside our camp. I just
wanted to road-test it before we left on the Ashes tour.

Instead of gripping the ball along the seam as fast bowlers have
traditionally done, switching your finger position to bowl either
an off-cutter or leg-cutter, you hold it across the seam so that
rather than travelling through the air proud, the seam wobbles.
Now I don't know whether you have noticed but that seam thinga-
majig is actually made of rope and is not smooth, so if it lands on

it, rather than travelling on straight, it more often than not changes direction. The idea behind wobble-seam as opposed to traditional seam bowling being that if the seam is wobbling about, it could hit either edge of it on impact with the pitch. Now if I don't know which way the ball is going to jag off the surface, then how on earth will the batsmen know? To my mind, if you are hitting a certain spot on the pitch regularly and the batsman knows it can go one way or the other, or indeed straight on, you are always in the game as a bowler.

It took a while to get used to bowling wobble-seam because it is a totally different grip from the one I use when I am trying to swing the ball. Whenever you swing the ball you are trying to accentuate its flight path with a combination of your wrist, hand and fingers, all working in unison to encourage it to bend in a certain way. The wrist is right behind the ball, almost pushing it in the required direction, whereas in contrast when I am bowling wobble-seam I want the ball to travel as straight as possible, so the cock of the wrist – to get any pace behind the ball it has to snap on release – has to be straighter and my grip will be one with fingers spread.

It is not something I have ever been coached to do; there is no method to be passed on in a conventional coaching context. With swing bowling there have been books written on the subject and you can teach someone the steps of doing it but with this there is no right or wrong way of doing it. It's something I have tried to figure out my own way by finding something that both works and feels comfortable, rather than make a technical assessment of how to deliver it.

When a spin bowler has a variation or two, he immediately becomes more dangerous because it is not only the movement of the ball that can cause a problem. The uncertainty of the batsman in playing it can also prove terminal for an innings, and the most heartening thing for me was the size of the reaction I got from our batsmen during my experimentation in the nets.

'What were you up to then? The ball looked totally different when it came out of your hand and when it came off the pitch.'

Obviously they were so used to me swinging it that anything else was a surprise. Those kinds of comments encouraged me to keep practising it, tinkering with it and improving it. I found it was particularly effective in England because I could bowl a few of these straight ones that might nip off the seam a little bit and then follow up with a big outswinger. If you throw in the odd one that swings among your wobble stuff, it makes it even harder to line up, and sometimes a straight ball can be more effective than a genuine inswinger, so to be able to control a ball like that offered another potential wicket-taking delivery.

For years I'd proved effective at international level whenever the ball was swinging but had not developed an attacking plan B. Previously, my fallback position when there was no aerial movement on offer was to be disciplined, go for as few runs as possible, which was effectively playing for time. This was a much more proactive alternative, which, if executed well, gave me a genuine chance to take wickets when the ball was not hooping about – exactly the thing that Australia, and its 20 million inhabitants unanimously claimed I could not do. Now, this extra string to my bow gave me the confidence that I would be threatening in Australia, whatever conditions confronted us.

Despite a raft of ex-Australian players writing me off in the build-up, the honest truth is I never doubted I would be successful because I knew that I was a much better bowler than I was even in 2009, let alone the one who had struggled through the 2006–7 Ashes. Fast bowlers tend to peak towards their late twenties, I guess, because by that stage you have learned just about all you need to know about your own game, and I had certainly learned a lot over the previous couple of years about myself and the game in general. During that period, if you've got anything about you, you put everything together and should become somewhere near the finished article. Personally, I recognized that in the past eighteen months something had clicked.

Bunkum to what others thought. To have three weapons filled me full of belief, and these days it means I am generally unflustered about bowling in any conditions anywhere in the world. I have become accustomed to thinking positively about my bowling because it is my job to hunt wickets – and you need twenty of them to win a Test, of course – but that's not to say that bowling defensively is not profitable on occasion. We had proved that by starving Mohammad Yousuf and the rest of the Pakistan middle order of runs, bowling to a 7-2 field, to give ourselves an outside sniff of victory in the fourth innings at the Kia Oval the previous summer.

Rather like a footballer scoring a great goal, for a bowler it feels very satisfying when a plan comes off that you have been working on for maybe six or seven overs. On the occasion in question, we came out after lunch on what was the fourth and final day, with a team ploy to bowl really wide of off stump.

Pakistan were 115 for 3 and needed only 148 to win but we dried up the runs and got the ball reversing a little bit. I had conceded only a single and a wide in my first four overs, when I produced a straight yorker that cartwheeled off the stump. Fast bowlers always like to see stumps flying, of course, but the fact the plan came to fruition was equally pleasing. Wickets like that – ones you have worked really hard for by being calculating – stick in your mind. In that situation we knocked Yousuf out of his thought pattern with some intelligent bowling.

Mentally, I was in a good place during the countdown to take-off, although the same could not be said of my physical condition after our infamous pre-Ashes boot camp. It is fair to say the squad was full of scepticism when we were informed that we would be off on a team-bonding mission in an unspecified location, and that we were to bring our passports with us. When you hear the words *boot* and *camp* in the same sentence, your mind starts to create images of some bull-necked skinhead ranting in your face – unless you are Stuart Broad, who probably envisaged a few days in the sun with Louis Walsh giving his best interpretation of Prince's back catalogue.

Reg Dickason, our Australian security adviser, organized the four-day trip and it was all very secretive. Pretty much all we knew was that we had to be at Gatwick at four in the morning on 24 September. Unfortunately, this was not just any morning but the one that followed the Professional Cricketers' Association dinner at the Hurlingham Club in London. The frustrating thing for us was that it was the first time for a couple of years that we had been able to go to our own dinner, and you really do appreciate being able to catch up with guys who you don't get to see socially very often any more – guys we grew up playing age-group cricket with or county cricket against. It's a real chance to let your hair down, so we were not best pleased to have to cut it short. A group of us literally dashed from the bar to the airport via a whistle-stop at the hotel to change into our England track-suits.

Upon arrival, we were shepherded on to a red-eye flight to Munich and greeted at the other end by two Australian ex-police-men, who drove us deep into the Bavarian forest. For the next seventy-two hours they abused us – I suppose having two Aussies do that prepared us rather well for what we were about to experi-ence – beginning with us being stripped of all mod cons. Watches, mobile phones, laptops, anything from which you could tell the time, were confiscated and stashed away for a few days. All our valuables were collected and thrown into bags; they were taken away and all we were left with was the clothes on our backs, a couple of sets to change into, and a toothbrush. Chocolate bars and sweets were also contraband, so there were no secret stashes.

Our clothes were shoved into backpacks along with a bowl, a spoon, a torch (the ones that go on the top of headlamps) and off into the forest we went. As soon as we got into our clearing, they had us running straight away. Soon we got our first taste of the exercise routines – sets of fifty press-ups and sit-ups – meted out as punishment for failure to call each other by the most formal names. For example, I was Mr Anderson and if anyone dared call me Jimmy, we were all forced down for a collective fifty count. When you're used to calling people by their nicknames, sticking to these ground rules can be tricky but it did not stop scathing looks being cast at perpetrators for every set of fifty.

From the very moment we got there it felt like torture. Grumblings – we were still feeling rather dusty from the night before – were rife and no one enjoyed the initial hours there. But as time drew on the majority of guys got into things, inspired by the challenges set us by these two Australian taskmasters. As a competitive sports team, we are generally the sort of blokes who relish taking part in any sort of contest.

Put into small teams – my team-mates being Monty Panesar, Steven Davies and Tim Bresnan – our first task was to put up our six-man. In comparison to our menu for the week and wet-weather apparel – it was packet noodles, and plastic ponchos were distributed – these tents were fairly luxurious, the sleeping quarters split in two, with a communal area to store the bags, although its accessories stopped shy of a TV room or hot tub.

But it was not long before the competitive juices began to flow. Set a number of challenges, our first was to build a stretcher out of wood and rope, and then carry one of our group members through the forest, stopping at certain stations along a designated circuit, to carry out specified exercises. Soon everyone was getting stuck in for each other, much like you do on the field, because in a team environment if three guys buy into making things work and a couple don't, the fact you are letting mates down kicks in. In that situation, the minority tend to snap out of their sulk pretty quickly, and get pulled along by the majority.

For each of the tasks we were set, starting with the stretcher race, there was a prize at the end of it for the winners. Because of the competitive nature in a group like ours, you just don't want to come last; that is the first thing that goes through your head, and as time went by, there became extra motivation to win. After several bowls of muesli and some fairly basic *nasi goreng*, my mouth tasted like the bottom of a budgie's cage, and I became intrigued as to what the culinary delight might be for the victorious team. I guess it was a little optimistic to assume we might be given a roast dinner, but even a fun-size Mars bar – the prize for the opening challenge, and not one shared between the whole group I am pleased to report – was an attraction well worth aiming for. Some of the shrewder lads decided to keep theirs, rather than immediately tuck in, in case they could pawn them later for something better.

Sure, some of the guys didn't enjoy all this, but I genuinely got into it, and there were some nice moments during the few days we spent together. Each evening we lit a bonfire, sat around on logs and chatted, which definitely helped us get to know each other that little bit better before our biggest challenge as an England team. Our talk was not just of cricket but of life in general and it was quite nice to share that external kind of stuff because we don't get the opportunity very often. One of my highlights came on the first of these evenings when we saw the two Andys, Flower and Strauss, the two guys who had sanctioned this trip, really cooked. Physically, they looked the worst out of the lot of us, and had aged fifteen years each.

It was all good fun, until, that is, the boxing challenge on the second day. Head gear was dished out and a ring created by everyone sitting round in a circle. Two by two guys were called into the middle and given two minutes to spar, with blows to the head forbidden. We were restricted to pounding each other in the stomach and chest under the guidelines, and this made for some comedy moments when in the early bouts some guys were struck accidentally on the chin or on the nose to choruses of oohs and aahs.

It was all very jovial as opponents were paired up according to their height and physical size. In a squad of sixteen, matching in this kind of way should be a fairly straightforward exercise but, in our group, there were nervous glances towards Chris Tremlett from the moment it was announced we would be boxing. You could almost see the thought bubbles emanating from the top of people's heads: 'Please, just don't let it be him. Anyone but Tremlett.'

Then came the moment we had all been dreading.

'Tremlett and . . . *Anderson.*'

How on earth had I been paired with our fast-bowling behemoth? The sighs of relief seemed like they were in surround sound.

Once kitted out, I made the judgement to hit him as hard as I could in the hope that it would distract him from hitting back. It proved a flawed tactic, however, and although he was probably not throwing his best shots, he was nevertheless hitting me really hard in response. Put it this way: it was harder than I could ever hit him.

In among the flurry came a single punch that I was not to forget in a hurry, and one that everyone else got to know about in the coming days, doubling me over as a result of its force. I am proud to report that despite this meaty connection, I didn't go down, as I stumbled backwards gulping for breath. After a brief pause, I even continued the bout and it wasn't until I was sitting back down, clapping and cheering the subsequent fights, that the discomfort really struck me. Trying to shout was absolute agony, and soon afterwards, as I spoke between deep breaths, it became evident there was some significant damage.

Dr Nick Pierce was among the support staff with us, and although he gave me paracetamol to take the edge off the pain, there was not much more he could do until we got back home. I managed to get through the rest of the activities, including abseiling – which was quite interesting because I am not a massive fan of heights – but was in need of assessment as soon as we were back in the UK.

Once home, general day-to-day stuff like picking Lola up was a real problem and it was no real shock when they found a cracked rib at my hospital check-up in Chelsea. Despite that discovery, however, the encouraging thing was that the medical advice, both from the ECB staff and the specialists, was that it should be fine within just a couple of weeks from rest alone. You learn to trust these kinds of judgements over the years, and so, despite the gloomy forecast being reported in newspapers that, amid heavy criticism of how the injury was incurred, some of the speculation even suggesting that it might even put me out of the start of the Ashes, I was always confident. It was a proper crack but once we arrived down under there was never a problem.

On this tour there was real intent about us from the word go, and we had definitive plans about what we wanted to achieve on it from a cricket perspective. In the past we had lurched into the first Test after warm-up matches played with an intensity of a glorified net, hardly ideal preparation for a series of such magnitude. For example, in 2006–7 one of our practice matches was a one-dayer, which we lost, in Canberra. What on earth were we doing playing a fifty-over contest as preparation for five Tests against Australia, for heaven's sake?

This time, we decided to treat our first-class programme before the first Test in Brisbane like a self-contained three-match series. We spoke about winning all three games, as if our prospects in the series proper depended in some way on them, and that attitude represented a massive sea change from previous tours. It was not something we made a song and dance about publicly but in our preparation meetings we were clinical about it, and everyone bought into it.

By the end of our first match, a victory against Western Australia in Perth, our intentions were fairly explicit. We had entered it with our strongest possible XI, couldn't have started any better than with a couple of early wickets for Stuart Broad, and by the time we arrived in Adelaide to face South Australia it was public knowledge that we meant business in these matches. Rain prevented us forcing a result there, which signalled the first-choice attack's final run-out before the first Test in Brisbane.

Myself, Stuart Broad, Steven Finn and Graeme Swann headed to Queensland alongside bowling coach David Saker to acclimatize while the back-up bowlers had a run-out against Australia A in Hobart. Again, splitting the squad up was a change in tack for an England tour down under but every decision we made was taken to give us the best possible opportunity of beating Australia in the main event. Saker, our Australian bowling coach, had twigged from a long way out that sending us to Tasmania's very British-style climate immediately before the opening Test match in tropical Brisbane was tactical on our hosts' part.

Our counter-punch was to get used to the weather conditions we would experience during that opening contest. This move showed a lot of faith in us because we could have gone there, and got on the sauce for a week. We repaid it by knuckling down and training hard, and although we didn't get to practise at the Gabba itself, we really felt ready for the series to begin after a few sessions just down the road. One evening we all went out for dinner as a group, and talked about bowling with Sakes, who had been a consistent wicket-taker with the new ball for Victoria and Tasmania between 1995 and 2002.

Although the scorecard will not relay the fact, I began the series with what is quite possibly the best spell I have ever bowled – well, certainly the best I had ever bowled up to that point in my career. It came during the first hour of the third day, which, after rain on day two, Australia resumed on 220 for 5, a deficit of forty runs. I felt in total control of things: what I was trying to do, where I wanted the ball to go, yet for love nor money I just couldn't get Mike Hussey and Brad Haddin out.

From my twelfth ball of the day, I had Mike Hussey given lbw by Aleem Dar, only for the decision to be overturned on review as it was shown that the ball was pitching outside leg stump. I had bowled pretty well on the second day, for figures of 21-9-40-2 but never felt as fluent as I did in those opening seven overs that third morning. I bowled them at a cost of seven runs, and we would have had Hussey in the eighties but Dar turned down a leg before shout that we considered plumb – it would have been overturned had we not already used up our two permitted reviews. In that situation it's important to stay calm, not to allow frustration to get the better of you, and hope your luck changes. Unfortunately, it just didn't happen, and although Haddin later said it was the best spell of bowling he had faced in Test cricket, he and Hussey shared a triple-century stand.

Of course, you would rather be taking wickets, but if you are constantly in rhythm, and the ball is moving about, you know they will come. Sure, two wickets in the match wasn't a great return in the end column but it was nice to know I was in good form.

From a team perspective, it was equally pleasing to discover that Cookie was in nick; having made sixty-seven in the first innings, he followed up emphatically, after we went in a second time 221 runs in arrears, combating the stories being written by the press in the build-up that he should not be picked in a most authoritative manner. I am not sure anyone in our dressing room would ever have countenanced such a notion – we always consider him one of the first names, if not *the* first name on the team sheet, and it's always nice to see your mates prove their character, and others wrong.

Of course, there would have been no issue regarding his place in the team had he been reeling off hundred after hundred against Pakistan that summer rather than suffering a period of poor form. But we all go through those kinds of cycles – Stuart Broad being a prime example twelve months earlier when a sword was called for to lop him one month and knight him the next – when your place is all too hastily called into question.

In my opinion, one of the reasons the England team became more successful during this period was that players in possession of the shirts were given extended time to prove they had the necessary quality. It is a much better selection policy than turfing people out after a couple of bad games with bat or ball, and has definitely contributed to players doing better in the long run. There is enough pressure on the team as it is without having added worries about your place, and from my own experience I know that the natural reaction to having faith shown in you is a willingness to repay it.

The most pleasing thing from a personal perspective after my display in Brisbane was that I built on it by utilizing any early-morning juice in the pitches at the other venues. There was a little bit in it in Adelaide the first morning, and that played into our hands when we lost the toss. There had been a lot of focus on my role as attack leader up until this point – I guess because the other bowlers were nowhere near as experienced as me – but it didn't add any extra pressure because I was bowling well. Being in good form made me feel like I was justified as the leader, and that always helps. When you're bowling well you also feel as though you can offer advice, whereas when you are bowling a pile of shit, you don't want to be telling others how to do it. You've got to be able to practise what you preach.

An attack leader's primary job, however, is to take the first over of a match, and try to set its tone, and having the expectation on me to do so actually helps me focus. At the Adelaide Oval, though, it was Jonathan Trott who set that tone for us with an amazingly alert piece of fielding. Running someone out in the first over, with a direct hit having had only one stump to aim at – yes, it is exactly what we practise – is quite something in a match situation. Our ethos under fielding coach Richard Halsall has been to prepare to take that first catch, or take that first run-out chance whenever it presents itself, and here was an example of someone doing it, for us to get rid of Simon Katich.

Halsall has made a massive difference to this England team because he has placed a much greater emphasis on the effect good fielding can have on a game. Everyone has to get involved in the business of trying to improve because, as we have witnessed, little differences can add up to something big: a run-out means the bowlers have to take one fewer wicket, saving six runs through a couple of sprawling stops can be the difference in matches that go to the wire, and in Trott's case here, he provided an incision into their batting at a venue considered to be one of world cricket's premier locations to bat.

It preceded a crazy few minutes on that opening morning, and to say I was pleased to locate the edges of the bats of Ricky Ponting and Michael Clarke is one of the understatements of the decade. Australia, having won the toss, were 2 for 3, and we had to keep telling ourselves not to get too carried away. We constantly reminded each other that it was going to be a hard day for us, and to stay sharp so that we were prepared for any opportunities that came our way.

We eventually bowled them out for 245 and that innings set the tone for the remainder of the series. It was more or less the average score (257 to be exact) Australia made in their final seven innings, which was an incredible effort. We stuck to our plans, never changed anything we came up with in our team meetings, and remained as patient as we possibly could, convinced we had the game plan for success.

It might have been a surprise to outsiders that we were able to maintain our threat with the ball despite changes being made. You always have to be ready for injuries or loss of form to alter selection, and it made it more special that the whole of our squad made an impact on that series. We lost Broad to a nasty side injury during that innings victory at the Adelaide Oval but with runs on the board – 620 of them to be precise, thanks to a double hundred from Kevin Pietersen and a staple contribution from Cookie – we knew we had the firepower to complete the task.

Steve Finn was the leading wicket-taker on either side until getting dropped after the first three matches, and Chris Tremlett and Tim Bresnan made impressions from the moment they were called in. To come in halfway through and perform the way they did was incredible. When you are drafted in mid-series everyone around you is up to speed, so to get to the same level with a click of the fingers is highly commendable.

Their ability to perform from the off spoke volumes for the environment we had created, and the backing we got as a team on that tour extended beyond the management. The support from the Barmy Army was phenomenal: they believed in us 100 per cent. It was nice to share some special moments with them, such as the final morning at Adelaide when Michael Hussey mistimed a pull to me at mid on. My natural reaction was to turn and celebrate, fists raised, with the fans who had been urging us towards victory.

It was not only our own supporters who recognized that we were the better team as the series progressed, either. The Australian public was definitely different in their attitude towards us this time – certainly a lot different from how they had been to us in 2006–7 – almost from the moment we landed and definitely from the moment we went 1-0 ahead. Every time you switched the TV on there seemed to be a debate over which team they were going to pick, and because there was a bizarre snub of Nathan Hauritz going on, the identity of their spinner.

This was all completely different from the previous tour, almost a role reversal, when they were deconstructing England in the same way. Who were we going to select? Not that it mattered anyway, they told us, because we were no longer the team we had been in 2005. Until I witnessed it, I would have thought it was inconceivable that the Australian public, and the country's media, could be so negative towards their own team.

However, in a five-match series against another major nation you will receive a jolt, and I was fully aware that if it came in Perth, I might bear the brunt of it. My decision to return home before the third Test to witness the birth of Ruby was a no-brainer for me. I was always going to be at the birth, it was just a question of how, and where.

My elder daughter Lola was born in early January 2009, immediately before a ten-week tour of the Caribbean, so that was easy to organize. But this one, given that I was going to be in Australia, took considerabie forward planning. Of course, I accept that being away from family goes with the territory when you are an international cricketer, and there are members of the old school who believe you should stick on tour once there. Bob Willis and players of his era were only too willing to let me know through their media outlets that they would have stuck it out in their day. Then again, their wives washed their whites, too. They want to meet Daniella!

Dissenting voices were never going to put me off placing family first. The England management were accommodating as soon as we realized the due date, and because they knew it was my express wish to be at the birth, potential options were discussed well in advance. The first option we considered was for Daniella to fly out to Australia thirty weeks pregnant, the latest she could do so under medical recommendations, rent an apartment in Perth, and travel around with me until we got back there for the third Test.

However, that plan fell foul of the strict rules regarding families on tour under Andy Flower's regime, and Daniella and Lola were not allowed to stay with me outside designated family time (which was for Christmas and New Year in Melbourne and Sydney). Therefore I would have had to stay in the team hotels, and they would have been required to stay at another location. Breaking the protocol for one player would have set a dangerous precedent, and although Daniella was not overly chuffed about the ruling, and we would be denied spending the last part of her pregnancy together, they were prepared to sanction an alternative: me to return home for three days, witness the birth and then fly back again.

From a professional viewpoint I felt like I could cope with those few days at home, and I really wanted to be there both for myself and for Daniella, and there was a window in the itinerary that allowed me to do it. All that I would miss in my time away from the tour was a three-day game against Victoria, one that I would have been rested for anyway, so it worked out perfectly.

It was almost like clockwork. Daniella's waters broke within seconds of me walking through our front door at seven o'clock in the evening, and after I had shoved a plate of shepherd's pie down my throat, we were heading for the hospital. She was going to be induced the following day anyway but the fact the birth started naturally meant we were a few hours ahead of schedule. Daniella slept as well as she could once we got there, and I sat up and read Stephen Fry's autobiography *The Fry Chronicles* cover to cover through that night. It took me seven hours – he does know some frightfully long words – so I was grateful for the part that he played in keeping me awake.

Ruby was born in the early afternoon on 9 December, and we headed home that night. Two full days later I was on a plane again and made it back to Australia for 13 December, as planned. I'd found it hard to leave, to be honest, having just experienced the joy of having another child, such a special moment in our lives for Daniella and me, but at the same time I was excited about going back because of the way the series was shaping up. We were 1-0 up, and having touched down in Perth on the Monday morning, I was running in to bowl at practice twenty-four hours later.

I never envisaged my trip having a negative effect on either myself or the tour but I was wary nevertheless of letting my form drop in that third Test match. Quite simply, I didn't want anyone using my personal circumstances as a reason for a poor performance. I am a stubborn so-and-so when I want to be and I'd resolved not to give anyone lining up a gratuitous dig the chance to unleash it. Thankfully, when I arrived back in Australia, although I didn't feel 100 per cent, neither did I feel like I couldn't play in the game. The adrenalin from the events of the previous week kept me going through the pre-match practice sessions, and the key for me had undoubtedly been staying on

Australian time despite travelling halfway across the globe. Not going to sleep on the outbound flight meant I didn't feel jet-lagged upon return.

Defeat at the WACA stood out like a sore thumb on this tour, a batting horror show comparable to our capitulation at Headingley in 2009. But if there were any positives for us at 1-1 with two matches to play, they lay in the team's recent history. We knew that as a team we not only responded well to set-backs but usually came back with some of our strongest performances in the immediate aftermath. Recovering well from defeats or being behind in series is something we had done well in all forms of cricket over the past couple of years, so we were confident we could turn it around.

During our post-match debrief, the batsmen admitted they hadn't given Mitchell Johnson sufficient respect – they hadn't expected him to swing it, or certainly not to the devastating extent that he did in taking six first-innings wickets. Take nothing away from him, he bowled very well, but part of our downfall was self-inflicted because we underestimated him. We vowed not to let that happen again and, as a result, we headed to Melbourne, fully expecting Johnson to bend it around corners at speed from ball one. The batting unit adjusted their approach towards him because of that but we also reaffirmed during our team meetings in the run-up to Christmas that one bad performance should not detract from the fact that everyone remained in pretty good touch.

Spirits were high in the camp on Christmas Day, although personally it was hard to be away from my family. Swanny's wife, Sarah, had also gone home by this point as she was heavily pregnant, so we spent the day having our faces painted, and making one of his on-line video diaries. For the team dinner, we sat on the singles table, and captured perfectly on film the deathly silence one would expect to dominate a Christmas Day meal involving half a dozen bored blokes. As much as I love them, pulling

Christmas crackers with Swann and Monty Panesar was hardly a barrel of laughs.

When you are away for months on end, you have to find ways to amuse yourselves and these video diaries actually provided something to focus on off the field. I quite enjoyed letting my creative side out, and we would sit at the back of the bus to the ground each day discussing what we could do next. That wasn't too taxing because the basis for all the stuff we put to tape was either re-enacting incidents that happened earlier in the tour, or showing people back home the kind of pranks we ordinarily get up to away from the TV cameras.

One of my favourites was a re-enactment of an incident that had taken place earlier on the tour. Swanny was talking to Sarah on Skype one morning, when I sneaked into his bathroom and re-emerged with just a towel on my head, excusing myself in a camp voice. Swanny was adamant we should re-create it for the diary.

Of course, Swann took all the credit, and he has even tried to deny my other big contribution to the 2010–11 Ashes, other than the twenty-four wickets I took. You see, despite him crediting Paul Collingwood for turning it into a major feature of the tour, it was me who was at the heart of creating the sprinkler dance craze.

During a warm-up game against South Australia, I had said to Matt Prior: 'If we go out after this match, I'm going to do the sprinkler.' He asked me what on earth I was on about, so I showed him. It was a dance move I had seen years ago, and I started doing it as a piss-take. Before I knew it, Swanny was filming every Tom, Dick and Kevin doing it for his diary.

Well, everyone except me, initially. Although I was quite happy doing it on a dance floor in a bar or nightclub, I was reluctant to do it on video, particularly as Swanny was pointing his camera at us in a sports hall where all the British press were having coaching lessons 20 yards away as part of a sponsor's set-up. I'd have happily strutted in the privacy of my own room – and you can probably tell by my moves that was something that had taken place on many occasions – just not in a place where I would be scrutinized by the media lot. Swanny claimed it was vanity that led to my reticence but shyness was closer to the truth.

However, all my inhibitions had gone when we performed the sprinkler in front of thousands of travelling fans at the MCG, an image that will be synonymous with the 2010–11 Ashes. To me, it represened what that trip was all about. Our supporters were with us all the way, and we genuinely enjoyed our cricket as Australia struggled to contain us.

We forced the kind of issues that used to trouble English touring sides on to our hosts: they didn't really have a spinner they could trust, when they got behind they started to try different batsmen and by the end their selection process was very un-Australian. Not that I had much sympathy for the Australians. Let's face it, they had been doing it to us for years. So it was lovely to go over there, win so convincingly, and share that success with team-mates and fans alike. It was also nice to get some respect from the opposition and their public. All we were really interested in was winning the series, of course, and that is what we did but it did feel like there was an acceptance that England were deserved winners and a superior team to Australia, which is not something that I had experienced before.

The pivotal moment in my opinion came on Boxing Day when we bowled them out for less than a hundred and were 157 for 0 at the close. It is certainly the day I look back upon most fondly.

Having looked at the MCG pitch, Andrew Strauss threw open a debate as to what we should do first if we won the toss. Us fast bowlers thought we should bowl first because if there was anything in the surface it would be on that first morning. It was a big decision to be made in the event of the coin coming down our side, with the series balanced at 1-1, and we were quite vociferous in putting our view forward, which is not something bowlers normally do.

As a rule I am fairly quiet but as the senior bowler I wanted to speak up, and there were a few guys who believed the same thing. It showed how far we had come as a team, though, that people were being asked, and were fully willing, to get involved. Graeme Swann is probably the only one who ever thinks you should bat first when winning the toss, and if you have any doubts about whether your decision is the right one, bat anyway. Batting first is the textbook way to go about winning Test matches but the fact we were vocal swayed Strauss's thinking.

This highlighted that even though we had just been beaten at Perth, we were still being positive in our decisions. Bowling first was the most proactive thing to do because we believed that we might get some assistance, and even if we didn't get as much as we thought, we were bowling that well as a group that even if we didn't dismiss them that first day, even if it turned out to be the flattest pitch in history, we were still confident we could restrict them to a reasonable total. In contrast, if you bat first and it does go all over the place you can be 40 for 4, the game is gone and there is no coming back.

As things turned out it was far from a minefield – the true nature of the surface was put into context when we batted – and we had to remain disciplined to create our chances, even missing a couple of tough ones when Paul Collingwood dropped Watson in the first over, and Kevin Pietersen failed to cling to another sharp one. We stuck at it, though, and had four wickets before lunch.

The wicket of Michael Hussey, nibbling at one outside off stump, immediately before an interval brought forward by a morning shower was a big one for both me and the team. Hussey had become Australia's most reliable source of runs, so whenever we dismissed him it undermined their efforts. And from a position of 58 for 4, the wickets really started tumbling. It was another day when it didn't really swing; it was just wobbling and nipping off the seam.

Without trying to big up our efforts too much, if there was anything in the pitch, we managed to locate it and bundling them out for 98 was put into context by the fact we didn't lose a wicket in response on that first day. Oh, and we completed our task with an attack quite different from the one that started the series in Brisbane. Chris Tremlett and Tim Bresnan are just no-fuss guys who get on with their jobs, and who have got to know their own games inside out over a decade as first-class cricketers.

Tremlett is very quiet but has confidence in his ability, and he knew conditions out in Australia would suit him. Critics said he first dropped off the international radar because he lacked 'ticker', and disappeared in games that were tough. I must confess that is never how I saw things, but there is no doubt his reincarnation as an England player was as a far more vocal, confident and assertive guy on the field. We complement each other and, if the ball swings, his ability to push batsmen back works for both us. The extra bounce he extracts from surfaces means he is always in games regardless of conditions.

Bres's biggest weapon is the fact that people tend to under-estimate him. Only after he had played ten Tests and won every single one of them did he gain the respect he deserves, or was it recognized exactly how good he is. He is not afraid of competing in anyone's company and that is probably his best characteristic. He keeps things very simple when he bowls – it's all about aiming for the top of off stump with him, and if your aim is any good you will naturally get success. It's not a bad game plan, especially when the odd one hits the seam, and is a fairly uncomplicated one, which is probably a good job because it is easy to confuse a lad from Castleford.

Simple Bres is much loved but also the butt of our jokes, and he doesn't help himself at times. A case in point was in Melbourne in the second over after tea on the third day when he was rewarded for his perseverance with a leg-before appeal given out by Tony Hill. Shane Watson had left one too close to his off stump for comfort but opted to review it. To a man we were confident that this was a futile exercise but as we were watching the replay on the screen, Bres turned around to the rest of us, shook his head and yelped: 'Oh no!'

'What's up, Bressie lad?'

'It's hit him outside the line!'

Cue tumbleweed as we all looked at him quizzically to check whether or not he was being serious. Unfortunately he was, deadly so.

'Bres, he's not playing a shot!' came the chorus.

That just sums him up. His record will tell you he's a natural talent but it's a good job we don't rely on him to interpret the laws of the game. Or for a summary of conditions: he came out with a belter in Sri Lanka in 2011–12 when the humidity was stifling. 'It's just so sweaty isn't it?' Swanny said after our first practice. 'It's no sweatier than England,' Bres countered. Of course, we had forgotten about the microclimate around Headingley. Silly us.

Tremlett and Bresnan were outstanding at the back end of the series victory and, equally, Steven Finn had played a major role at the start. Lest we forget, he took six wickets in the first innings of the series to dispel any nerves and highlighted the firepower our bowling arsenal contained.

Finn was actually at the centre of an incident at the Gabba that showed how different this England team was from others that had toured Australia in recent times. When Brad Haddin was batting, every time Steve walked back to his mark, Haddin would chirp from the non-striker's end: 'You're shit. Shit, mate, you shouldn't be here.'

He just didn't stop niggling at him throughout the morning session, and, being a youngish lad, Finny didn't let on to the rest of us until lunch. It was decided as a collective to nip this in the bud, and so as soon as we returned to the field we went as hard as we possibly could at Haddin. He was literally still walking to the crease, when a group of us were around him: 'What do you think you are playing at? You don't say a word to anyone else, and yet you are picking on the young lad who has played a handful of

Tests. Why don't you grow a pair?' We would have told him to pick on someone his own size of course but that hardly applies when you are dealing with someone like Finny.

The harder we went at Haddin the more apologetic and defensive he became, to the point where he suggested he hadn't said anything at all. Haddin is like that, he wants to be everyone's mate, and he got out soon afterwards. That was a good example not only of getting someone out of their comfort zone but also of where we were at as a team, not letting someone suffer on their own. We were very much about sticking together.

Our collective desire to be successful meant we remained focused heading into that last Test in Sydney. Many people would have considered it job done given that we had achieved our target of retaining the Ashes with victory in Melbourne, and that was true enough, but there were a number of other things on the agenda over and above that for this team. We had not lost sight of our desire to become the number one team in the world, and knew that victory would help us towards that, and also felt completing what had been a good series for us with another strong performance would be just reward for our efforts.

There was also a will, driven by Andrew Strauss, to win the Ashes rather than just retain them. If you are an England cricketer you should want to win every single game you play regardless, that goes without saying, but there was a determination in this particular situation to finish what we had started. Some England cricket supporters would have been satisfied with going down under and coming back with the urn but we wanted to go that little bit further for our own personal pride, so we were not going to cut ourselves any slack.

It was therefore fitting that we were able to finish off with an almost complete all-round team performance. We just played really well, implementing the same formula that had made us successful in the previous Tests. We bowled Australia out for 280 and 281 on what was a peach of a batting track, and in between our top seven put plenty of scores on the board. Alastair Cook and Jonathan Trott were inevitable contributors and Matt Prior weighed in heavily as well.

Statistically it was my best performance of the series, but the best of my seven wickets, or at least the most enjoyable, came in the second innings. The abrasive nature of the SCG square took its toll on the ball, and so I managed to get some reverse swing going, one spell at Michael Clarke, when I was hiding the ball, proving particularly enjoyable. I like those kinds of contests when conditions allow – trying to get a top-class batsman out, who is having to work hard to judge which way the ball is going – especially when I win.

There hadn't been much socializing while the series was alive this time – our bowling coach David Saker sneaked out for a beer with the Australians a few times – although afterwards the rest of the lads did the traditional thing and knocked the froth off a few with the Australian players. My absence was explained by illness striking during that game, resulting in me losing my voice. During a post-match interview for ECB TV I could barely speak, and within half an hour of getting into our dressing room I fell asleep in the corner. Everything had caught up with me: the illness, the physical exertions of the past few weeks, jetting across the globe midway through the series. When I awoke, all the families were there and the champagne was flowing.

From there, us players reconvened on the square at the SCG, to share a beer and reflect on our favourite memories of the tour. My offering was rather non-specific because the whole package meant so much to me – just being involved in a successful tour like that was special. Being involved in a winning team in Australia, one that got on so well, was a once-in-a-lifetime experience (although it is our intention to blow this theory apart very soon) and an accomplishment that no English cricketer could ever forget. The sense of achievement when a team works in unison over such a long period of time to reach its goal, and does so, is incomparable, and for me it is the time that you share your success alongside your colleagues that sticks in the mind rather than the award of individual medals. One of the things we talked about was that whatever happened to us all from that moment on – teams tend to evolve quickly in the modern game – we would always be able to share that ecstatic feeling of winning in Australia, and few England players can lay claim to that. Those who put the emphasis on Australia's perceived weaknesses would be doing us a disservice. Whatever the so-called experts said in the aftermath, the Australians were still a good team in my opinion and still very tough to beat in their own backyard, as their record over three decades testified.

When I reflected on my own return, the fact that I took twenty-four wickets and didn't take a single five-wicket haul was pleasing rather than disappointing because it showed how incredibly consistent I had remained throughout the whole series. In that respect, it was undoubtedly the best series I'd ever had, and, coinciding with Ruby's arrival, a great period in my life. Let's just say, if I was being asked to prove a point or two, I had done so. Two dozen Ashes wickets is something I will always remember, and I reckon I will be able to recall each one forever.

My only regret was a minor one. Because I'd fallen into slumberland straight after the game, I missed out on the tradition of victorious visiting players scribbling messages on the wooden lockers before they leave. I felt that even more months later when someone tweeted that they had been on a tour of the SCG and had read Swanny's and Matt Prior's marker-pen inscriptions. Matt's was my favourite because it said it all so succinctly: ASHES 2010–11 JOB DONE!

16

Top of the World

We had worked so hard to win the Ashes that by the end of it I was physically drained. Everything had just caught up with me, and it was a good job a ten-day holiday, representing some rare family time, had already been pencilled in my diary by order of the England hierarchy. It meant that I missed the first two one-day internationals of seven against Australia but I truly needed the rest, as I had nothing more to give. When friends tell me how emotionally sapping it is to watch an Ashes series, I always suggest they try playing in one.

Physically I was down on my usual levels, and this time when I got back to Australia, unlike the relay for Ruby's birth, I felt out of sync. Lethargy consumed me and although I bowled okay in that Commonwealth Bank Series, I had certainly lost some of my snap. However, only once was I disappointed by a poor performance and that came in Sydney when I conceded 91 runs and we failed to protect a 334-run target.

But I was not the only one struggling to replicate previous glories by the time we arrived at the World Cup. The whole atmosphere was rather jaded, and when people are tired, and you stop winning, as we had done at the back end of the Australian tour, there is a tendency for people to get shitty with each other. Everything gets a little bit fractious and there is more angst around the team. Thankfully, on this occasion, that didn't happen – everyone was getting on well and training well – we just could not replicate the intensity that had served us so well across five Tests.

I was fortunate but other guys had only had two days at home in those past four months, a schedule that they had not experienced before. Such an intensive build-up to the Ashes was perfect preparation at the time but you could factor it in as a reason for the fatigue we now felt as a squad. Some of us had played seven or even eight games of Test-match intensity, having been on the road from the start of November, and were now adding one-day games to the equation. In India the intensive workload started catching up with us. Not just for the players but for the coaches as well. It undoubtedly took its toll on everyone.

Exactly what good playing a seven-match series in Australia does to prepare for the slow, low tracks of Asia I have yet to comprehend. It doesn't really make any sense to warm up in such alien conditions. If the England football team were preparing to play a tournament in somewhere like Mexico they wouldn't go for a pre-tournament training camp in Iceland. For cricketers, to practise on those bouncy Australian pitches, ahead of a competition we were expected to win, and wanted to win, was far from ideal. I don't tend to have much sympathy for Australians as a rule but even I could see that it affected their chances, too. No wonder our two boards have switched the Ashes cycle away from World Cup years ahead of the next event in 2015.

There is room for improvement out in Asia, both for me personally and the England team, as we have seen over the past two years, a period which has otherwise encapsulated incredible success. It is the one territory we have yet to conquer in world cricket, and as I enter my thirties I feel it is a place where I have still got a lot to prove. Hopefully I've now got more skills to enable me to cope with any given conditions because in previous series I have played on the subcontinent I have not really been confident about having anything else to fall back on if my plan A has failed. I don't have any height to give me that extra bounce, so on certain wickets you become very hittable – the ball tends to skid on, and you need to come up with ploys to combat the periods when you are being targeted. Unfortunately, I didn't have the answers with me at the World Cup.

Once again we displayed the capacity to go toe-to-toe with the tournament favourites and be kicked up the backside by tournament outsiders within days. In 2009, we suffered the ignominy of losing to the Netherlands and then winning the Ashes, and here we opened with more struggles against the Dutch. I went for seventy-two runs from my ten wicketless overs and, although we won that match in the penultimate over, it caused us considerably more discomfort than anyone would have estimated.

We've always struggled against minnows and to be fair here they caught us at just the right time. If you are going to play teams of superior quality you want to do so when they are weary, and our lack of cutting edge was highlighted in the defeat to Ireland in our third game when, at 111 for 5 midway through the Irish innings, the game was all over. Or so it appeared, because it was from that point that Kevin O'Brien played the innings of his life, with his six-infested, fifty-ball hundred. Bangalore is one of the best batting pitches in the whole world, and we had witnessed evidence of its true nature during our tied match with India only days earlier when we matched the world champions' 338 all out, and should have surpassed it, having been 281 for 2 with plenty of overs up our sleeve.

Even when I got things right, I didn't tend to get the rub of the green, most notably when I had Virender Sehwag dropped at slip and edging into no-man's-land in the opening over of the match against India. I knew I wasn't bowling well, and although you will by now be only too well aware that I hate being dropped, I would have dropped myself at this World Cup a game or two earlier than

Andrew Strauss actually did. I didn't feel strong, and I was bowling too many loose balls on surfaces where even your best balls can get thwacked. If you're not bowling any of those best balls, you are on a hiding to nothing.

Of course, I really appreciated the faith shown in me, and Strauss made a point of coming up to me regularly before a match to tell me: 'Keep going, Jimmy, we are going to stick with you. I really want you in my team.'

It was a massive confidence booster at a time when mine was diminishing rapidly. But ultimately, because I wasn't bowling as well as I could, I felt as though I was letting the team down. If you're experiencing those thoughts, it is a horrible place to be in. Perhaps Strauss recognized this and was trying to drag me out of my malaise. Perhaps he thought a four-wicket haul might just do that.

The first time he came up to me to have one of these chats was the day before the Ireland game. 'I know you can do a good job for us,' he reassured me. I did an okay job as it happened but I definitely wasn't feeling 100 per cent physically. I was going downhill and could not apply the handbrake.

There were some brief glimpses of my best form, with my spell against South Africa in Chennai, when I got the ball reverse swinging and bowled AB de Villiers and JP Duminy in quick succession, being a case in point. But if evidence was required that neither myself nor the team were on top form, it came just a few days later when Bangladesh were eight down with fifty-seven runs still required in their chase. For a team that prides itself on being clinical, it was criminal to allow them off the hook. We lacked the spark to finish them off and went down by two wickets. That just isn't us.

In truth, I had been running on empty from the halfway point of our group games, and had little gas left beforehand, so considered my exclusion for the winner-takes-all encounter with West Indies back in Chennai almost inevitable.

The only pride we took from that tournament was the fact that England games were so exciting to watch. It was a subject that came up among us at the time. We were playing really entertaining cricket which meant sometimes we won and sometimes we lost. Of course, we would have preferred to have been dullards and won every game but it just wasn't to be. During a World Cup, you tend to watch most of the other games to check on the opposition but there was nothing like the entertainment that we were serving up on offer on the box. Even when we lacked energy, we didn't lack fighting spirit, as we showed in those victories over West Indies and South Africa when defending under-par scores; we came out on top after it looked as if our opponents were coasting. But stepping up to Sri Lanka's level in the quarter-final in Colombo proved too big an ask.

Although still well short of where we wanted to be in limited-overs cricket, we made no secret of our ambition to push to become the best Test team in the world, and knew that the minimum requirement against Sri Lanka and India during the summer of 2011 would be to win convincingly. Our desire was to win 3-0 and 4-0 respectively.

To get there before the end of 2011 we would have to produce results not achieved by an England team in history, so our intention was not to give Sri Lanka a sniff or let them settle into the series. We wanted to hit them hard from the moment we got on the field, whether it be with bat or ball, but unfortunately the start of the English summer proved a real damp squib. We tended to spend more time off the field than on it, and my darts had definitely improved by the end of our 1-0 win.

My part in our success was limited following a side strain picked up in the first Test at Cardiff that prevented me bowling in the amazing second innings. The game appeared to be drifting towards an inevitable draw when the efforts of Tremlett, Broad and Swann turned it on its head. It was rather surreal at the end, as I watched one of the most dramatic final sessions of a Test unfold alongside no more than another hundred-or-so supporters. No one had turned up because of the horrendous wet weather but those that did got good value for it as we ended up bowling them out for 82 to win by an innings.

Victory was completed in the nick of time after Andrew Strauss had shown his softer side to allow Ian Bell to become the third batsman in our first innings to register 100. It was rather unlike us to be sentimental about landmarks – we are more often than not proactive about moving the state of the game forward – and indeed Strauss had a change of heart because that is what we were going to do when we talked about our plans on that morning. It was only when rain further restricted the contest that there was a change of heart.

Thankfully, my injury proved to be little more than stiffness and when I went for subsequent scans it showed the most minuscule grade one tear. Within two weeks I was fully healed. Sidelining me was precautionary and I thought things were taken a little too far when I was left out of the next match at Lord's. I felt strong enough to play but the management simply didn't want to take any chances with my fitness.

And I seemed to be at the oche more than the crease during the rain-affected draw in Southampton. Cookie, the other big arrows fan in the team, organized one of the dart manufacturers to get a board dispatched to the Rose Bowl and so we had something to keep those rain breaks interesting. Of the England team, it is only really me and Cookie who are massively into darts, and although he's the better player, it is clearly because he has time to practise at home. My best checkout is 149, so that might tell you how good he is. I am also an armchair fan, and get down to watch live whenever I am given a pass-out. If ever we've got a window between series, it's great to get down there and have a few beers. Of course, Broady has never been because they refuse to serve gin and tonic.

Although the inclement weather ensured the victory over Sri

Lanka remained low key, the same could not be said of the series against India, billed as a fight for top spot in the world Test rankings, and a fight we were confident of winning. We actually needed to win by two clear matches to get there, but fancied our chances in combat·with any team, particularly in our home conditions.

To perform as clinically as we did for such a sustained period was extremely satisfying. Our formula was the simple one that had served us so well over the previous nine months. The batters scored big runs – we took our team tally to twenty-two hundreds in a dozen Tests from the start of the Ashes onwards, and the bowlers kept chipping in with wickets.

But the big feature of the 4-0 whitewash that surged us to the summit was an ability to wrest the initiative back from India whenever they were in the ascendancy. There were several incidents in the series where they could have taken games away from us, and we simply refused to let them. Our victory at Trent Bridge in the second Test contained a particularly good example of that, when the Indians got into a first-innings lead with only four wickets down. It was at that point that Stuart Broad, who had already revitalized our first innings with a stunning, counter-attacking ninth-wicket partnership alongside Graeme Swann, produced a hat-trick that instigated a collapse.

Having helped us up to 221, his influence with the ball helped restrict the deficit as India plunged from 267 for 4 to 288 all out. That match could quite easily have slipped away from us without that kind of magic, but we did our best to support it by fighting back as hard as we could.

Within this England set-up, players like Broady have been encouraged to play their natural games and it has proved an essential ingredient to our success. In Nottingham, we prospered from Broad and Swann showing their love of a good counter-attacking opportunity. Give them nothing to lose, and they play like there is lots to gain. Whereas some teams might go into their shell when they are reduced to 124 for 8 and attempt to nurdle their way out of trouble, we try to slash our way out of it. A big point has been made of allowing people to indulge themselves if that is their most natural way of playing. If someone has attacking instincts we do not try to curb them, and that applies to both batsmen and bowlers. And Broady also had something else to prove, having been the odd man out in a selection equation for a one-day international against Sri Lanka in Manchester just a few weeks earlier.

The series had begun against a backdrop of expectation that Sachin Tendulkar would complete his 100th international hundred in the opening match at Lord's. It was hard to ignore the hype, and I am sure the world and his wife thought that Tendulkar was destined to achieve the feat at the home of cricket. Little did anyone suspect exactly how long his wait would continue.

How much of a distraction this little sideshow caused I am not sure, but in every innings throughout the whole series the same question came up: would this be the one? The answer was emphatically no as he kept making thirties and forties. When you are bowling at someone like that you have to be very patient and keep putting the ball around off stump. Good balls will always ask questions of even the best batsman, and it is just how they deal with them. Someone like Tendulkar rarely makes mistakes, and when he is in touch you can see some decent deliveries disappear through midwicket that you consider have no right to be hit there.

But we were able to play on his mortality. Our approach to Tendulkar was to try our utmost to stop him scoring, by being as accurate as we possibly could be for a concerted period of time. You have to accept that certain top-notch batsmen can do things to you that you do not like, and he is one of them.

For example, I know I have a decent record getting Sachin out but the funny thing is – I really do not like bowling at him. Most of my brethren would say that, I suppose, given that he has made mincemeat of international attacks for twenty-odd years. But he is very difficult to bowl to because he plays all around the wicket. Those are the batsmen who are the hardest to overcome. He sees length so quickly that if you are out by the merest fraction he will punish you. The same if you miss your lines slightly: you can be punished either side of the wicket. Too wide, that famous punched drive comes out. Too straight, you will disappear through the leg side.

The fact that I went in having dismissed the little master five times in our previous six meetings in Test cricket didn't mean a great deal to me, to be honest, because I have learned that things can change drastically from series to series. It actually surprises me when I hear that certain bowlers like bowling at certain players because I have never really enjoyed bowling at anyone in particular.

During 2011, he would hit me for twenty runs – a handful of fours off me – in no time at all. Yes, people will say that I won the personal contest by getting him out on a couple of occasions but, believe me, I didn't enjoy the journey getting there. In international cricket you know if you don't bowl well you can be dealt with, and dealt with comfortably. The fact that I don't particularly enjoy bowling at any one individual keeps me focused on what I need to do, and that is to keep hitting the pitch where I want to hit it.

Of course, it feels that extra bit special to get someone like Sachin or Ricky Ponting out, because they are a couple of the game's greats and I am lucky to have been able to compete against them as much as I have, let alone dismiss them. But as a bowler it is even nicer to get someone out when they are having a really good series themselves. Like Michael Hussey in the 2010–11 Boxing Day Test. Claiming his wicket at a time when he had stacked up a shedload of runs in the first three matches of the series was a moment to treasure as a bowler. It is why I went mad when he nicked behind. The rest of the team appreciate moments like that, too, and when you get such a joyous reaction from everyone else, you really feel like you've contributed to the team effort.

Tendulkar was fairly representative of the rest of the Indian top six in that they regularly scored fifties but unlike our batsmen they failed to convert their starts into big runs. It was only Rahul Dravid who ever got away from us, and as the series drew on it became a realistic prospect that we could win the series by at least a two-Test margin, and in so doing depose India and assume their Test crown. That was a real incentive not to let up at any stage and we stuck to our goals brilliantly.

However, we are fairly pragmatic as a team and since making a horlicks of things at Headingley in the 2009 Ashes have been aware of not getting too far ahead of ourselves. Sometimes, if you take your eye off the bigger picture and think about winning a series before you have even won the match you are heading for a fall. One thing we have always done well under Andy Flower is not to think too far ahead. We genuinely do think about winning one hour, one session, one day at a time. You have to add up lots of little processes to win a game of cricket, and we weren't about to fall into that trap again. You have to have respect for exactly how hard it is to win a Test match, and never lose that respect.

Because of India's stellar batting line-up, there were some great scalps to be had over the four matches, and, without doubt, the highlight for me was completing the returning Virender Sehwag's king pair with a jaffer at Edgbaston. The following morning, I sent back Gautam Gambhir with the first ball of the day, and added Dravid and Laxman to my list of victims before lunch. The innings victory, which sealed the series and our number one status came on the afternoon of Saturday 13 August, the fourth of the match.

Only Dravid's extraordinary appetite for a fight delayed the whitewash at the Oval. He carried his bat in the first innings for an unbeaten hundred, although his efforts could not prevent India being asked to follow on.

Without doubt, he has been one of the great ambassadors for the game during my time, and it was partly his diplomatic touch that averted the one flashpoint of the series developing into something altogether more fruity. Of course, I refer to the infamous run-out of Ian Bell in Nottingham on the stroke of tea on the third day, when during a moment of confusion as to whether the ball had gone for four, and therefore whether it was the start of the interval, the Indians claimed Bell's dismissal and initially refused to withdraw their appeal.

As the crowd bayed for blood during the interval, the message that came back from the Indian dressing room was that they wanted to uphold the decision. Andrew Strauss and Andy Flower were heavily involved in discussions, and went downstairs to address Duncan Fletcher and Mahendra Singh Dhoni, India's coach and captain respectively.

The information that came back to us was that Fletcher and Dhoni wanted the decision to stand, arguing that he was going for a third run and it was the senior players within the dressing room, Dravid and Tendulkar, who really pushed for Bell's reinstatement. It became like a pantomime for a couple of minutes when the Indians emerged for the evening session to a cacophony of boos, only for them to turn to cheers as Belly walked down the steps. I think that reaction showed the Indian team that they had made the right decision.

The 2011 season offered double cause for celebration for me, with Lancashire crowned county champions outright for the first time in seventy-seven years. My role in that success was minimal, playing just two of the sixteen games, but it nevertheless meant something to me. The club has been a major part of my life, they were kind enough to award me a benefit this year, and it is my intention to pay them back through my performances whenever I get the opportunity.

I have become accustomed to toasting success with England but to be part of Lancashire's entourage to Buckingham Palace in the autumn offered a different kind of day for me – a chance to raise a glass to team-mates who I grew up with, and blokes who I have come to respect and admire in equal measure. These blokes had been involved in the guts of the Championship win and I could sit back and observe from afar. It was lovely to do so.

Our wives and partners accompanied us as we met Prince Philip, and received our medals. Phil looked me up and down and told me he was surprised I had not put on an ounce of weight since I started playing cricket.

But the 2011 season was certainly not about me. It was about several other club stalwarts and a hungry crop of emerging local talent. I considered Glen Chapple and Gary Keedy to be grumpy old men when they first tried to prise words from me in the Old Trafford dressing room. Chappie was honoured by being named First Division player of the year but typically of the person he is, he thought there were more deserving winners of the award from within our own team: Keeds for his sixty wickets, and Kyle Hogg for his fifty-odd.

But above and beyond his all-round contribution with bat and ball, Chappie had an extra quality. He filled the team with belief, and a strong collective spirit. He squeezed every last ounce out of his team for them to succeed where others of modern vintage, those containing players of the calibre of Michael Atherton, Wasim Akram and Muttiah Muralitharan failed. Certainly when Murali was around we should have won it but we just didn't play well enough. Perhaps too much was expected of him.

In 2011 everyone contributed. Of those to have played at least half of the sixteen matches, only openers Stephen Moore and Paul Horton averaged in excess of thirty-five with the bat in Division One. But people dug in when it mattered, never more so than in the final game of the season at Taunton when the entire XI got double figures.

Obviously, when you become established as an England player it becomes more difficult, but I always love going back to play whenever I get the opportunity. To be a part of it, even though it was only a small part, was brilliant. It was an annual occurrence once on the staff to be asked how long it had been since Lancashire had won a County Championship title, and each April you would add a year to the number. It was a bit like the wait Manchester United endured before they won the Premier League in 1993.

Because I don't get to play that much, I am always fully committed to doing well, and to contributing to positive results. The way I've tended to look at it is that whenever I am freed up by England to go back for a game or two, it means someone else misses out, someone who could be a key member for the team for the whole season. Thankfully the club accommodates me every time I'm available, and a good example of that came when I asked England if I could play a one-day game against Glamorgan in a bid to get some more competitive bowling behind me.

At some counties, getting their international players back can be a little strange to the team, especially if they have been operating with a settled XI. Bringing someone in as an outsider can be a disruption, but I have always cherished the opportunity to make a telling contribution to Lancashire's fortunes. In between home and away series against West Indies in 2009, I got a game in against Sussex at Hove and managed to develop the good form I showed in the latter half of the four Tests in the Caribbean. It was late April, the ball swung nicely and it is probably the best I have bowled in a Lancashire shirt. My match figures were 51-15-109-11 and we won the game by eight wickets. That was my solitary appearance that year and, in contrast, my 2011 return was just five wickets in two outings.

The 2011 season was a bit like a throwback in time for Lancashire. It was the first time in a while that the club could justifiably claim to have a predominantly home-grown team, and it coincided with a first pennant since 1934. But this was just a by-product of the troubles behind the scenes at Old Trafford: the redevelopment of the ground and general lack of investment meant we had not been able to spend money on high-profile signings from overseas and the financial uncertainty caused while fighting the Derwent Holdings court case even restricted the potential to attract domestic signings.

Unable to splash out on new players meant the focus turned inhouse, as new coach Peter Moores put his faith in lads from Blackburn, Blackpool, Liverpool and Ormskirk. It was not necessarily by choice, if we are brutally honest, but the way it worked out was fantastic. And it was a fitting finale that on the last day it was two Lancashire lads knocking off the winning runs to beat Somerset.

The two overseas lads we did bring in – Pakistan's Junaid Khan and Farveez Maharoof, of Sri Lanka – were hardly box-office names but made significant contributions to the team when selected. In fact, in one of the two games I played, the Roses match at Liverpool, Maharoof got us over the line with some clean striking in an outstanding finish. At times like that, he played with the same kind of passion that the Lancashire-born players did. His fist-pumping as supporters ran on to the ground, after he smacked the winning runs to get us to our 120-run target inside fifteen overs, showed how much he was caught up in it.

He was not always selected but performed whenever he was called upon, slotted in really well, got on with all the lads and gained admiration for the hard work he put in. To be honest, sometimes overseas professionals come, take their cheque and leave, so it was nice to see someone who put in that extra effort to just be one of the boys.

My own will to win became something of a talking point in that Roses match when I got involved in a heated exchange with Andrew Gale and Joe Sayers. But that is just me when I am on a cricket field. Whether I'm playing for England, Lancashire, Burnley or in a benefit match, I always want to win.

That pitch at Liverpool was pretty flat and on the final morning the game was drifting along, they were batting quite well and I just tried to ruffle a few feathers. I don't see anything wrong in trying to put the opposition off a bit. Tension hung around that game following some comments by Gale at the start of the season, when live on Sky Sports News he dismissed Lancashire's title chances after a couple of early victories, suggesting that he expected us to be relegation fighters rather than being involved at the business end of the table.

I had a few things to say to him and I had also been quite verbal towards Joe because I felt he had nicked one the night before. Initially, Gale resisted the temptation to get into a verbal joust but then suddenly snapped in response to one of my quips from slip. The very next ball he edged a delivery from Gary Keedy straight to me, and we understandably got excited as a team.

From the game going nowhere, we had opened up one end, and although my aggressive conduct got close to the line, it is what I would expect of a hotly contested Roses clash. Both sets of supporters want their players to show passion, and I can't imagine another county match that would have made me like that.

But we still had to shift Joe, one of those batsmen who can be very frustrating to bowl at because he is so dogged, gets stuck in and is willing to bat a long time. He looked well set and dismissing him was crucial to our chances of winning, so we hoped to unsettle him in any way we could. At one point, he brushed passed me, rubbing my shoulder as he went by. I simply stood my ground and stared at him.

Afterwards, Martyn Moxon, Yorkshire's director of cricket, collared me and told me there was no need to shoulder-barge opponents, that I was a better cricketer than that. I was adamant that I had not done what he was accusing me of. Emotions were running pretty high – we had just knocked off a ridiculous run chase – and although there is a limit when it comes to on-field conduct, and I sometimes get too close to it, I was quite content that I had not been too physical on this occasion.

We won both matches I played but the celebration at Aigburth was a lot more animated than it was at Edgbaston for victory versus Warwickshire. We were on the balcony going berserk when Farveez hit the winning runs, and I couldn't remember the last time a county match had finished with supporters running on to the pitch to celebrate. A couple of hours earlier we thought the game had gone.

It had swung this way and that – from them looking as if they were saving it, to us looking as though we would finish off their tail quickly, to them resisting once more – and it took a ridiculous catch from Steven Croft at gully off my bowling to take the final wicket. Moments like that are the ones that win you the Championship. Because when games are fizzling out, you need something special to change them, and provide the difference between sixteen points for a win and a handful for a draw. He took that catch right on cue because if it had been any later we would have been into the final hour, lost another couple of overs between innings and not had enough time to reach our target. When you win from that position fills you with a confidence that you can win from anywhere. It also provided us with momentum.

Lancashire were undoubtedly lucky to have a coach as positive as Peter Moores. England's loss was definitely our gain, and, looking from the outside, never did he earn his corn as well as he did when we lost the third from last game to Worcestershire inside two days. It was a pleasant surprise to see the way the team came back against Hampshire to force another last-minute win, and then perform as they did against Somerset in a match with so much riding on it. Whether it was Moores's influence alone or that of Glen Chapple, everyone managed to keep their calm at the most crucial period of the season, and maintain confidence that they could win.

Lancashire allowed Moores to repair his reputation post-England. He obviously knows how to win County Championships; how to get the best out of cricketers; how to help them improve; and how to form a competitive team. He showed as much at Sussex. Given time, I believe he could have done a great job at international level.

His ethos has pretty much remained the same. He has taken some young players, the likes of Tom Smith, Steven Croft, Simon Kerrigan and Gareth Cross and brought the best out of them. These were all guys who were showing potential but not fulfilling it. He finds a way of bringing talent out of you. It is undoubtedly his best quality as a coach.

He can be one of the lads and has a very old-fashioned work-hard, play-hard sort of ethos. If you put all the hard work in over four days of a game he will be happy for you to go and celebrate when you win. And he will more likely than not be there celebrating with you. He is so passionate about the game, and loves winning. That attitude appeals to players. But it is not to say that he doesn't have a serious side. If you play badly he will let you know, and he has the potential to go off on one.

But what Mooresy does better than anyone I have ever met is lift people when they get down after a loss. You will all go away from the game thinking about where you went wrong but he always comes back the following morning with a fresh, and positive, perspective. He will have worked out how things will be put right and if he is down for a bit after we lose he never really dwells on it. The fact that he is able to move on quickly helps the team do the same.

His sides tend to battle for everything they get – it was clear that Lancashire did that in 2011. There are times when you need to scrap, when it's not about looking pretty and playing a nice cover drive. Sometimes it is about fighting on behalf of your team-mates and playing the situation of the game. That is something he drums into people, as is the understanding of the club's rich heritage. He has tried to get us to play with a passion befitting the history, and with a passion for the area that we represent.

My own attitude has been developed from observing those

around me. In my early days at Lancashire, I used to watch Carl Hooper prepare to bat. He'd get his pads on, be fully kitted up, then nestle the rest of his clobber left on the floor – spare shirts and jumpers – into a pillow and fall asleep. He'd have to be nudged with 'Hoops, you're in' and would walk out without a care in the world. He taught me that cricket is a relaxing as well as intense game.

Chappie is another great role model on how to play the game. Certainly, the way he plays is the way I would like to see myself come across. He plays with so much passion, really wants to win, yet always conveys that in a controlled manner. I freely admit that whereas I sometimes overstep the mark he never does. He goes about his business in such a professional manner, and that is how I would like to be thought of by people.

Even at thirty-seven, he could still bowl close to 90 mph. He captains the team superbly, and the rest of the squad really look up to him. He leads by example rather than with words. He is not the biggest talker in the world and will not say things for the sake of it. He only speaks if something needs to be said. Come 1 November, when it's time for players to start up again after a month's break, he will be in the gym working as hard, if not harder, than anyone else, and will continue to do that right up to the start of the season.

Worryingly, I was also part of the Lancashire group keeping up fitness that month after England informed me that I would be rested for the five-match one-day series in India. While I appreciated the time with my family, without any further assignments until early 2012 I was to endure an unusually long down period, and would have preferred to have been given the opportunity to prove I could bowl in one-dayers in Indian conditions, that the World Cup was a blip, and that I could continue to be successful in both Test and limited-overs cricket.

Andy Flower's insistence that I put my feet up ahead of the tour of the UAE to take on Pakistan was a compliment of sorts, suggesting on face value because of my age and career record that I had nothing to prove. But you are always conscious that others have the opportunity to further their causes at your expense when you are absent, and it was indisputable that, despite passing the 200-mark in one-day international wickets against the Indians in September's home series, I had dropped behind Steven Finn in the pecking order for one of the two new-balls in ODIs by the time the England team returned home for Christmas.

17

Surplus to Requirements

Being left out of a one-day series was one thing but missing a Test match when I considered myself fully fit created an altogether stronger reaction from me. I was angered by the prospect of having to sit out the final Test of the series against West Indies at Edgbaston in June 2012 when feeling in both good rhythm and good form.

A sportsman's lot is to compete. From the moment you sign your first professional contract, getting into XIs and into sixteen-man squads becomes part of your day job. You never want to be on the outside. So the phone call I received on the afternoon of Friday 1 June 2012 got my blood up. If Andy Flower is ringing you less than forty-eight hours before an England squad is announced, you have a fairly clear idea of what's coming. So I was braced for what he had to tell me.

That's not to say that I was prepared to accept my fate – which was to sit out the dead rubber in Birmingham, with the more prestigious series against South Africa in the second half of the summer, and career longevity in mind – without airing my displeasure. The previous few days had prepared me for what was going to happen.

When Andrew Strauss mentioned the need for rotation in his captain's post-match press conference following victory at Trent Bridge, I had taken it as no more than the customary line offered after every Test or one-day series success – players are monitored regularly to make sure they are not thrown into games when fatigued or carrying niggles. I had been troubled by stiffness in my thigh in the win that put us 2-0 up in the Wisden Trophy with one match to play but, following confirmation that there was no significant damage, didn't read anything more into his comments.

However, twenty-four hours later it occurred to me that there was clearly something behind the words when I learned that David Saker, the bowling coach, had spoken openly in another press conference about the possibility of Stuart Broad and/or me sitting out at Edgbaston for the good of our top-level careers. It was, he said, something that would be discussed between himself and Andy, and the other selectors ahead of the third Test squad announcement on 3 June.

Now Andy explained their thinking: there was a hectic summer schedule in front of us, including limited-overs series against West Indies, Australia and South Africa, followed by a World Twenty20 and an important tour to India at the end of what was shaping up to be a long year (if I played in every form of the game).

I listened to what he said but could not shake my utter disappointment. I told him I didn't want to miss *any* Test cricket for England, that although I loved playing one-day cricket, the form of the game in which I made my international debut, and was desperate to get back in the Twenty20 team as well, I could not escape the fact that Test cricket was, is and always will be my priority.

Test cricket retains its primacy for me, and it didn't go well with me that I was sitting out when available. There are lots of other things on world cricket's menu these days but for English players it remains the priority. That much is quite obvious. For example, if you had asked Alastair Cook then he would have said that Test matches come above everything else even though he was one-day captain.

To his credit, Andy told me he fully understood and that in the same position he, too, would hate to miss a Test. When he played, he said, Test matches were the pinnacle for him.

But, as team director, he had a responsibility to manage his players. He explained that he didn't just want me to play through everything, waiting for injury to form a natural break in my chain of matches for England. His theory was that if he oversaw things well and took opportunities like this, in removing me from what was effectively a dead rubber, it might prevent injuries for a while and also prolong my career at its back end.

But I remained miffed that I had not been consulted before-hand and, from my point of view, when in good form you want to keep bowling. It's the only way to stay in good form, in my opinion. This was only a couple of Test matches into the international summer and I had been restricted to just one game for Lancashire in the series build-up, so I did not feel overburdened by my work-load at that point.

But Andy maintained his argument that, while I was naturally concentrating on the here and now, in his position he had to have one eye on the future. He told me that he didn't want another sit-uation developing like the one he had just experienced with Kevin Pietersen earlier that week. It had been only a matter of hours since Kev's retirement from all limited-overs international cricket had been announced.

Andy said that he didn't want another scenario developing where a player was having to retire from one form of the game because the overall schedule was proving too heavy.

'If I keep missing Test matches then I'll have no choice but to seriously consider retiring from one-day cricket too,' I replied.

Idle threat or not, it showed that this really wasn't a subject I was taking lightly. I was looking for a vehicle to carry my frustration; a way of expressing to Andy just how pissed off I was. The last thing I wanted was a situation developing whereby every time we went 2-0 up in a three-match series I missed the third and final Test.

To be fair, I got the vibe that Andy expected and understood that I would be annoyed, and I knew he was taking it all on board. It was a conversation neither of us really wanted to have, I guess, but he had made his decision and he was sticking by it. So, with his mind made up, it didn't matter how well I argued my case. I had expressed my disappointment in the strongest terms but concluded that batting things back and forth was not going to get us anywhere.

'What else I want to say is not going to change the situation, so let's just leave it at that,' I told him.

By the time I arrived at Edgbaston on Saturday 9 June, for a pre-arranged fitness session, I'd had a few days to calm down and began to see the other side of the argument. If they wanted me to play one-day cricket then it probably was a sensible option. All I considered initially was that I had spent such a long time trying to secure a place in the England team and now, with it almost cemented, I was being removed. It felt like a major blow.

But from Andy Flower's point of view, his remit as team director is to make England better across all three formats of the game, and if he wants the England one-day team to improve, to climb up the rankings, he needs his strongest side out for fifty-over matches. So, although Test cricket was once considered sacrosanct, that can no longer be the case. If Andy rests people from one-day cricket all the time, we will never get better, and he let me know that our fluctuating fortunes in limited-overs cricket is something he wants to change.

At the end of the day, Andy's job is not to keep people happy but to get results, and while there were people messaging me on Twitter upset that they had forked out £60 for a ticket, and therefore wanted to see the best XI playing, it might be the sign of things to come.

Previously, it had never been a part of English cricket's culture to rotate players; it has always been about playing your best team, and, to be honest, in previous eras we had never had the strength in depth to do it. But Andy has long been an advocate of individuals taking physical and emotional breaks.

Now we have incredible strength in depth, especially in the bowling, and that only exaggerates your sense of paranoia when you're left out. Realistically, we could play any three seamers out of as many as six, seven or eight blokes. Whereas in the past we have had players come in to replace injury victims, and they've done a job, we did not have that tried-and-trusted quality. These days there's a surplus of bowlers who would genuinely get into most other international attacks. That in itself maintains the pressure on you to keep performing, and if you do take your foot off the gas then someone is going to take your place. Simple as that.

I had to take all I was being told at face value, but I had considered over the previous months what a very fine line it can be between an established player being rested, and being dropped. That one-day tour to India in the autumn of 2011 proving to be a case in point. I couldn't help asking myself: 'Are they trying to ease me out of the fifty-over side? Or do they genuinely want me to rest?' Bearing in mind that I had two months off ahead of me, I couldn't help think it was the former. However, there is nothing you can do about it once that kind of decision has been made and if they want to rest you that is the management's prerogative.

My suspicions appeared to have foundations when, on the eve of the first ODI against Pakistan in the UAE in the new year, Alastair Cook and Andy took me to one side to tell me I would not be playing. That was particularly galling; I got a sulk on, and didn't talk to Cookie for about three days (remember that he's one of my best mates).

I was told that they were intent on a pace attack of Steve Finn, Tim Bresnan and Stuart Broad. But during the first warm-up game against the Lions it was obvious that Bres was struggling with his lingering elbow injury, and when it came to the opening match of four in Abu Dhabi they decided he wasn't fit and that I would play after all.

Naturally, I felt I needed to prove a point when given this chance, and did just that in the second match when, with Pakistan 207 for 5 chasing 251 to win, I began the forty-fifth over to Shahid Afridi. A yorker second ball accounted for him during a wicket maiden, and forty-four off five overs was a tall order on a pitch of limited pace. As a fast bowler, you want to turn games that are getting tight towards the end and it's very pleasing when that sort of thing happens.

This was the kind of performance I've always had in me, and was a continuation of what I viewed as good form in all formats over the previous few months. Others recognized that fact, too, when I was named England's player of the year at an awards dinner in the Long Room at Lord's in early May 2012. Of course, after the winter our batsmen had endured, it kind of narrowed the field! But it was nice to be recognized by the media as the best player for the twelve-month period, not least because this award is not just for performances in Test cricket. It's for everything.

Looking back, I would consider it to be as consistent a year as I had experienced as an international player. There were a couple of five-fors among my forty-six wickets in eleven Tests, but I didn't get big hauls, which meant that there were lots of threes and fours, showing sustained consistency. The same was true in ODIs, with my dozen appearances including eighteen wickets at fewer than twenty-six runs apiece, a return significantly lower than my career average of thirty.

It was a period when everything came together for me as a fast bowler. As you get older, you realize your optimum pace to operate at, and in Test matches generally I am bowling within myself these days. First of all, that provides a lot more control and increases accuracy. Secondly, you are able to bowl longer spells, and don't tend to feel as tired when you come back later in innings.

Of course, you are still trying to bowl a decent pace, and there is still a quick spell in me if I need it but I don't tend to go there in Test cricket. It's in one-day internationals that I tend to slip myself. Partly because of operating in shorter spells, I run in a bit harder, and partly because if you are bowling in the low eighties in terms of miles per hour, just trying to be accurate, you can get lined up quite easily.

I have always liked thinking about the game, what I am doing, how I am trying to take wickets, and after ten years of it with England things have started coming together. Let's face it, there has been a lot of trial and error in my career, and I have got rid of a lot of stuff that didn't work for me, so in Test cricket I have narrowed it down to bowling within myself, and with patience.

Tactically that worked for me in the United Arab Emirates and Sri Lanka during the Test winter of 2011–12, even though the pitches offered limited encouragement.

When we headed to the UAE to face Pakistan in January, we did so as favourites to win the series, we knew that. People went as far as saying we should win comfortably but we knew it wouldn't be that easy for us because we had seen some of the previous series that Pakistan had played out there against Sri Lanka before Christmas, and they played really well. Watching those matches, it seemed like they had all bases covered. Given the make-up of their side – two seamers and three spinners – we also got lulled into thinking we would be faced by subcontinent conditions.

We were not, and unfortunately, unlike recent tours elsewhere, such as to Australia, we did not hit the ground running. This time, both warm-up games were at the ICC's Global Cricket Academy Ground. In the first, against a representative XI of associate and affiliate country players, we did not play well and had to declare 96 runs behind on first innings. In the second we scrambled to a total, and although we strung two wins together, there was little fluency to our play.

Nevertheless, we had been through so much together that, despite not starting off as we wanted to, we remained confident in our ability. I guess we got a bit of a shock with Pakistan's mystery spinner Saeed Ajmal. He bowled brilliantly, and we didn't play him well at all.

We shouldn't really have been surprised by their spinners – Ajmal, Abdur Rehman and Mohammad Hafeez – as we'd watched them and pre-planned. We knew that they all bowled quicker than your usual twirlers but we were exposed by the differences in theory and practice. Because they bowl that little bit faster there was reduced reaction time when one misbehaved off the surface: the odd one spun and the odd one went straight on and that caused us problems.

The effect of the Decision Review System was also noticeable. Since it has come in it has forced batters to think a little bit differently: whereas before they were quite happy trying to get their pad outside the line of off stump, they are now wary that DRS might show that they are not quite outside, increasing their sense of vulnerability. Five of Saeed Ajmal's seven wickets in our first innings of 192 at Dubai Sports City were lbw and the uncertainty caused problems to several players with top-class records. Now they were having to think about playing spin in a completely different manner from what they had been used to in the past.

We seemed to have been caught cold in that opening Test, one that was over inside three days, after we were dismissed for 160 second time around, but because the ten-wicket defeat was followed so quickly by the final two Tests, there was not a lot of time to address things. One of the things Andy Flower prides himself on is ensuring this England team is immaculately prepared but on this occasion we were not and there was a need to go back to the drawing board.

Although guys weren't making wholesale changes to their techniques, they were looking for better methods of playing as the series progressed. The problem was that Ajmal, Rehman and Mohammad Hafeez attacked the stumps so much, and also bowled with very flat trajectories. Sending down these 60 mph darts made it difficult for someone like Kevin Pietersen, who enjoys coming down the pitch, and like a number of other guys that negated his release shot – the one that gets the scoreboard ticking and throws the challenge back at the bowlers.

Time in the nets was spent devising other methods of scoring against these spinners, a trio very different from the other spinners around the world. It took quite some getting used to, and I am not sure we ever did. In one way it was easier for us tail-enders because we kept walking in with such low totals on the board. In that scenario, particularly with someone else from the lower order for company, you are given licence to swing from the hip, and occasionally a hack will be worth a dozen runs or more. Only when there is a frontline batsman at the other end is there a responsibility on you to stay there and support.

That was not often the case, and summed up how utterly outplayed we were during that series. There was no doubt Pakistan adapted much better to the conditions, and any frustration we felt as a bowling group stemmed from the fact that we so desperately want to win every game we play. It is not right to blame the batsmen in a situation like that – you just have to hold your hands up and admit that you have been beaten by a superior team.

Yes, from a bowler's point of view, when you think you are doing your job it is a major source of irritation when the batters are not doing theirs. But having said that, the batsmen were amazing in the previous twelve to eighteen months, playing huge roles in the Ashes win and the home victory over India. And you cannot have everything your own way as an international team. We had a period of two years in which a lot had been going our way, and this was a major slip-up for us.

People pointed to the fact that this was our first game since being named the world's best Test team and that the pressure might have got to us. That we had begun to believe our own press. But being number one or not was irrelevant. To produce a performance like that at any time would still be unacceptable. We set ourselves high standards as a team and we fell well below them.

We just couldn't counter the Pakistanis' threat. Arguably, our top order was not ready for what they were faced with but not adapting is no excuse for the world's best. We had been preparing ourselves for slow pitches, catches in front of the bat and a hard slog against probing spin. Yet the threat was more encompassing. There was always some encouragement for the fast bowlers – the new-ball period remained a crucial part in the game, and there was some reverse swing in Abu Dhabi – and the spinners hunted wickets more aggressively than expected.

At times they were all over us, and at others they overturned situations with spectacular success. First, in pulling back a position in the second Test when we were 166 for 1 in reply to 257, then in the final match, recovering from being dismissed for 99 on the opening day to secure a 3-0 whitewash.

A 4-0 win in the one-day series proved that we could prosper in those conditions but things were to get worse before they got better for us in Test cricket.

Galle, scene of the first Test against Sri Lanka in late March, possesses a notoriously flat playing surface, so I felt well rewarded in claiming five first-innings wickets. The heat can be punishing in the extreme, but dismissing Sri Lanka for 318 meant that we limited our time in the sun. I claimed two wickets with the new ball, then got one with some reverse swing before picking up two tail-enders with the second new ball. All in all, given that we were competing on a pitch of relatively low bounce and one minus any demons initially, it was a decent start to the two-match campaign.

With little spin in it either, we thought we might be able to post a big score. We needed to go significantly beyond Sri Lanka's first innings to give ourselves a good chance of victory. Instead, we failed to get anywhere near credit and were left with a significant deficit. In those conditions, you need to make the most of your first innings, knowing that the wicket is going to deteriorate.

And this one did. It is very difficult to bat last on Sri Lankan pitches, so we knew we were up against it when set 340 in the final innings. Even then, Jonathan Trott showed us what could be done on days four and five with discipline and a trusted method of batting. The only problem at that stage, on a surface like that, though, is that you always think there is a ball that will do for you – one that has your name on it.

With that in mind, it would have been a monumental effort to chase those runs down, and although we never stopped believing we could do it, the freak dismissal of Matt Prior, probably our best player of spin, turned the game decisively in Sri Lanka's favour.

Trotty had just brought up his hundred when, later in the same over, Matt swept at left-arm spinner Rangana Herath and Lahiru Thirimanne clutched the ball in his midriff, falling backwards. There were still 107 runs required when that latest moment of misfortune struck us – had Stuart Broad, hardly a big no-ball merchant, not overstepped towards the end of Sri Lanka's second innings, we would have been chasing forty-odd fewer, and little things like that change games – and it proved too many.

However, that second-innings effort and Trott's 100 in particular was arguably a big turning point for the batting group because it showed them how to play, and the fact that we could make runs in those conditions.

Heading to Colombo for the second Test, we had to avoid defeat to stay top of the rankings. But that is not something we generally talk about heading into matches. As you will have seen, we tend to break things down into as many small parts as possible. We would never talk about not losing, rather the importance of the first half-hour of the match, whether we were batting or bowling. As we have found in our rise to the top, it is doing all the small bits well that gets you there.

And the opening half-hour was successful as it happened. Although it was another ridiculously flat pitch, and you had to bowl extremely well to get wickets on it, a new-ball spell can be crucial anywhere in the world, and so it proved at the Tamil Union Ground. There was minimal lateral movement, so my policy was to get the ball into an area to create pressure. It worked, eventually.

Tillakaratne Dilshan got a few away off me in the opening overs, before I managed to nick him off. Then I got Kumar Sangakkara first ball for the second time in the series, and when I pinned Thirimanne in front, Sri Lanka were 30 for 3, after winning the toss.

In the circumstances, making those early inroads was crucial, because once again we found Mahela Jayawardene in freakish form. His 180 in the first Test was majestic and when he is in that kind of nick it genuinely feels as though he is not going to get out whatever you try. He seems to have a lot more time to play the ball than anyone else I have ever bowled at. My speed through the air might have dropped as the mercury rose to inhumane levels but he makes you feel about 10 miles per hour slower still. Again, he played brilliantly for his second hundred in as many matches but we kept the home team to 275, which was a magnificent effort.

With Sri Lanka in range once more, this time there were no mistakes. And at 213 for two when he walked to the crease – a deficit of just sixty-two runs – KP had been provided with the perfect platform. From that point he well and truly took the game out of the Sri Lankans' reach by playing one of the innings that has made him as popular as he is with England fans. He absolutely destroyed the opposition. The Sri Lankan spinners couldn't bowl at him; they didn't know where to bowl at him. He was sweeping, reverse-sweeping, coming down the pitch. It was a brilliant, match-winning innings.

One of the beauties of our team is that the two Andys, Strauss and Flower, have always advocated us playing to our individual strengths, and doing what comes naturally. What comes naturally to Kevin is going out and being as dominant and as arrogant as possible, and so when he took the game to the opposition they had nowhere to go. This was something of a role reversal to his duels with the Pakistan spinners a month or two earlier because Rangana Herath and Suraj Randiv are bowlers who rely on flight. When they gave it some air, it meant he could come down the pitch and strike them aerially.

Herath had been their match-winner in Galle, and although we always give a lot of respect to the opposition we play, the collective feeling was that we gave him too much respect in that first Test. Sure, he bowled well but at the same time we didn't play him very well, and at the end of the day he's a left-arm spinner with no real mystery to what he does, so he shouldn't be taking twelve wickets in a match against us.

The positive vibes given off by KP's 151 were contagious and, after restricting Sri Lanka to a sub-300 score for the second time in the match, we set off on the chase of 94 at a gallop. In Abu Dhabi, when we had to chase 144, we made a right hash of it, and I know for certain that was in people's minds. Our start against Pakistan was block, block, block, and we basically dug ourselves into a rut.

They say the sign of a good player is someone who learns from past experience, and this time Alastair Cook was not going to fall into the same trap. Despite losing opening partner Andrew Strauss in the first over, he maintained his intention to play some really attacking shots: he didn't slog, he simply showed intent to create a tempo more like a one-day innings. In that size chase, once you get to fifty you realize that even if you lose a few wickets it only takes a couple of twenty-run partnerships and you are there, so Cookie's attitude settled us down, and after four consecutive defeats, ensured a strong finish to the winter.

Because of the scheduling, our summer assignments followed

just five weeks after we returned from the 1-1 draw against the Sri Lankans. And, suddenly, Andrew Strauss's position was becoming a topic of national debate. The question came up a lot in press conferences, and just about everyone in the team had been asked about it by the time we met for the first Test against West Indies at Lord's. But it was never considered by anyone from within that our captain would ever miss out. He was one of the main reasons why we had been so successful in the last few years.

By focusing on his eighteen-month period without a Test hundred, his massive influence on the team was being overlooked. Let's face it, it wasn't as if his eyes had gone or he had forgotten how to bat; he just hadn't scored the runs the media would have liked him to.

So when he got his hundred in the first innings of the 2012 summer, it provided a chance to witness how much he was respected, not just in our dressing room but among English supporters. The whole ground erupted when he got to three figures, and the entire dressing room was out on the balcony clapping him. It's really nice when people act spontaneously like that towards a fellow player because it doesn't always work like that in sport.

His 122 would have taken some weight off his shoulders. Everyone in this England team has been through one of those periods where the pressure is on you and you are not getting the runs or wickets. So we know how he felt; there was definitely relief for him and you could see it.

It must have been lovely for him to receive the ovation he did, and the welcome back into the dressing room emphasized the fact that there were ten other blokes appreciative that he was doing things right. Everyone gets their own reaction from the rest of the team when they've done well and for Strauss we tried to make it like a public school environment. When he did well, you could bank on a lot of handshakes, stiff upper lips, and 'well done's. It was always a lot more subdued than when Cookie gets one, that's for sure. Then, you can expect big cheers and high fives.

I played with Strauss for more than eight years at international level, and came to recognise man-management as one of his great strengths. So it wasn't a huge surprise to me when, having added a twenty-first Test hundred to his collection in the series-sealing win over the West Indians in Nottingham, I received a phone call from him regarding the decision to rest me. The Test team is his baby, and he wanted to have some input. Leaving it a couple of days before ringing me was a wise thing to do. He certainly wouldn't have got anything constructive out of me if he had chosen to call on the same day that Andy Flower had informed me of the decision. He knows I am quite grumpy, and always dealt with everyone differently. He learned that, while some needed a dressing down, others merely required a quiet word in the ear.

While Strauss did not surprise me, one man who did during that 2-0 Wisden Trophy success was Marlon Samuels. I was really impressed with him. I thought he was the tourists' best player by a distance. People might think I have overlooked someone here but, no – you see, Shivnarine Chanderpaul always seemed to give us a chance, would edge one through the slips or something like that whereas Samuels was pretty chanceless throughout the first two games.

Certainly given his reputation, and the way he played in the Indian Premier League, we thought he was a bit of a dasher. But he got stuck in and batted for long periods of time, which led to some verbal exchanges between the two of us. You generally end up talking to people who stick around in the middle, and so there were several periods in which I chirped away at him. It's fair to say that he gave as good as he got.

At one point in Nottingham, I asked him whether he was ever going to play a shot. 'People have paid good money to come and watch runs and wickets,' I told him. 'Will you actually do something?'

'Don't be like that,' he replied. 'You're my favourite bowler!'

I enjoyed the contest. He plays with aggression, plays to win and I do the same. So after he got to his hundred on the first day, I shook his hand as he left the field. I appreciated his efforts. Later, we were both put up for the post-play press conferences. Marlon was in the squash courts behind the pavilion, and I was standing, in his line of vision, behind the Perspex wall, when he was quizzed about our on-field exchanges. He didn't miss the opportunity to have a joke at my expense and we shook hands again as he left the room.

He will have gone up in a lot of people's estimations as a cricketer, and I presume other teams around the world will have watched the series and been surprised by his performances. He will now be held in a lot higher esteem and be more greatly respected by opponents as a result.

It seems a weird thing to say but it can actually be a nice feeling when you've had a battle with someone and they come out on top. If you have given your all, and know you've competed at your very best, then respect goes to your opponent. Samuels got scores in four of his five innings in that series. I genuinely hope he does well for the rest of his career. He has obviously worked really hard at his Test game, and he deserves to reap the rewards.

It is during these kinds of skirmishes that people see my split personality. You see, on-field I am always in character – whenever I cross that white line I become Jimmy. Then, when the bails are removed, I become James once more.

This bloke Jimmy is a warrior, and warriors are aggressive by nature, people who will do anything they can to win a battle. That is who I am when I am out on the field. The competitive animal comes out in me: in chuntering away at opponents, in my body language and in my facial expressions.

Part of the work I do with Mark Bawden, our team psychologist, focuses on flitting between the two sides of my life. He regularly talks to me about switching between the character and the real me because what I don't want to do is dwell in that confrontational place when I come home to my family. That is something I have been guilty of in the past. For example, because I have a short fuse, there have been occasions when Daniella has asked me to do the washing up, and I have told her to do one. Or words to that effect. That kind of behaviour needs to be left in the middle.

It is all about getting my work–home balance right, and I want to be James whenever I walk through the front door, never Jimmy. Mark recognized the split in me a couple of years ago, and we have worked on transferring from one to another ever since. For example, sometimes Mark will tell me he has seen too much James on the field, and if there is too much James, and I am too friendly, I don't bowl at my very best. I need to create that intensity, and slip into my other skin, to succeed in my day job. I become ultra-confident with a fiery temperament. I become that tough fast bowler with a rhino-hide skin. I become Jimmy.

18

THE CHANGING OF THE GUARD

Without doubt England's success in Test cricket over the previous couple of years had been in no small part due to stability within our team. However, events of the 2012 summer disrupted that and brought significant change to the set-up. During the space of just a few weeks we lost Kevin Pietersen temporarily and Andrew Strauss, our highly respected leader, permanently.

Some people have speculated that one might have spawned the other, that the protracted Pietersen issue might have been a factor in Strauss's decision to quit, but while I concede it was not ideal, he was thinking about retiring before the South Africa series started; it wasn't something that just developed halfway through. That sort of indirect issue just wouldn't influence a man like Strauss.

It was a measure of the man that his reasons for giving up the job were all about what he felt was best for the England side in the longer term. As I said earlier, we all knew his runs against West Indies meant a great deal, but although he had displayed glimpses of form, with eight years' experience and 21 Test hundreds behind him, he knew better than most what it took to succeed and to continue being successful at this elite level.

Some might have reconsidered walking away after the 2-0 loss to South Africa, preferring to wait until after a series win before going. But typically, Strauss was thinking in the interest of the England dressing room rather than a personal last hurrah. Undoubtedly, what he viewed as the best course was the opportunity for a new captain to get his feet under the table well in advance of the 2013 Ashes.

There was a real touch of class about his departure, too. Leaving a team is always much harder than joining one, I imagine – and you will know by now how difficult I've found the latter – so it would have taken a concerted effort for him to explain his decision to each and every one of us in personalized, hand-written letters. Each piece of correspondence related to specific shared experiences, and I find it only right to keep the full contents of mine private between the two of us. However, the gist of it was that he was proud of us as a team and that he had many great memories to take with him into retirement.

One thing was for sure: the England dressing room was going to be a little different from September 2012 onwards. A good deal quieter for a start.

You will no doubt be aware that Strauss possesses one of the loudest voices in the northern hemisphere, and that when interviewed by Sky Sports' roving reporter Tim Abraham somewhere on the other side of the planet, it has been known for them to have been heard back in the studio in London ... without use of either a microphone or a satellite.

His booming tone was just one thing he was regularly ribbed about. You see, he was always a good sport, a willing butt of others' dressing-room jokes. His education at Radley was decent subject matter too, as was his up-and-at-'em public schoolboy nature.

It was Matthew Hoggard who first christened him Lord Brocket, before settling for Posh Twit (at least I think it was Twit). Swanny, of course, called him plenty else besides, but the quality I appreciated most about Strauss was his willingness not only to take it but give it back, too. Sometimes when a player becomes captain he loses the ability to josh and remain at the hub of the team's camaraderie. Not Strauss.

Neither was he fearful of taking the mickey out of himself, or joining in the banter whenever we got the opportunity to let our hair down. Nights spent out on the town in celebration of successes were always richer for Strauss hitting the dancefloor. After a few drinks he would transform into an embarrassing uncle at your cousin's wedding, mesmerizing those around him with his moves. Check out his input into our post-MCG win sprinkler dance on YouTube for one delicious slice of comedy gold.

Physically his co-ordination let him down on such occasions, but seldom did he make the wrong move in his time as England captain. His greatest asset, as I highlighted with both his treatment of me in the 2011 World Cup and with my omission for the Edgbaston Test against West Indies the following year, was to read a situation and react accordingly. As a communicator he was second to none, whether the appropriate course of action was a rousing speech in the privacy of the dressing room or a light moment on the outfield before the start of play when, with television cameras in the vicinity and a match situation in the balance, tension hung in the air. In the latter scenarios, he would crack a joke or leave us baffled by a Chinese proverb. I'd always wondered how he had passed his time at university.

In fact, whatever situation he was confronted with, and whatever the state of his personal game, you always felt that his number one priority was the welfare of others. That is the trait of a natural leader.

It was a shame we couldn't have paid him back with just a smidgeon more on the field. On the eve of that Lord's Test against South Africa, a match in the spotlight as much for the furore surrounding KP as the delicately balanced scenario of the series and Test cricket's world order, he had asked us to keep fighting all the way to the end. The fact that we got as close as we did to what would have been a record run chase, with Swanny swinging hard into the final throes of the match, was a tribute to him. We never stopped believing we could do it, and that was Strauss's mantra for the team.

What was evident post-series was that Strauss was tired, and he had every reason to be following the situation that had developed publicly in the aftermath of the drawn second Test match at Headingley. What was said in the post-match press conference by Kevin has been well documented, and certainly snowballed into what became a draining period of time for the England captain. In the heat of the battle cooked up by a series between the top two sides in the world, it must have been deflating for him to have to be drawn into such off-field matters. By the end of the season, there would also have been the attraction of being able to spend more time with his young family.

The question about Kevin's future availability cropped up all the time in the media and at every press conference. And, after trailing 1-0 courtesy of losing the opening match, the distraction provided after Leeds was one we could have done without, too. Our status as the number-one team in the world had been hard-earned, and suddenly there were headlines being written about off-field activity rather than the action on it.

The issue seemed to drag on far too long, and all we wanted was for it to be put to bed so we could concentrate on the task in hand. Kevin talked openly about it being 'tough' for him in the England team environment, but after he announced he was quitting one-day international cricket in mid-summer we had just got on with things.

When he chose to retract his withdrawal of labour via a YouTube video on the eve of the third Test squad announcement, there were still issues unresolved – the press highlighted text messages (actually, to be completely accurate, they were BBMs) he had apparently exchanged with members of the South African touring party as a problem.

So, although dropping a player capable of winning matches on his own, and one who had scored 149 in his last appearance, was nonsensical on face value, the selectors exercised their right to highlight that no one is ever bigger than the team. And certainly, from what I have experienced in my career, you need all eleven players pulling in the same direction.

Of course, we had coped pretty well without Kevin a few weeks earlier when Ian Bell was drafted into the 50-over team as his replacement at the top of the order, and Alex Hales filled the hole created in the Twenty20 side brilliantly, so we knew we had good depth. It was equally encouraging to see James Taylor's mature debut at Headingley, taking advantage of Ravi Bopara's absence, to bat alongside KP for such a long period.

At Lord's, it was Jonny Bairstow's turn to show off evidence that we can look forward to an infusion of new blood at some stage, with a majestic 95. To be honest, it was an innings that deserved a hundred. Everything about him that week was positive.

However, the bottom line is that you want your world-class players playing when they are fit, and from a cricket perspective it was disappointing not to have Kevin around. We had worked so tirelessly as a unit to get to the top, and could have done with being at full-strength at a time when our status was being snatched away.

There was no doubting it had been a strange few months to be an England cricketer, and we didn't deal with things particularly well at the time. So a lot of credit has to go to Kevin for the manner in which he returned to the fold for the tour of India. It is fair to say that we found a way around previous difficulties on both sides. As a group we welcomed him back, and in turn his reaction was as if he hadn't been away, and there had never been a problem. We looked forward rather than dwelling on the recent past.

In life, not everyone is always going to get on with everyone else, but it is how you deal with that. From that perspective we were very professional. As long as we all share a common goal then nothing else really matters, and when we returned from India victorious, I reflected on what a pleasure it had been to be a part of the dressing room over the course of that four-Test series.

Winning in India for the first time since the England team of 1984–85 was quite a way for Alastair Cook to kick off his captaincy. To be honest, though, you get used to Cook doing amazing things. It was Strauss's great strength to have the respect of his team, and the same can be said of Cookie. So while I bet there were a number of guys who would have loved to have inherited the post, there was not a single quibble about him having the right credentials.

As Strauss's understudy and more recently as one-day international captain, he showed himself to have a good cricket brain, and to always be up for the challenge. And as challenges go, they don't tend to come any bigger than winning in India. The Australians called it the final frontier for good reason, and the fact that it had been 28 years without an England victory there showed the magnitude of what lay ahead.

When we last went to Australia it was against a backdrop of two and a half barren decades, and I guess the opportunity to make history yet again spurred us on. Motivation was also generated by the knowledge that even some of the staunchest England cricket followers would have had doubts about our credentials to succeed in India.

So, sat down at the airport a couple of days before Christmas – we flew home immediately after the fourth and final Test – we really couldn't believe the enormity of what we had achieved. Especially after people had said, following our defeat in the first Test, that we were going to lose 4-0. It was a really euphoric feeling to have beaten India 2-1 away; a result on a par with the 2010–11 Ashes.

As a group we knew all along that we had the personnel and skills to succeed out there. It was just a case of putting it all into practice on the pitch. Even after the first Test in Ahmedabad when we were obviously disappointed by the result and the performance – matches tend to go only one way when you trail by 330 runs on first innings – privately, we nevertheless thought we had shown enough in periods to prove we could be competitive. When we analyzed that nine-wicket defeat, it was obvious that we had played much better in the second innings. There had just been too much damage done in the first.

We didn't need anyone else telling us we had not played well, but when people from outside do start saying things, such as predicting whitewashes given our struggles against subcontinental opposition earlier in the year, you want to prove them wrong. Primarily, of course, we wanted to prove to ourselves that we could play out there, but the doom-mongering gave us a little extra motivation to show it.

Cook's batting in the second innings of that first Test, a determined 176, showed everyone else in the team two things: firstly, that he was going to lead from the front, and secondly that the way to prosper out there was to believe in your own method. He showed us all that you could succeed by implementing whatever personal plans had worked best for you in the past. As a batsman, Cookie has many qualities but resilience and durability are chief among them, and he used them aptly during his brilliant 176 on the fourth and fifth days' play in Ahmedabad.

As captain, he asked us to maximize our own potential from that point forward – to get the most we possibly could out of ourselves in the middle by playing our most natural games in those conditions. That meant, for example, Kevin Pietersen being as aggressive as possible because aggressively is how he plays when at his very best. He had shown us the way, and the ongoing challenge was for the rest of us to get the best out of ourselves, and ultimately the best out of the team in the remaining matches.

It was always going to be a difficult task to follow Strauss, but Cook managed to put his own stamp on things, carrying on seamlessly from the job he had started as captain of the England one-day team. Some of his decisions in the field were mightily impressive. It's quite different playing cricket in India, and a lot of captains might be tempted to change the field just for the sake of it once batsmen are on top, but he never got dragged into that trap. There was no ball-following, and he implemented his own ideas on when to attack and when to defend. He got the balance of that spot on, so that we went for the kill or bided our time at exactly the right points. Also, when you go to somewhere like India, it is not only the contrasting conditions that prove a challenge. As an England captain, it is rare to be operating with a four-man attack incorporating two frontline spinners, so rotating the slow bowlers around the two seamers is a task in itself.

His leadership was nearly perfect on that trip. Not absolutely perfect, because he still foamed at the mouth when speaking to the group, but coming from someone else who is also not a natural speaker either this is no slight. I know how intimidating it can be to address others, and Cookie became more comfortable with it, and will get better at it still. The only problems he encountered were from one of his closest allies. Graeme Swann continued to be a menace because he preys on every little mistake.

Just as in Ahmedabad we lost the toss, but this time at least I was able to force an early breakthrough with the dismissal of Gautam Gambhir, lbw second ball of the match. And although we struggled to dislodge first Test double centurion Cheteshwar Pujara, Swann and the recalled Monty Panesar both bowled beautifully on a receptive surface to keep India in check with regular wickets.

They shared nine between them, in fact, and a second partnership, of 206 runs with the bat between Cook and Pietersen, set up a significant total. That helped secure a healthy if not massive lead on first innings and our spinners' threat did not diminish second time around. With pressure exerted, India were dismissed for 142 early on the fourth morning, which left us with only a minimal score to negotiate for a ten-wicket win.

Suddenly, with a comfortable victory behind us, everything looked different, and the complexion of the series changed overnight. Typically after such a result, the calls for change began in the local media. We didn't need to be picking up the papers every day to know what was being talking about. Every time you switched on the telly there was a debate on whether they should start dropping their senior players, and the issue was pretty much unavoidable in a cricket-mad country like India.

This provided a distinct feeling of *déjà vu* for me. This talk around players like Virender Sehwag and Sachin Tendulkar was exactly the same sort of stuff that was being said about Australia's old guard when we played them two winters earlier. In years gone by the Australians would never have asked questions of their own team. Their international XIs had always been so nailed on, and the same went for India.

Now when there are doubts about players' form like that, it's natural that those doubts creep into the team environment and onto the field. From experience, we knew that when that happens it gives the opposition an edge, and we were able to play on the uncertainty throughout the whole series. It didn't really manifest itself on the field in any noticeable way but as a team, we have learned that once you're on top of your opponents the challenge is to stay on top of them – keep them down while they're suffering.

Cook was the one at the forefront of this, with his third hundred in as many matches setting up the win in Kolkata. Once again, it came after losing the toss but securing first-innings bragging rights, and once again involved chasing a modest target. With India now unable to win the series, their selectors axed Yuvraj Singh, Harbhajan Singh (who had also missed the third Test) and Zaheer Khan – three of their best players in the modern era. Yuvraj is as destructive a batsman as goes round, Harbhajan was the leading active wicket-taker in Test cricket and Zaheer not long since one of the best pace bowlers on the world circuit. It served to show that when you put some pressure on the opposition, they can do things that are a little bit out of character.

We knew India would come hard at us with the ball in the last Test at Nagpur, and there was a bit of chat in the field after they took two early wickets. But a partnership quelled all that, and put them back onto the back foot again. Nullifying momentum is the best way to keep chirpy characters on the other team quiet and we managed to turn them quiet very quickly.

Although a draw was all we needed to pull off an historic series win, we were desperate to make the margin 3-1. Unfortunately, the nature of the pitch did not allow it. I am not sure that was the pitch that India actually wanted, either, and they would have been as disappointed as we were with its lifelessness. With the scoreline as it was, they would have favoured a result pitch, too.

There was nothing in it at all for the fast bowlers, no pace or bounce whatsoever. I actually don't know what's wrong with me – perhaps I need to give my head a shake – but I get a huge amount of pleasure bowling on those kind of surfaces. You know before you tread onto the turf there that hard work is in store and so you are kind of prepared for it. With that in mind, you can probably imagine how I felt when I got a wicket with my third ball. That's how precious new-ball wickets are out there, and Sehwag is always a big scalp, so it was a real shock to knock back his off-stump. Emotion took over, which is why I almost cleaned KP up as I ran off in celebration.

Dead pitches require you to bring out some of your other skills once the ball goes a bit softer, and certainly both here and in the match at Kolkata, I found the challenge of reverse swinging the ball to set batsmen really enjoyable. It is a real test to get what you prac- tise so much right in games, and when you do it feels good. So to take four for 81 in India's only innings felt like a real feather in the cap, as did winning the man of the match award and being singled out by India captain Mahendra Singh Dhoni as the difference between the two teams. I didn't see it like that, but you cannot get higher words of praise than those from the opposition captain. Getting that kind of seal of approval was nice because I so wanted to be considered effective out there. I knew taking wickets would be difficult, especially so after the first two games when I had only two to my name, so it was pleasing to reach the levels I did. I have standards that I want to keep no matter where I am playing or who I am playing against and that is important to me.

The final one of my dozen victims in the series, Ravindra Jadeja, leg before, was special because it took my England career wicket tally to 528, matching the number Sir Ian Botham managed in his illustrious career. I went to sleep that evening in the knowledge that no one had taken more wickets than me in an England shirt. In all honesty, it takes some getting your head round. It is incredible that I have found myself in this position.

Take Beefy out of the equation a minute. The fact that I had reached 528 international wickets is phenomenal. It certainly seems like a huge amount to me, and something I would never have dreamed about before my first international call-up.

Of course, I want plenty more wickets yet and while I am fit and youngish I will endeavour to keep taking them and contributing to a successful England team. The numbers will take care of themselves, and I will let guys sat in the press box talk about milestones and things like that if they wish. Maybe one day when I'm sat up there next to them, we can have a chat about it, but while I remain on the field, I just want to focus on taking the wickets to contribute to us winning.

This was the thirteenth Test series win out of the twenty-six I had been involved in, and while the personal landmarks are there to be acknowledged, the memories will be of my mates in the dressing room after such triumphs. In Mumbai, we stayed behind for about four hours after the game, chatting and listening to music. Having a beer together, as we did on the outfield at Sydney, outweighs any of our own personal highs.

This team has a huge year ahead, too, and you don't really need to set any goals when you have got two Ashes series within a year on the horizon. As an England player, what more motivation do you need than the opportunity to beat Australia again? We know exactly what we want to achieve: to complete four consecutive Ashes series wins would be such a great achievement, and one not completed by an England team since 1887.

Having experienced one win Down Under, a repeat is definitely something I have an appetite for. The majority of our team grew up in an era when Australia dominated. Throughout the 1990s they won series after series, so it would be nice if we could flip history, and become the dominant force for a few years. I am sure that would give a lot of pleasure to a great number of cricket fans of my generation.

Acknowledgements

There are a few people I need to thank who made this book possible:

Richard Gibson, for helping me write my life story (so far!), my editor Rhea Halford, publishers Simon & Schuster, Jonathan Conway, of Mulcahy Conway Associates, and Luke Sutton and Gaia Bursell from Activate Sport Management.

I would also like to thank my parents, grandparents and the rest of my family for all their love and support.

Daniella for always being there and for the two most beautiful and precious things in the world, Lola and Ruby. I love you all more than words.

And thanks to all the people from Burnley Cricket Club, Lancashire County Cricket Club and England that have shared, helped and believed.

Index

Note: 'JA' denotes James Anderson. Unless otherwise indicated, names of countries refer to cricket teams. In subheadings, Test matches against Australia are listed under 'Ashes'.